THE FAQ
MANUAL OF STYLE

THE FAQ
MANUAL OF STYLE

RUSSELL SHAW

MIS:
PRESS

MIS:Press, Inc.
A Subsidiary of Henry Holt and Company, Inc.
115 West 18th Street
New York, New York 10011

99 98 97 96   4 3 2 1

Associate Publisher: Paul Farrell   **Executive Editor:** Cary Sullivan

Editor: Andrew Neusner   **Technical Editor:** Michael Banks

Copy Edit Manager: Shari Chappell   **Copy Editor:** Bud Paulding

Production Editor: Maya Riddick   **Assoc. Prod. Editor:** Carmen Walker

Dedication

To my supportive parents, Ted and Ida, and sisters, Janet and Phyllis. Sharing your DNA is a badge of honor.

And to Anicia, who graced my life and graced the Earth with her life force for too short a time, but who now rides the Kentucky wind forever.

Acknowledgements

Debt in the face of friendship, faith through failure, services, and good deeds rendered is no vice. Thanks go to many, including Angela Gunn, mentor, networker, door-opener, and right-minded human being; Tommy Bass, who configured the computer system this book was written on; Jim and Mary Ellen Pettigrew, for their advice, tolerance, and encouragement; Dana Blankenhorn and family, for being there.

Also to Robert Hertzberg, editor of *WebWeek*, whose assignment to do a story on FAQs led to this book; Wendy Woods of *Newsbytes*, whose faith in me opened up many doors; Rod Kuckro of Business Research Publications; Betsy Edgerton of *Electronic Media*, quite possibly the best editor this journalist has ever had; to Michael Banks, for working with me to make this book better; and to Andy Neusner, the best editor this new author has ever had, who saw a book project even before I did.

And finally, to all the FAQ writers on the Web and Usenet, undercompensated, unappreciated and sometimes, uncompensated tutors of cyberspace who do their best to try to teach. I promise I'll do my best to learn.

Contents

CHAPTER 4: INITIAL FAQ LISTS AND TIPS 35

CHAPTER 5: WHEN DO YOU DIVIDE
AND HOW DO YOU RUN YOUR FAQ? 45

CHAPTER 9: CHANGING TIMES, CHANGING FAQS 105

CHAPTER 10: LEARNING FROM LINKS 127

CHAPTER 11: MAKING MONEY, SAVING MONEY 155

CHAPTER 12: SITE-TO-SOFTWARE INFORMATION FAQs . . .183

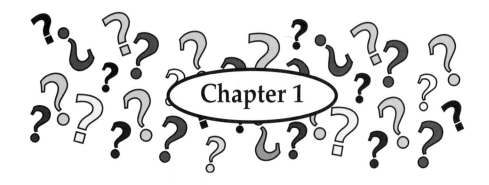

What Are FAQs?

In this chapter, you'll learn…

- How did FAQs develop as a concept?
- Growth of the online world has spurred FAQ development
- What is a FAQ maintainer?
- What can a well-constructed FAQ do for your site or newsgroup?
- Online resources for FAQ writers

Just a few short years ago, when you would buy a computer or a software program, it would come with an indecipherable user's manual. The marketing managers for these products had multi-millions of dollars invested in advertising campaigns intended to demonstrate their practicality and user-friendliness, but the approach involved in writing manuals that were easy to understand for the common person had not yet permeated the insular world of product management.

Hence, manuals for these goods were written by "techies" for "techies." We all remember printed software guides where installation Step 11 didn't necessarily follow installation Step 10, or even refer to it. Books had tutorials accompanied by indecipherable drawings, referring to procedures or parts that should have been explained and defined, but were specified poorly if at all.

The result was a long string of calls to customer service, where outside personnel, often with little understanding of the product to begin with, vainly struggled to answer questions posed by irate customers, who not only had tried in vain for six hours to get the newly purchased product to work, but who has also listened to listless string music while on hold for 30 minutes waiting their turn.

Many questions were being "asked frequently," or at least, more than other questions. The concept of counting which questions were commonly posed, and then arranging them in printed form in some kind of logical sequence began to dawn on people with enough clout and vision to make such a practice a reality. Not only would such a methodology be helpful to customers by showing a significant degree of "we care about you" to them, but it has, in the age of downsizing, enabled corporations to economize on the number of customer-service reps they carry while freeing the ones they retain for more complicated questions. Perhaps most important, a list of "frequent questions" included in a product brochure can prevent some frustrated-buyer hostility long before it has a chance to fester.

MORE SURFERS, MORE QUESTIONS

At the same time, the growth of the online world in the early and mid-1990s exponentially expanded the numbers of people who needed quick answers to relatively easy questions. The growth of online services, and then, of course, the explosion of new users for the different parts of the Internet drove this need. We've all asked the same questions, frequently. "How do I install this telecommunications program to work in Windows?" "I've plugged the new modem into the back of the serial port, but it's not dialing." "How do I send the same electronic mail message to multiple recipients?" "How do I download a transcript from a chat session?" "How often is this Web site updated?" "Are there options for text-only delivery? "What does 'VRML' mean?" "What is the purpose of this newsgroup?" "Will you let me post an advertising message on it?"

So, whether we're talking about software applications that run on computers, telecommunications programs that access the Internet, navigating the body of content on the Internet, or just simply getting that new $2,000 machine to work in the first place, people are bound to pose a lot of the same questions, very often. If you are a product manager, a Webmaster, a bulletin-board system operator, or a newsgroup moderator, there's a way to marshal these queries into a logically organized, helpful, easily-available hierarchy that will be to your benefit: a list of Frequently Asked Questions, or "FAQs."

THE HISTORY OF FAQS

The history of FAQs goes back well before the dawning of the mass information age, however. With almost every movement, someone has to be first. Back in 1982, the first FAQ was put up on the ARPAnet (the Internet's predecessor) by Eugene Miya. He was the National Aeronautics and Space Administration's designated liaison to the *SPACE[- Digest]/net.space* ListServ. He thought that some answers to some questions were not especially helpful and a waste of time, so he gathered up some of the most common questions and posted them monthly in the companion *net.space* newsgroup. Snail mail addresses and phone numbers of NASA centers were some of the first FAQ questions to go up. ARPAnet is now the Internet and has grown by factors of thousands, but this ancestor of all FAQs is still being maintained today.

The last few years have seen an explosion of FAQs, both in printed form and online. There are tens of thousands of them, and hundreds more are written and posted each week. Behind every FAQ is a FAQ writer, and probably a FAQ "maintainer" as well. Sometimes these are one and the same, but at some companies, Web sites, newsgroups or mailing lists, the FAQ writer has moved on, leaving the "maintainer" to tend herd over the flock of questions, weeding out ones that become obsolete, migrating new ones to the FAQ list when they, well, are asked "frequently" enough to merit inclusion, occasionally anticipating questions in advance, and cleaving up the FAQ list into several lists when the list itself becomes overly long and complicated.

Thus, with all these attendant issues, an ironic paradox is raised. When they are completed and then printed, posted, or both, Frequently Asked Questions lists should be easy to understand and simple; yet while striving for simplicity, the act of writing them is anything but simple. In terms of timing, assembly, composition, and administration of a FAQ, there aren't many standard rules. It will be the purpose of this book to provide a guideline for FAQs, how they should be written, and how like grapevines in a vineyard, they should be nurtured and watered.

WHAT THE FAQ?

"FAQ," as we have shown, is an acronym for a Frequently Asked Questions list. There are no hard and fast rules for what constitutes a "list." I've seen some Web sites with as few as three questions in their FAQs. Others have dozens of subsections and thousands of words— probably too unwieldy in most cases. Yet regardless of the numbers of questions in a FAQ, their very presence results in an appearance on a FAQ list, or on Usenet, a FAQ "article."

If the reader will permit a bit of pretzel logic here, the initial question many people ask about FAQ is, "how do you say it?" Saying it the wrong way in studied circles brands you as a newbie. Worse yet, uttering the word FAQ by pronouncing the "A" as a Britisher would say the "a" in the word "fast" might brand you a cussing fool, if said in the company of those who don't know better. You should instead think of the term "FAQ" in its phonetic translation, which is "fak" or "fack." The plural of this, of course, would be "facks"—too close to "fax" for my taste, but distinguishable from it if given the proper preamble context; e.g., "there are four FAQs on that Web site and they are all helpful."

The term FAQ has gained acceptance on the Internet as the first place to go to get answers to your questions. There are two qualifiers that need to be stated at the outset, though. First, some lists of questions are FAQs— only they are referred to by different names. The most common of these are Help menus written in the style of FAQs. Some help menus are close enough to FAQs to really be FAQs, despite what their writers say. Besides the title, the main difference I can think of is that they will have most of the answers a similar FAQ would have, but without the attendant questions—sort of like the hit television game show "Jeopardy," wherein answers are stated and the contestant has to guess the question.

At other times, especially on Usenet newsgroups, FAQs are less a compilation of questions and answers and more a policy declaration. Such FAQs are called FAQs, and may even have questions and answers, but are more declarations of a newsgroup's mission, policies, and procedures than a road map to the group itself. Does calling this list a FAQ automatically make it so? That's a question which could be debated for hours. Might make a fun subject, but it's a bit outside our mission here.

ALL FAQS ARE RELATED, SOMEHOW

Before we talk about how some FAQs in some places necessarily differ from each other, perhaps we should mull over their basic similarities. The most basic of these is that, at least in a perfect world, FAQs are composed of queries that are either asked the most, or will be asked the most by the people using the product or accessing the newsgroup, Web site, etc. They aren't necessarily the most intelligent questions, or the most basic, but they should be the most common.

As we'll see by specific example in several of the following chapters, questions "come" to a FAQ list through a variety of sources. FAQ writers say that often, initial FAQ lists come from their own intuition and experiences. If it's a FAQ for their product, a customer service or product manager will already know the kinds of questions that are being frequently asked. A Web site with a mail-to option may use a mechanism for monitoring questions posed via Email and phone not already on a FAQ—and then migrating them to the FAQ after they get posed a certain number of times. A software upgrade, a major expansion to a Web site—these have the inherent potential of complicating matters. The intuitive FAQ list maintainer will anticipate this and draw up questions even before they are asked. A bit of preventive maintenance, you might say.

Properly and cleverly done, FAQs will make life simpler. It's not a cure-all for the pain-in-the-neck factor; some people new to Web sites will instinctively push the panic button and ask questions even if the answer is right in front of them, in a FAQ that is just waiting to be accessed. That's why it is critically important for people to be able to locate your FAQ.

WHERE IS IT?

The question of accessibility has different implications for different formats. On a Web site, for example, the initial indication that there is a FAQ, or FAQs, should come via a quite visible home page presence. This might be nothing more than hyperlinking the term "FAQ" or "Frequently Asked Questions" at the bottom of the page. If yours is the type of site likely to attract a large number of inexperienced accessors, maybe the iconed term "FAQ" would be a bit too arcane. I would suggest that you icon the phrase, "Frequently Asked Questions," or better yet, "Help." After all, "help," or its equivalent in other languages, is an exclamation of distress common to many of us. Once they click and are transported to the "Help" page, you can hit them with all the alphabet soup you want.

I've got an even better idea, though. Why not have a visual representation of your FAQ feature on your home page? If you remember your school days or are still in school, you know that some people are ashamed to ask questions. Take the shame out of it, by putting up an icon with a drawing of a perplexed individual and then a big question mark over his or her head. You can put the hyperlink under the picture, or better yet, in the picture. Also, if the FAQ icon is one of several theme-setting icons on your home page, it will make your site more user-friendly, and even cut down on the "where do I find" questions you may feel obligated to place on your FAQ page.

In product manuals, FAQs can either be at the beginning of the guide, or at the end. Placing them at the end would serve readers who have taken the time to read through the whole booklet but still have questions. Putting them at the start would serve as a clear map of purpose and intent at the outset, making the rest of the instructions easier to understand. Obviously, wherever you put your product-info FAQ, it should be referred to in the table of contents and the index, if you have one.

Usenet newsgroups have particular elements of their culture that make frequent reposting of FAQs mandatory. Most newsgroup postings only stay up a few weeks, and most of the newsreader programs people use to access their favorite groups have a similar short-term lifespan. There is nothing more futile than to put up a well-crafted FAQ, only to have it "fall off." There are a number of Web sites and newsgroups which attempt to palliate this problem by acting as archives, or repositories, for FAQs. This is important news for Web and Usenet FAQ writers, because going to these FAQs provides a ready tutorial on how other people have written theirs.

In Usenet, the most popular initial gathering spot for FAQs is at the *news.answers* newsgroup. An archive of all postings in this group is at the *rtfm.mit.edu ftp* site. See Figures 1.1 and 1.2.

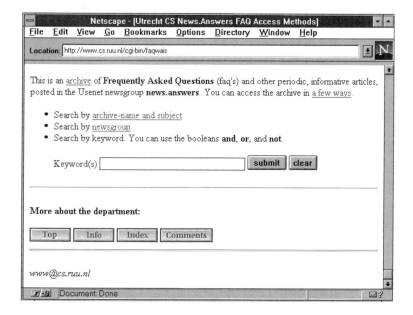

FIGURE 1.1 HOME PAGE FROM THE USENET FAQ LIST.

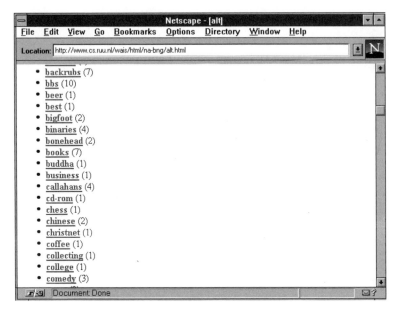

FIGURE 1.2 SAMPLE PAGE FROM THE USENET FAQ LIST.

There are several mirror sites as well. When you get there, looking for a FAQ that you might want to model yours after, you can search in several ways.

By subject line:

/pub/usenet/news.group.name
/pub/usenet-by-group/news.group.name

By subject category:

/pub/usenet/news.answers
/pub/usenet-by-group/news.answers

and for the other *.answers* newsgroups:

/pub/usenet/.answers (e.g., comp.answers, sci.answers, rec.answers)*
/pub/usenet-by-group/.answers*

By newsgroup hierarchy:

/pub/usenet-by-hierarchy/news/group/name.

This directory is organized by hierarchy (*sci., comp., alt.,* etc).

New postings are posted and stored at */pub/usenet/news.lists,* and can also be retrieved via Email as a *list listserv* through *mail-server@rtfm.mit.edu* and keying in the term "help" in the message (not subject) line.

There are also several FAQ archives on the Web. The three most common repositories for these are:

http://www.jazzie.com/ii/internet/faqs.html

http://www.cs.ruu.nl/cgi-bin/faqwais

http://www.lib.ox.ac.uk/internet/news/faq/by_group.index.html

BE CONSPICUOUS

Some Web FAQs reside on these archives, but most of these postings are Usenet FAQs. This fact of life presents a potentially frustrating but highly solvable conundrum: To a FAQ writer, these postings are invaluable resources; yet your subscribers, end-users, etc., will almost certainly lack the knowledge to go to a place like *http://www.jazzie.com/ii/internet/faqs.html* and fish out a FAQ that has fallen off your newsgroup. That's why it is *imperative* to repost your FAQs frequently.

There really ought to be a central library for Web FAQs, but alas, there isn't. Why? The answer is simple, really. Despite the wide range of newsgroups out there, Usenet has more of a community culture, but the Web world is more akin to many thousands of people off doing their own thing. If you're a Web FAQ writer or want to be one, there are options, however. See how other people, particularly those in your or allied business sectors have written their FAQs. Your key is a search engine. Web indexes like Yahoo! won't be good places to find FAQs, because the body of searchable site text they allow is limited to short comment fields that are not likely to say that a FAQ, or FAQs, reside therein. The beefier search engines are better. Stay away from the unabridged ones like Alta-Vista; you'll get too many unrelated hits. Open Text and Lycos are the best, because searching is easy and citations are accurate. Lycos, especially, gives you rich detail about each hit. Role models are then just a click away.

CRAWLING THE WEB FOR MODEL FAQS

Say you are the would-be FAQ writer for Amalgamated Widgets' new Web site. Your four corporate competitors are Republic Widgets, American Widgets, Wonder Widgets, and Williams Widgets. Key in the terms REPUBLIC WIDGETS FAQ (don't put an "and" between them) and see what you find. If three out of your four competitors have FAQs, click to them and either print or download them. This should be a big help in writing your own, but make sure that for copyright reasons—as well as of course, the fact that your widget is better than theirs—that you don't emulate their FAQ too closely.

Yes, copyright is a big issue. These are litigious times. Many, if not most, Web sites have a copyright designator which you would ignore at your own peril. Some Usenet groups put anti-copy disclaimers up as well. Some CD-ROM vendors like to scour up Usenet FAQs and sell them commercially; while this may not be illegal, it's seen in the newsgroup world as highly improper. FAQ-copyright law—and Internet copyright law, for that matter—is in its formative stages and is still evolving.

FAQ-writing requires a commitment of time and thought. But before you write one, you should decide if you need one. We'll discuss this issue in the next chapter.

DO YOU NEED A FAQ?

In this chapter, you'll learn…

- When do you need a FAQ?
- When don't you need a FAQ?
- The Web site–newsgroup FAQ connection
- FAQs are time-and-money-savers

The fact that you are reading this book indicates that you are at least thinking of starting one. There are few, if any, hard and fast rules here. Perhaps the best way to start would be via the old process-of-elimination route, i.e., when do you *not* need a FAQ?

In my career covering the online world, I have "visited" thousands of Web sites, have contributed a weekly column to one of them, have lurked in hundreds of Usenet newsgroups, and have bookmarked dozens. Surfed there, clicked that. Based on my hopefully well-considered cybertravels, I've concluded that you *don't* need a FAQ if:

- Your Web site is extraordinarily simple, such as a home page with a CGI (Common Gateway Interface) order form. If your Web site basically has photos of your beau, your cat, and your garden it might be fun to write a FAQ, but you really don't need one.

11

- Your newsgroup content is just a series of opinions without any standard-setting or taste-maintaining apparatus in place. This almost always means that your group is not moderated. Most likely, such a group will be in the *alt.* or *rec.* hierarchy.

- You don't have the time to write one. If you regard having a FAQ on your Web site or newsgroup as a mildly interesting idea but a pain in the neck, you will probably not want to run it right. Putting up a half-baked FAQ will cause your hit count to nose-dive. On a Web site, especially a *.com* one, that certainly won't help your company revenue. In a Newsgroup, your threads will wither if people find a more user-friendly atmosphere elsewhere. Arrested development of a product FAQ would be yet another mutation of CMS (Convoluted Manual Syndrome).

"No, that's not me. I really think we need a FAQ," I hear you saying.

So why write one? It could be argued that the most powerful reason is societal. People are more rushed these days. They have shorter attention spans and less patience to go from Point A to Point B via Point N. Inculcate such befuddlement on your Web site and they won't be back.

Couple the attention-span problem with chronic information overload—so many sites, so little time—and it will almost always be in your interest to create as friendly an environment as possible. I know it sounds hokey, but taking time to write a FAQ shows that you care about the people coming to "visit" you.

FAQS CAN BE GOOD FOR BUSINESS

One of the best-known FAQ writers, Russ Hersch, addresses the issue in "FAQs about FAQs," which he posts monthly to several newsgroups. "A FAQ is a good way to help lots of good folks at the same time," Hersch says. The first FAQ that I wrote was as a result of my search for information on Intel 8051 microcontrollers. I couldn't find anything for a long time. I used Archie, Gopher, and lots of other methods that I either read about or that friends recommended. In addition, I scanned the appropriate newsgroups. However, all that I could find were the same questions that I was asking. I nearly came to the conclusion that the Internet was a waste of time.

"After compiling a few facts," he adds, "I put them together in a small article (under 5K) and posted it to a few Usenet newsgroups that seemed to have a reasonable connection to the subject matter. In a short time I was inundated with Email. Readers of my FAQ from all over the world sent additions and corrections for the FAQ, requests to post to other newsgroups, kind words of appreciation, offers of free software and literature, and even a job offer. Today the FAQ is over 100K in size and two other FAQs were born from the leftovers from this first FAQ."

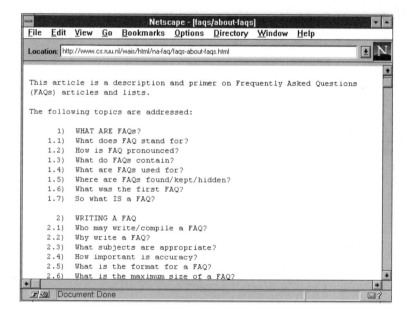

FIGURE 2.1 THE FAQS ABOUT FAQS FAQ.

"As a result of this modest effort," Hersch continues, "I have learned a lot. I have more than enough information about the 8051 microcontroller, I learned my way around the Internet, and I have made connections with a number of really nice people. Even more, my FAQ had a snowballing effect."

In Hersch's view, this "snowballing" has markedly served the greater good. "Several other people are now either maintaining or starting FAQs on other microcontrollers," he notes. "In a short time, if a new-comer to the Internet is looking for information on microcontrollers, a pile of information will be immediately available, without the need for months of searching. Hopefully, the same will be true about the subject(s) that you are interested in."

The much more mercantile world of the Web has its own imperatives for the existence of FAQs. Webmasters say that two key rules apply:

- If your site is becoming increasingly complicated and sophisticated, you definitely need at least one FAQ.
- If your "human" answering apparatus—customer service or marketing—is becoming overwhelmed answering some basic questions, that should serve as a clear indicator that you need a FAQ.

"If we decide to post a significantly technical subject, I'm sure the building of a FAQ would be part of the process of placing it on the Web," says Susan Chatman, Webmistress of the Silicon Studio site since its launch in October 1994. Silicon Studio, which provides high-tech production resources for the entertainment industry, is a wholly owned subsidiary of Silicon Graphics International (CGI). Figure 2.2 shows the Studio Central FAQ.

C/net, a major computer-related Web site that uses multimedia tools for a daily Web-delivered radio broadcast and produces its own weekly 30-minute cable television show, has an increasingly complex business model. For them, it's always FAQ-spawning season.

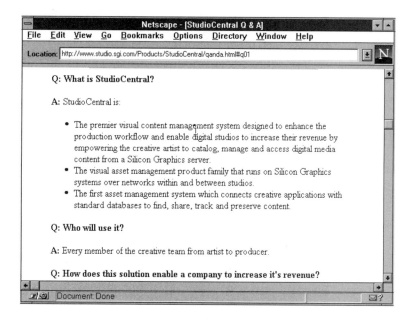

FIGURE 2.2 THE STUDIO CENTRAL FAQ.

Frank Voci, vice-president of production and creative affairs for c/net, has a system in place for FAQ-page justification. The point of possible conception is monitored through an Email address, *support@cnet.com*. Every message that comes to this address is logged and answered. A database of which questions are getting asked often is created and a decision is made whether they are worthy of a FAQ, he says.

A good, useful, and universal rule for determining whether you need a FAQ is via e-mail, snail mail, phone calls, fax, or smoke signals, are you and your staff being asked the same darn questions over and over? And over again? In short, frequently?

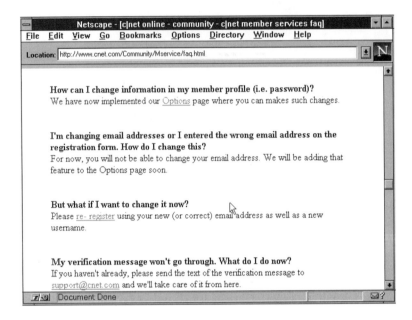

FIGURE 2.3 THE C/NET FAQ HOME PAGE.

"Generally, if the same questions keep coming up time after time, you need a FAQ," says Dave Mordor, an automotive expert with his own Web site, *http:///www.mordor.com*. Mordor is also a regular figure on numerous automobile-related newsgroups. "While I created the FAQ for newsgroups, my Web site generates the same questions. I now also have a filter; when someone clicks on my Email address, they automatically go into a Web page that advises them to check the FAQ before asking me a technical question. I estimate that half of the questions I used to get were in the FAQ, and about one-quarter to one-third of those that appear in the newsgroups."

Dave Dennis, who maintains the Internet Provider FAQ at *http://www.list.amazing.com/internet/faq/html*, says that reading the inquiry-frequency meter is a practical way of determining if you need a Frequently Asked Questions page. "In the case of the Internet Provider FAQ, it was fairly obvious from mailing list traffic that a FAQ was required," he says.

CROSS-POLLINATE YOUR FAQS

An expert on Internet FAQs, Dennis has a surprising revelation that should be a big help to corporate Webmasters. Many major companies have nonaffiliated, but nevertheless companion, newsgroups with areas of identical interest. Dennis has observed that the FAQ maintainers at many companies will lurk there, cataloging questions about their products that are posed in these newsgroups, and then—if the questions are asked often enough—start a FAQ on the Web site and import FAQs from the newsgroup to the site itself. This way, an "allied" newsgroup acts as a kind of filtering agent for a *.com* Web site FAQ page. "Most FAQs are created from the grassroots of Usenet or mailing lists, and not as part of a vast organization like Silicon Graphics, Inc. or Sun. The SGI FAQs are the most professional I've ever seen, but even they are written by outside people, not SGI. SGI's Web site links to them, but they are definitely not organization products," Dennis says.

When FAQs on a .com Web site are first "hatched" as reactions to newsgroup traffic, there's another, more ephemeral, benefit. There's an impression, however much or little deserved, that the company listens to the concerns of its most devoted and inquisitive customers, the part of the customer base most likely to "hang out" in Usenet groups. Dennis also thinks that Web site FAQs first posed in newsgroups are likely not to have the stigma of overly-commercial artifice like the questions that are first hatched by an overeager yuppie in the marketing department.

SAVE TIME, WRITE A FAQ

The most compelling reason for starting a FAQ page is to save time. Whether you operate a customer-service department for packaged goods, moderate a listserv or newsgroup, or run a Web site, this time represents money saved or lost. Unnecessary inquiries to your Webmaster or to customer service can be labor-intensive. It's a lose-lose situation; not answering questions posed to operations with a FAQ runs you the risk of being branded, aloof but getting bogged down in such minutiae keeps you from potentially more productive tasks.

Should you be in the listserv or newsgroup universe, you are likely running the operation on your own time. The same time-is-money axiom applies.

"I personally got tired of writing the same things over and over, so I created a little text file that I started sending to people, and then I decided to do it right and created a FAQ. This sequence of events took about six months," says Buzz McDermott, maintainer of the *rec.models.rockets* newsgroup. "In the case of *rec.models.rockets*, I noticed the same questions being asked over and over. There also comes a point where you start seeing multiple 'there ought to be a FAQ for this group' posts."

Raising the profile of your site or group is another reason to start a FAQ. As the 1990s wear on, the proprietary online services are still an initial and frequent point of entry for people new to cyberspace. All of the major ones have several dozen of their own discussion groups with similar themes to corresponding newsgroups on the Internet.

The potential of a FAQ to cross-pollinate interest among Web site, online service, and Usenet audiences is cited as a powerful attraction by Dean Radin, director of the Consciousness Research Laboratory at the University of Nevada in Las Vegas. In addition to writing the Parapsychology FAQ on the *sci.skeptic* newsgroup, Radin's group has a Web presence at *http://eeyore.lv- hrc.nevada.edu/~cogno/cogno.html*.

"We were getting three or four requests a day for the same information," Radin says. "The FAQ is now hit about 1000 times a month, and it is growing rapidly because it has been mirrored in several other locations, translated into two other languages, and ported to CompuServe and AOL newsgroups." The Parapsychology FAQ is shown in Figure 2.4.

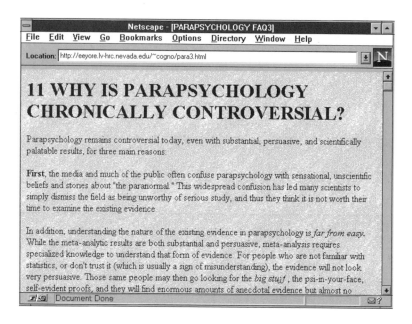

FIGURE 2.4 THE PARAPSYCHOLOGY FAQ.

"Any group needs a FAQ. I've never seen a group that didn't need to respond to questions of some kind. a FAQ provides a convenient reference to eliminate the need for endless repetition of the same information," agrees Ellen Armstrong, a film buff who compiles the Kenneth Branagh FAQ, which appears on the newsgroup *alt.movies.branagh-thmp-sn* and Web site *http://users.aol.com/luvvy/kbfaq.htm*. She also writes the Colin Firth FAQ for the Colin Firth listserv, which also appears on the Web site *http://www.iupui.edu/~rogersc/firth.html*.

Simply having a FAQ is not enough. It has to communicate answers cogently. It not only has to serve as a "Frequently *Asked* Questions" list, but also as a "Frequently *Answered* Questions" list. Either way, a FAQ requires time and effort but will save you both. This is a classic means-to-an-end connection, which we will spell out in the next chapter.

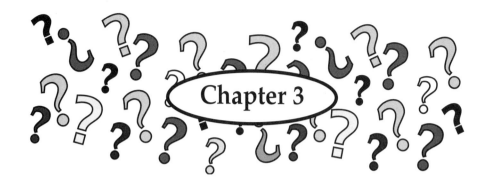

WHAT MAKES A FAQ GOOD?

In this chapter, you'll learn…

- How to tailor a FAQ to your site's sophistication level
- Some basic style and grammar rules
- Making and keeping your FAQ accurate
- In what order should your questions be?

The best FAQ writers have a co-dependent streak about them: they draw their strength from helping others understand their Web site, Newsgroup, or product, but they want to make sure their particular page draws enough traffic to justify its existence. In short, they want to be accepted.

There are many kinds of FAQ lists. They vary in where they are placed, in size, tone, and sophistication. Because of this, you might think that a set of common standards would be an implausible thought. Not so. The best FAQs, experts say, have several generic attributes. While these qualities may have to be adjusted proportionately, depending on the subject of the FAQ, there's some basic roots to start from when planning a quality FAQ.

KEY ATTRIBUTES

Here are some key attributes a "good FAQ" must have:

- It must be appropriate to the sophistication of the venue. Posting an intricately technical FAQ to a Web site won't work if that Web site is likely to draw a lot of traffic from people new to the product or technology that is being announced on the site.

- If you feel the need for multi-tiered levels of complexity, it might be a good idea to "split up" your FAQs. It's not wise to mix in simple questions with complex ones. It would have the same affect as a freshman in college being forced to take a graduate level course along with a regular class load of three or four "101" classes: too much gear-switching and strain on the brain. You'll risk intimidating your less experienced FAQ readers; if they want more, tell them where they can get it (for example, another FAQ in a different part of your site). There's more about this subject in Chapter 5, "When Multiple FAQs Are Necessary."

- In the Usenet Newsgroup world, avoid spamming your FAQ. This cheapens the value of your FAQ, and may land it in groups where it would have to be substantially retailored to be helpful, or doesn't belong in the first place.

- People must know where to find it. Go for what I call "cross-pollenization." If you're a newsgroup FAQ writer, use a search engine to see if there is a like-themed Web site and offer your FAQ there. They should appreciate it, and the exposure will help. Likewise if you've written a FAQ for a Web site, use a search tool like the excellent Deja News (*http://www.dejanews.com*) and see if there is a similar newsgroup and whether or not they have a FAQ. In most cases, cross-pollenization will serve the greater good. See Figure 3.1.

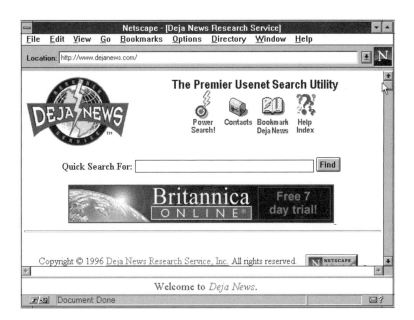

FIGURE 3.1 THE DEJA NEWS SERVICE IS A GOOD PLACE TO SEARCH FOR FAQS.

- Organization, organization, organization. Russ Hersch, one of the highly-regarded writers in the FAQ world, recommends grouping your questions via a numbering system, or by letter, i.e., "A," "B," "C," and so on.

- Indent. Hersch's FAQs, as well as most of the better ones I've seen, use indentation. This causes centering of the copy, which helps it stand out. Odds are the FAQ copy will need this attention. After all, it is likely to compete with cool graphics, colorful Icons, and enticing top-of-the-page Toolbars for your eye's attention. White space—which there is more of when whole lines of monitor real estate are not full of consonants and vowels—is easier on the eye and frees the rest of the brain up for absorption of the material being communicated.

"A FAQ should have clear, concise writing, good organization and a flexible structure. It must provide accurate, timely, useful information in a format that makes retrieval fast and convenient," says Ellen Armstrong, maintainer of the FAQ for the acclaimed Irish actor Kenneth Branagh on the Web at *http://users.aol.com/luvvy/kbfaq.htm.*

IT MUST BE ACCURATE

Too many FAQs are put up in a mode charitably describable as the formalization of hearsay. This is especially true in the newsgroup world, where a volunteer without a thorough understanding of a given subject cobbles together a FAQ based on nothing more reliable than the postings of other group members. Putting the inprimatur of a FAQ on a set of data bestows a certain prestige, even beatification, which shouldn't be taken casually. Besides, misinformation can spread fast.

There's a far greater potential for harm in an inaccurate FAQ than just being flamed. Sticks and stones and flames can hurt your feelings, but lawsuits can result if the information is erroneous and causes harm to property. There are hundreds of FAQs about software, for example. Many of these are written by self-styled experts. Some of these FAQ writers really are experts; others suffer from at least a bit of delusion about their expertise.

If, as a hypothetical, you are writing a FAQ about an upgrade to the Windows95 operating system, and your wrong or imprecise piece of advice causes a faithful reader's system to crash, pray hard. That crashed system might have held a Power-Point-enabled sales presentation she or he is making to a key client next Tuesday. Now, here you've come along and ruined things. Once their system is back up and running, the person whose sales presentation (and potential six-figure deal) you ruined will certainly blame you, get their lawyer to write you a threatening letter, and possibly rat on you to Microsoft. With this danger in mind, the best FAQ writers check for accuracy.

As automotive FAQ writer and site maintainer Dave Mordor points out, if your FAQ has a reputation for accuracy, "you're taken as the last word, you gain lots of credibility, and people quote you all the time. Maybe one of 100 people who uses the FAQ will tell you about their experience and how they spent two minutes and 15 cents and didn't need to do as 3 mechanics said and replace their entire engine and/or transmission. On the other hand, this means you must be very careful and sober, because people WILL listen to you and do what you say. I also suggest a legal disclaimer at the top to limit your liability because people MAY sue!"

KEEPING A WEB FAQ ACCURATE

Challenges to accuracy can pop up on Web sites as well. The potential problems can come from several sources. If you know where these travails take root, you can take steps to make sure the roots don't grow. Here are some potential traps to avoid in Web FAQs:

- Get your spelling and grammar right. In the eyes of those who know something about a given subject, a misspelling of a key word in a FAQ tells them you don't know what you are talking about. Some people are more forgiving than others about typos, but don't assume that everyone is that charitable.

- FAQs written by technical types, even Webmasters, might not be appropriate for user-friendly commercial sites. The problem is not so much that of creeping jargonitis that techies are often guilty of, but of a lack of preparatory dialogue between the FAQ writer and the people who have made and sell the product. The FAQ writer must have a real understanding of how the product works. When you are washing a linoleum floor, how much water should you dilute your Brand X cleanser with? Pardon the thought, but do you put in less water if there are cat stains? In short, the FAQ writer must be one with every single, foreseeable aspect of how the product works.

- FAQs can become inaccurate through neglect. If you put up a FAQ when a product or service is introduced and don't change the FAQ to reflect brand upgrades or new editions, the body of information on your FAQ can become irrelevant. If a new version of a brand fixed a flaw, and the FAQ still gives information to customers about how to get around that flaw, the age of the FAQ shows. It is giving information about a problem that no longer exists. Therefore, it is inaccurate.

FAQ ARCHITECTURE

A good FAQ can be like a tree, with branches leading to twigs. The tree is the FAQ itself. The branches are the questions and the answers, and the twigs are the incidental but necessary addenda, like sub-sections of the same answer field.

Here are two tips on organizing the architecture of a typical FAQ:

- Call it what it is. The first part of the FAQ is the header, or title. Sounds like an obvious no-brainer, but it really is important. Since many search engines will look for a citation in the URL and the title first, you'll want to name your FAQ **exactly** what it is about. List the subject in the header line, the top of the page, and certainly in the URL.
- Decide on a plan for your question-order, and stick to it consistently.

ORDER, ORDER

Web and Usenet FAQs have a good bit of latitude in what order to place questions and answers. Basically, there are three approaches:

- Start with the simplest questions and progress to the most complex;

- Begin with the most frequently-asked Frequently Asked Questions and go down the popularity scale from there;

- Put your newest questions at the end, to give the hopefully true impression that you update your FAQ page "frequently" with new information.

Each of these approaches has its devotees. Which one is best? Like so many other decisions in life, it depends.

Some favor the simple-to-complex order because it facilitates the learning curve of new site and group visitors. Such is the approach taken by Vocal Tec's Internet Phone's FAQ, About Internet Phone (*http://www.vocaltec.com/faq.htm*). The first question is site-specific but about as basic as you can get: "What Is Internet Phone?" FYI, this is one of the products that permit Internet users to have real-time conversations with each other. See Figure 3.2.

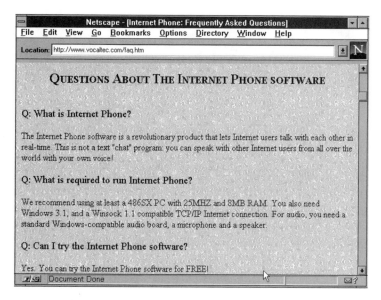

FIGURE 3.2 INTERNET PHONE'S FAQ STARTS WITH THE BASICS.

The next several questions increase in complexity, dealing with topics like necessary bandwidth, security, and compatibility with Local Area Networks (see Figure 3.3).

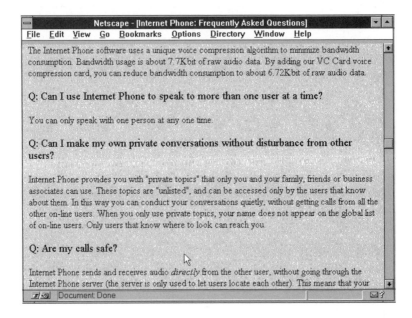

FIGURE 3.3 LATER INTERNET PHONE QUESTIONS ARE MORE COMPLEX.

Matthew Wall, a Webmaster at the M.I.T. Student Information Processing Board site, also favors a hierarchical approach. "Answer the questions in levels," he says. "The first paragraph should be an overview. The following paragraph should be more detailed, with lots of details at the end or pointers to where the details can be found. "Much of this," he thinks, "depends on the audience. But its better to err on the side of too much info rather than too little. A detailed FAQ saves you a bunch of time answering questions later on." Figures 3.4 and 3.5 show good progression.

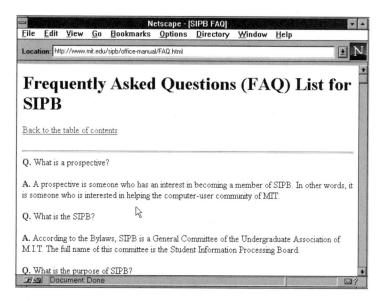

FIGURE 3.4 MIT's SIPB FAQ STARTS WITH THE BASICS.

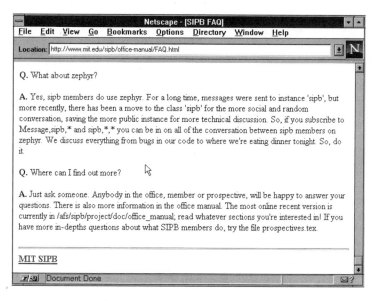

FIGURE 3.5 THIS FAQ THEN PROGRESSES IN SOPHISTICATION.

"I think the FAQs I do are based on something that might be called a natural progression of interest. The process of discovering an actor's work seems to follow a rather common path of basic-to-complex or readily-available-to-rare," says Ellen Armstrong, who also writes the Colin Firth FAQ for the *Colin Firth* listserve and also appears on web site *http://www.iupui.edu/~rogersc/firth.html*.

Buzz McDermott, maintainer of the *rec.models.rockets* newsgroup, agrees. "The current r.m.r FAQ is organized into sections much like a book," he says. "Each section represents what would be a 'chapter' of a book. It also starts with the first section having the most general questions. Areas having a number of general questions and also a number of very specific questions have two FAQ sections, one general, one specific. For example, there is a general section on questions concerning hobby rocketry in general: regulatory issues, names and addresses of organizations, book lists, pointers to archives, etc. Model rocketry, rocket gliders, and high power rocketry each have specific areas for questions about construction and flying those particular types of rockets."

Jordan C. Lund, author of the Dark Tower FAQ on *alt.fan.authors.stephen-king*, now puts the newer questions at the end. "I tried to place them (originally) in the order of what was most frequently asked," says Lund. "If a lot of people really want to know the answer to that hot question then they shouldn't have to wade through a lot of text to get there. After the FAQ got rolling, though, I found it easier to simply add the new questions at the end so there could be no confusion as to how new something was."

There's also a school of thought that, although a simple-to-complex hierarchy of questions is not necessarily bad, it would also be a good idea to put an "easy" summary-type question at the end. Sometimes, as in a commercial FAQ like the Frequently Asked Questions Page of Education Credit Corporation's Web site (*http://packetpress.com/ECC/eccfaq.html*), the last major question, "So Why Take Out a Private Loan," takes on the extra role of a sales tool. Sort of a digital deal-closer, you might say.

A FAQ SHOULD BE MORE THAN 'Q'S'

Some FAQ writers will put more than questions and answers into a FAQ. This approach broadens a FAQ page from a simple repository of questions and answers to one with general information as well. "Other" information likely to be found on FAQ pages includes phone numbers, Email addresses, posting advice, and links to other Web or Gopher sites.

SUPER FAQS/SEARCHABLE FAQS

Quicken Financial Corporation, makers of the popular Quicken and TurboTax packages, has a multi-layered approach to its highly-rated FAQ pages. There are more than 65 questions on its TurboTax for Windows FAQ. Realizing that such a number is unwieldy and cumbersome for some, it has taken about 10 of these questions and created a kind of "Super FAQ," which it calls Most Frequently Asked Questions. Both FAQs, incidentally, are accessible through the Home Page "Technical Support" Toolbar and are keyword-searchable through a configurable Technical Support Topic Search. See Figure 3.6.

FIGURE 3.6 THE TURBOTAX "SUPER FAQ."

BIGGER? NOT NECESSARILY BETTER

After you've assembled your FAQ, you might find it growing like a fungus. There's nothing inherently wrong with that, except a single FAQ that is too long might be hard for an inexperienced user to navigate. For Web surfing, not everyone has a Netscape Navigator browser and is fluent with the tool's handy "Find" command for local file searching. In the newsgroup universe, many older newsreaders cannot handle files larger than 64K, or even 32K. When you find yourself getting close to that number, you essentially have three choices: let the technologically-challenged people be damned; condense your post to a more manageable size, or split it up.

Hopefully, you now have an understanding of what makes a FAQ stand out, as well as the mistakes to avoid. The next chapter, "Initial FAQ lists and Tips," will show you how to get started with your first Frequently Asked Questions list.

TECH TIPS

Chris Lewis, author of "FAQs: A Suggested Minimal Digest Format," posts his suggestions every 20 days on the newsgroups *news.admin.misc*, *news.software.readers*, and *news.answers*. His FAQ is also available through FTP at *ftp://rtfm.mit.edu/pub/usenet/news.answers/faqs/minimal-digest- format*. On the Web, it can be found at *<http://www.cis.ohio- state.edu/hypertext/faq/usenet/ faq-format/top.html>*

His tips, some of which are highly technical in nature, are equally applicable to the Web and Usenet FAQ worlds. Some of his basic recommendations should be of interest to every FAQ writer.

These are excerpted below.

General FAQ Format

Most FAQs lend themselves to a format like:

```
<news headers>
<news.answers required headers, if the FAQ is registered>
<title and author>
<section>
<section>
<section>
<section>
```

While FAQs aren't always lists of questions and answers, they usually have "sections" of text—whether they be sets of lists, individual Q&A's, groups of Q&A, textual sections, or suchlike.

FAQ Page Section Format

A "section" is merely a block of text. In many FAQs they are simply the introductory paragraph, the table of contents, and each question and answer. Through the use of digest format, most newsreaders can skip from section to section using the convention presented here, and more sophisticated packages can hypertext them.

A "section" consists of:

```
<blank line>
<string of 30 hyphens>
<blank line>
Subject: <subject line>
<additional optional RFC822-like headers>
<blank line>
<text>
```

Subject Line

The subject can be any arbitrary string of text. You may wish to use a numbering scheme, for it makes it easier for your readers to "grep" down to the precise section they want.

Table Of Contents

The Table of Contents simply consists of the subject lines from the rest of the FAQ, excluding "Subject:", and preferably is indented. The subject lines should be exact copies of the section headers.

This is only a suggestion. There is no existing software that parses this data. The intent of using exactly the same strings as the subjects is to enable users to use search mechanisms to find specific sections. If the subject line is too long to fit into a Table of Contents line, it is suggested that you truncate it at a convenient point—the search will still work.

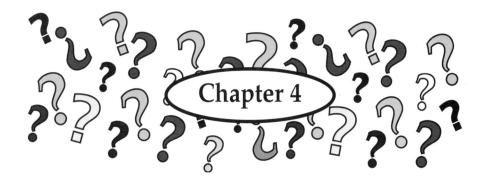

Initial FAQ Lists and Tips

In this chapter, you'll learn…

- Determining where you should post your FAQ
- How often you should post?
- Sources of content
- What level of sophistication should you use
- What are the potential legal issues?

You've now made your mind up to write a Frequently Asked Questions list for your Web site or newsgroup. It's like the mountain climber. Asked why he would ascend the icy, scaly peak, he, or she says, "Because it's there." You have a place on the Internet and you want to help your site visitors gain the experience of a user-friendly environment. Congratulations, because you are only about two percent of the way there.

Many decisions await. Five of the most important questions you'll need to answer are:

- Where should I post?
- How often should I post?
- Where should I generate my content from?
- Will I need to take any legal precautions?
- What general tone should I set: elementary, intermediate, or advanced?

Russ Hersch, who prepared the FAQ about FAQs list on several newsgroups and Web sites, including *news.answers* and *http://www.med.umich.edu/cgi-bin/ uncomp/faqs/about-faqs*, thinks that as a general rule, more is better. Using some of his recommendations as a base, and expanding on them for relevancy to the broader FAQ-writing community, some of the places where you might think about posting and distributing a FAQ are:

- Your own site or group, first. A no-brainer, huh?

- Newsgroups with interrelated missions to your own. You might take a look at the traffic in your newsgroup, and cross-reference some of the text of the messages to see if other newsgroups are mentioned to any degree. If a pattern emerges, it is accurate to assume that at least some of your crowd lurks there as well.

- Going along with the above recommendation, here's a fun trick I've just thought of. If you run a newsgroup, with, say 500 messages archived over the past two weeks, thread through them and see who the 20 or so most frequent posters are. Write down their Email addresses. Then go to DeJa News, the superb newsgroup search engine, and key in these addresses. It will tell you where else each of these people have posted in the last few months. Should there be several other newsgroups with frequent cross-citations, it would probably be right to assume a commonality of interest. Then go to that group. Do they have a FAQ? No? Would yours fit there? Post it and see what happens.

- Cross-post to Web sites and newsgroups. If you are a Web site FAQ writer for a branded product, computer program, or entertainment-industry entity, I'll bet you six ways to Sunday there is a compatible newsgroup. The reverse applies as well. That corresponding Web site or newsgroup might want to have a FAQ, but no one has had the time to write one. Be nice and offer yours. This is a great way to make new friends, get new customers, and build up a reservoir of both favors owed and karma due.

  This door can swing both ways. You can acquire as well as offer. If you are a FAQ maintainer for a site or group, you can go on fishing expeditions for compatible FAQs in other places, contact the maintainers, and ask them for permission to post their FAQ on your site.

Jan Hardenbergh, maintainer of the FAQ on the Oki Advanced Products Web site (*http://www.oki.com*), regularly surfs for FAQs on compatible Usenet groups. "I've found FAQs on the Usenet groups and mailed the author for permission (VERY IMPORTANT) and had them send me any more FAQs they wrote, plus I posted for all FAQ writers to send me new FAQs they have written," she reports. See Figure 4.1.

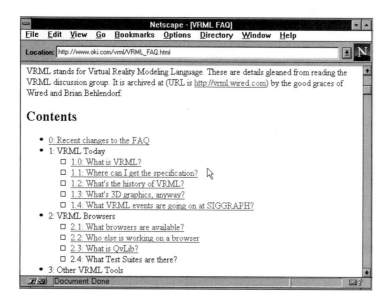

FIGURE 4.1 THE OKI VRML FAQ.

- Don't overlook the online services. America Online, CompuServe, the Microsoft Network, and Prodigy all have several dozen chat groups and subject archives that might be ideal perches for your FAQ.

- Bulletin Board Systems. There is a trend toward dial-up bulletin boards transforming themselves into Web sites, but the process is in the puberty stage; there are tens of thousands of bulletin boards that are local dial-up only. Some are toying around with telnet access, but not many of them. Local boards can be about mostly anything: especially business, games, or sex (one might argue that there isn't an impenetrable firewall between those three).

You might want to scour a database of local bulletin boards and see which ones might be topically close enough to carry your FAQ. They might appreciate it as a booster for their own traffic.

Finding local dial-up BBSes isn't as easy as locating Web sites or newsgroups, but there are a couple of effective ways to do so. *Online Access* magazine, widely available in better bookstores and magazine counters, prints a CD-ROM every six months or so with a list of BBSes searchable by specialty and area code. Computer Shopper Magazine periodically posts its BBS User Groups Directory on its Web site at http://www.zdnet.com/cshopper/bbs. Many of these have Email addresses and some are telnetable. An enlightened and growing number of them are mirrored as Web sites. Go there or contact them and offer to post your FAQ.

- Manufacturers' literature. Because numerous Web sites and newsgroups are about products, this is an effective exposure enhancer for Web and Usenet FAQs. Hersch says he has given his permission to several major corporations to include portions of his microcontroller FAQs in various product/technical documents. Hersch also suggests contacting authors or publishers with books or pamphlets coming out on the same topic your FAQ is about. Based on his experience, he says the response might be highly favorable. Many authors or publishers like to include portions of the appropriate FAQs in their works, giving the reader an easy way to find more information on the subject. I guess we're practicing what he preaches right here in this book.

How Often Should You Post?

As a general rule, post more often in Usenet than on the Web. I've seen some perfectly acceptable FAQs on Web sites that haven't changed in months. Leave it untouched for too long, however, and you are flirting with danger.

There's a rather fascinating, seldom-discussed paradox with FAQs on Web sites. You want people to come to your Web site often, and do whatever—gaze at new automobiles, play Tetris-clone games, do electronic commerce. But you don't necessarily want them to come to your FAQ page every session, because that would indicate a degree of confusion. You have to walk a very fine line between making your FAQ entertaining enough to draw frequent hits, but not having it serve as a convenient crutch.

Some people are forgetful and lazy, and need their hand held at every URL. If they keep coming back to your FAQ, maybe it wouldn't be such a terrible idea to add something new every once in a while, even if there isn't much new to explain. How often? Maybe once a month.

Usenet FAQ postings simply have to be more frequent, because as we've explained, they are prone to fall off after to or three weeks. You don't want to make the newbie mess with searching through an FTP archive to obtain your precious, missing FAQ, so take the path of least resistance and repost every couple of weeks. Who knows, you might even have new questions to add.

Because there are ways to repost newsgroup FAQs automatically, you may not have to do it yourself. The several *.answers* newsgroups, like *news.answers*, *sci.answers*, and *alt.answers*, have moderators that evaluate and approve Usenet FAQs. If you pass this test, you can use their FAQ-server to set up an automatic reposting to the given newsgroup without you having to do it yourself. Go to the specific *.answers* newsgroup in your hierarchy for more information.

There are also a number of FTP sites that might be willing to act as a repository. Look for them in Web directories like Lycos by keying in **ftp** and then the general subject matter of your FAQ in the search field. This will take you to FTP sites that are already disposed to storing FAQs, as well as to those who can be easily found by folks combing FTP sites for FAQs. After all, you found it, didn't you?

WHERE SHOULD YOU GET YOUR QUESTIONS FROM?

Another key issue is what sources should be used to generate FAQ questions. Most Webmasters say these come from an internal consensus of what it is important for your site visitors to know, combined with updating based on the "real" questions posed to customer support via Email or phone. Frank Voci, vice-president of production and creative affairs for c/net, says that a good start-up strategy for a new site FAQ would be to see what issues FAQs in similar industries address. "The best way to start making your own FAQ is to read as many others as possible to see what the recurring questions throughout the Web are. Make a list of those 'frequently asked-frequent asked questions,'" he says. In Voci's case, he found that many of those questions included the topics of downloading and playing multimedia files, using hyperlinks, and Email.

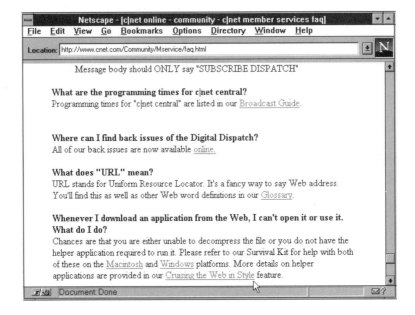

FIGURE 4.2 QUESTIONS ABOUT MULTIMEDIA APPEAR ON THE C/NET FAQ.

"We constantly monitor the traffic to the Web site, and the content of the feedback we receive. We would change the FAQ as needed. If we decide to post a significantly technical subject, I'm sure the building of a FAQ would be part of the process of placing it on the Web," says Susan Chatman, Webmistress of the Silicon Studio site since its launch in October, 1994. Silicon Studio, which provides high-tech production resources for the entertainment industry, is a wholly owned subsidiary of Silicon Graphics.

Sometimes, creating an initial FAQ list for a new site is a classic chicken-egg dilemma. How can there be "Frequently Asked" questions if there hasn't yet been a place to ask them?

The best way to get around this problem: listen to what is going on inside your head. You, the FAQ writer, should put yourself in the mind of someone who might want information about what you are writing about. You may not have written a FAQ before, but odds are you've had at least informal discussions with people about your area of coverage. Since some of them won't know as much as you do about their specialty, the odds are you already are being "asked" questions frequently without you realizing it's been going on.

Jordan Lund, maintainer of the *alt.fan.authors.stephen-king* group FAQ, has quantified this process more than most. Lund, whose FAQ has consistently earned high marks from most of the online site-rating services, believes that a FAQ can serve a wide range of sophistication without either being "dumbed-down" or going over people's heads. "The one thing I can think of is that once you start a list of Frequently Asked Questions and their answers, you can either set some ground rules or limits for yourself in advance or you will never stop answering questions. You need to define for yourself what constitutes frequently," he says. "If five people Email me and ask the same question I can bet it's on the minds of many more, it might merit dealing with in the FAQ, but I usually wait and see what is being asked in the public areas first, what questions are always generating public threads before I address Email questions. See if different people are asking essentially the same questions over and over again and see if other people are complaining `THAT QUESTION? AGAIN? WE JUST ANSWERED THAT!'" he continues. "Chances are that group needs a FAQ." Keep in mind that a FAQ isn't just for the benefit of the people that don't know all the answers yet, it's also for the benefit of the people who have been around for a while and are on the verge of madness because they keep seeing the same questions over and over again.

Back to the updating quandary for a moment; since his FAQ is on a visible, public figure, Lund monitors the news. When Stephen King announces a book tour, or a movie based on one of his books is cast, Lund will anticipate such questions (i.e., "Is Stephen King coming to Portland?"), and enhance the FAQ by anticipating the questions before they roll in. For many maintainers, this may mean establishing a line of communication with a celebrity's public relations representatives.

Maybe you also have questions yourself, like Dave Dennis did. Dennis, maintainer of the Internet Provider FAQ, initially approached his FAQ that way. "I thought about the questions I had a hard time getting answers to (i.e. `What is a router?' and `how does this all fit together?' and wrote them down. My first version of the Internet Provider FAQ was only 512 lines." Subsequently, Dennis continues, "I had more questions, and I put them and their answers in the FAQ on an ongoing basis."

Also, don't be reluctant to ask your peers for advice. This was the approach taken by Dean Radin, director of the Consciousness Research Laboratory at the University of Nevada In Las Vegas. The Parapsychology FAQ is on the *sci.skeptic* newsgroup, Radin's group, as well as on the Web at *http://eeyore.lv-hrc.nevada.edu/~cogno/cogno.html*. "The first draft I wrote was just off the top of my head," he admits. "I've heard so many questions over the years that I knew 90% of what anyone who ask. The other authors added some new questions and added significantly to the content, clarity, and balance of the FAQ. I don't think that any of my original questions were deleted from the FAQ, and we've only added one or two since the fifth draft was completed."

LEGALITIES

As stated in the Berne Convention, copyright automatically is assigned to the writer of the work. Putting a FAQ up on a Web site, newsgroup, or in product literature is protection enough. Several Web sites and newsgroups about Internet law can give you more information, including:

The Internet and Computer Law Assn., http://grove.ufl.edu/~cmplaw/, and Law of Electronic Commerce, http://www.infohaus.com/access/by-seller/Benjamin_Wright.

A disclaimer might be useful if your advice has the potential to profoundly affect someone's life. A FAQ on an investment-advice Web site that touts the growth potential of certain types of stocks might land you in hot water should the prices hit the tank and lose someone thousands of dollars. You probably won't be in any danger, but there are litigious sharks out there.

Hersch isn't an attorney, but he's respected and experienced enough in the FAQ-writer community so that his boilerplate exclaimer posted on FAQ About FAQs carries cachet:

"This article is provided as is without any express or implied warranties. While every effort has been taken to ensure the accuracy of the information contained in this article, the author/maintainer/contributors assume(s) no responsibility for errors or omissions, or for damages resulting from the use of the information contained herein."

STRUCTURE AND TONE

There is little agreement here, but a couple of rules generally apply:

- Start it simple with the basics, and progress to greater complexity from there.
- If you find yourself branching out into multiple tangents of increasingly complicated dialectic, it's probably time for a multiple FAQ.

There is no magical cutoff point that will automatically tell a FAQ maintainer to split the FAQ up into multiple ones. It's a judgment call, the nuances of which we'll explore in the next chapter.

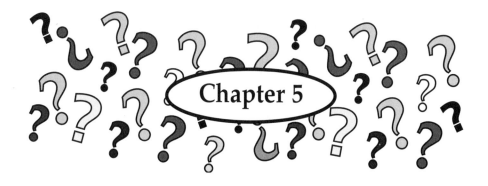

WHEN DO YOU DIVIDE AND HOW DO YOU RUN YOUR FAQ?

In this chapter, you'll learn:

- Whether you should divide your FAQ or keep it unified
- How your location on the Internet should influence your decision
- When is length an issue and when is it not?
- Breaking FAQs up into sections but keeping the FAQ together
- Who should administer your FAQ?

Suppose your Frequently Asked Questions list is a big hit in cyberspace. Thousands of visitors to your Web site or hundreds of newsgroup lurkers a day call on your creation, but you should consider that in time, you may become a victim of your own prosperity.

If you remember the splitting one-celled organisms you saw under the microscope in your high school biology class, you'll get the analogy. The primal creature is doing fine in its simplicity, until suddenly it grows too large for its cell walls and splits in two. Where once there was a portly protozoan, there are now two well-proportioned ones.

There may come a time when, like the protozoan, you'll have to divide to conquer. No hard and fast rules exist to guide you. It's more of a feeling you get that your list has so many subtopics and tangents that the central purpose of the thing—to explain the Web site, the product, or the newsgroup the FAQ resides on—is being buried under a decimal-point-ridden, overly long table of contents.

Two key matters to consider are: how to tell if your FAQ is a candidate for division, and if so, how to go about dividing it.

TO DIVIDE OR NOT: THAT IS THE QUESTION

The specific way you ask and answer these questions will have a lot to do with where on the Internet your FAQ is posted. At its starkest, this issue turns on the distinct differences between some *.com* Web FAQs, which are often written by marketing people as a guide to information about a company and its hundreds of products, and FAQs on newsgroups, which are there to explain a single issue or topic—most often without any commercial goal in mind. Use the following guidelines to help you decide whether to keep your FAQ unified.

- If your FAQ is on the *.com* domain of the Web, it's probably there to help the site explain, promote, or sell something. What is the nature of the business? Is it a Web site for an interior design firm, or the main online presence of a conglomerate with eight divisions and 37 brand-name products? A good model to follow is on the Magnavox site *http://www.magnavox.com*. With each linked from the customer support page, there are five separate FAQs, entitled "Television Frequently Asked Questions," "Audio Frequently Asked Questions," "Home Security Frequently Asked Questions," "Computer Frequently Asked Questions," and "Magnavox Frequently Asked Questions." Plainly, this is a textbook example of a situation in which divergent product lines dictate separate FAQs. See Figure 5.1.

- If your FAQ is on *.gov* or *.org*, what is the nature of the governmental unit or organization whose operations it is designed to explain? Whether it's an organization-run or government-affiliated federal, state or local site, such a FAQ will likely explore the various duties and divisions within the department. Does your organizational chart contain many branches? If so, it's likely that your FAQ will as well, creating the potential for bloatedness.

- If your FAQ is a *.edu* resident, especially one that is on a university site, it's almost a no-brainer that it ought to be split up, if it hasn't been already. A good university will have dozens of academic departments, with students and faculty in any given department who really don't give a whit about the others. Such FAQs are also likely to draw a significant amount of off-campus readership, such as from would-be applicants. Make it easy for them. Don't force them to comb through a jumbo subject tree for FAQ information about the course of study they want to major in, or the administrative procedure they need to follow to apply to that individual college.

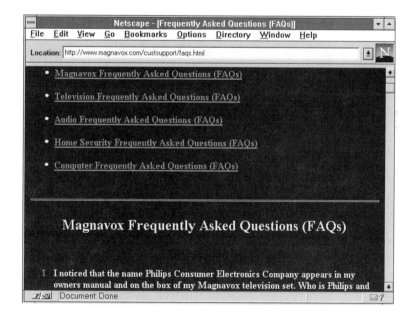

FIGURE 5.1 THE MAGNAVOX SITE HAS FIVE SEPARATE FAQS.

- If your FAQ is in the *.net* area, you have the most subjective decision of all your FAQ-writing Web brethren. Befitting the appellation, your site will likely have a significant technological component. If it's product-related, for example, how many products are you selling? If there's more than one, you must deal with a completely separate set of instructions. Should the instructions take more than a few pages in a hard-copy manual or more than a dozen or so screens of a HELP or README file, there will be too many questions to answer if you force this product to share a FAQ with every other one. There's also potential for customer good will here. A dedicated FAQ about an individual product can't help but create the notion that your company cares about each one of its brands and has taken the time to explain it thoroughly.

DIVIDING NEWSGROUP FAQS: THE ISSUES ARE DIFFERENT

Many newsgroup FAQs won't have to be divided. The reason for this is that by their constitution, a significant number of newsgroups deal with a topic that is so specific that dividing the FAQ up won't make any sense. Besides, where would you put it? You'd probably have to open up another thread. Since most postings stay up just a few weeks, that means running two FAQs on the same newsgroup will just overcomplicate your workload. It might not be worth your time, or you may not have the time. Judging from periodic conversations on the FAQ "Maintainers Listserv," hardly any newsgroup FAQ writers get paid for their troubles.

There are two exceptions to this, however: your newsgroup FAQ may be a viable candidate for break-up if it is too long, or if your group is general, with lots of disparate threads discussing widely varied topics. General newsgroups probably should have one sweeping FAQ dealing with posting policy, and maybe a couple more about hot subject areas that are most often discussed.

Sometimes FAQs grow because the nature of the postings change. This can happen for any number of reasons—the most common is that a hot new trend happens, engendering new threads that could cause the initial FAQ to swell and lose focus, but the new threads are close enough to the original intent of the newsgroup not to cause the group itself to splinter. In such cases, the most popular choice is not to break up the FAQ into different threaded postings, but to carefully subdivide it into distinct, separate sections. The "Netcom FAQ" is a good example of this. Netcom is one of the largest Internet-access companies, and operates a formidable national point-of-presence network. It also offers the NetCruiser Web browser; in providing both Internet access and navigability, there are a lot of questions to be answered and organized. A moderate-size, intelligently presented FAQ, it contains 33 questions in five subject fields. These include:

- Eight questions in the General section, starting off with "Where can I go for Netcom help and information?"

- Nine questions in the NetCruiser Accounts portion, leading with "Can I use the Windows 95 dialer to access my NetCruiser account?"

- Eight questions in the Shell Accounts area, kicking off with "What does the 'Password Adjunct' error mean?"

- Five more questions in the Macintosh Customers department, launching with "Does Netcom have NetCruiser for the Macintosh?"

- There are three more questions in a brief section entitled "Answers to questions not covered in this document may be found in..." Links are provided here to tech support resources and the phone number for Netcom's Fax-On-Demand service is also listed.

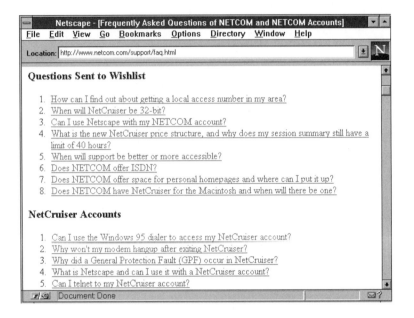

FIGURE 5.2 NETCOM HAS ONE LARGE FAQ BUT IT BREAKS UP INTO SECTIONS.

These links, incidentally, point out the difference between newsgroup and Web FAQs. Since the Web, of course, is more of a visual medium, FAQs can be split up and effectively put almost anywhere on the site. With a newsgroup FAQ, however, there are not too many places for it to go, or grow; either it serves as an impetus to start a new newsgroup and moves there, becomes a separate, periodically threaded post, or sits where it is and grows corpulent.

But there's a better way, according to Buzz McDermott, FAQ writer for the *rec.model.rockets* newsgroup. "Originally, the r.m.r. FAQ was in 1 section consisting of about 25 questions and answers. Its original intent was to be a reference document to point readers to other sources for complete answers. Over time, the interests of the *rec.models.rockets* group grew (i.e., first model rocketry, then high power rocketry, then amateur rocketry) and there was a corresponding increase in the numbers and range of questions being repeated every week. Also, international readership changed the scope of the group. At first, there was only interest in the U.S. form of the hobby. Now the groups get questions and posts from more than a dozen countries."

As a result of this prosperity, the current r.m.r FAQ has grown to 16 parts, just under 9000 lines, and takes up about 450K bytes.

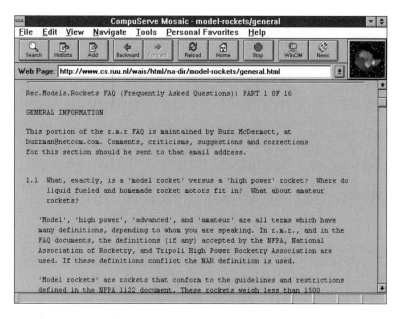

FIGURE 5.3 THE REC.MODELS.ROCKETS FAQ HAS 16 PARTS.

Bulkiness can present some problems for FAQ writers. In some circumstances, the size of the growing FAQ can be managed by putting in links as answers, rather than attempting a 2K general answer to a question and adding a link as well.

Plainly, this "rocketlike" growth presented McDermott with a dilemma. Something had to be done. "There were two reasons for going to multiple FAQs," McDermott says. According to him, these were:

- The size of the FAQ as a single document grew to exceed the capacity of some of the smaller Usenet sites to process. Around 50K seems to be a size where you start to see problems with document size at smaller sites.

- The FAQ was becoming too much work for me to keep updated by myself. I made the decision to solicit help from the newsgroup. Once I got an initial volunteer, we exchanged Email discussion of our areas of relative interest. It turned out we had a number of areas of non-overlapping interest. I broke up the FAQ along those lines. Over time, it has grown to where there are now eight FAQ 'editors' in seven countries around the world helping to produce the *r.m.r* FAQ. To facilitate that I broke the FAQ into more sections, and all but one section has a single individual entirely responsible for updates to that section.

Over time though, such corpulence resulted in a few inevitable spinoffs. These took the form of new, independent documents. "This has always happened at the specific request of an individual who felt the information contained in the document could best be presented in other than the FAQ question/answer paradigm that I try to maintain. An example is the *rec.models.rockets* glossary of hobby terms," McDermott continues. Posted within *rec.models.rockets*, "It started as several questions in the original FAQ asking about and explaining the meaning of a few terms. Another *r.m.r.* poster wanted to produce a much more complete glossary, so I replaced several definitions in the FAQ with a pointer to his new glossary document."

Size can get in the way in more ways than just the loss of clarity. Big FAQs can lead to technical problems. On the Web, that means longer transfer times and trying the user's patience. The transfer-time issue is also a concern for Dean Radin, director of the Consciousness Research Laboratory at the University of Nevada in Las Vegas. His lab has a Web presence at *http://eeyore.lv- hrc.nevada.edu/~cogno/cogno.html*. "We have one split into three HTML pages. It could be three times as large, but it already answers most people's questions. We split the pages because a single file would have been too long for people using modems," Radin says.

On Usenet, some newsreaders get anxiety attacks if they are forced to present very large documents. This is a common area of consternation for FAQ maintainers in all areas of the Internet.

"Speaking of size limits, I had an annoying experience," says David Roth, co-author of the "Hosaphone FAQ" (*rec.arts.marching*), a newsgroup dedicated to a trumpet-like instrument used by many marching bands. "I posted it to two Internet mailing lists that both use MAJOR-DOMO (a utility used by listservs to manage forwarding of new postings). I waited and waited, and it never appeared. No message was sent back to me or anything." Roth suspects that sinister forces were at work. "It seems the default limit for message sizes in MAJORDOMO which I believe is called maxlength or something like that is 40K. Nothing in the info about the mailing lists that use MAJORDOMO has this as info about posting guidelines," he says. Frustration inevitably resulted. "The most annoying part is I didn't get an error message or anything from either one of them when I tried to post the entire thing as one 42K FAQ. The owner would get the error, and would have to write to you and tell you what to do."

FAQ maintainers at software-related groups have an even more specific challenge when faced with the 64K size barrier. That's because some groups like to include sample selections of source code for programs or applets within a FAQ. Such code can eat up valuable space, as Vic Metcalfe will attest. Metcalfe maintains the UNIX-socket FAQ (*http://www/auroraline.com/sockfaq-unix-socket-faq*) a UNIX network-programming FAQ frequently accessed by Webmasters and software writers needing information about the Byzantine world of UNIX network programming.

"There is a section at the bottom of my FAQ which contains sample source code," he notes. "Samples are really important to programming documentation, as most programmers learn better from seeing a working model than from reading about one. But the last issue of the FAQ grew past 64K, and (his newsreader) wouldn't accept the posting, so I had to strip the source code from the bottom of the FAQ to make room."

Dividing the FAQ may be Metcalfe's best option. "I am thinking about making the source into a part 2 section of the FAQ," he says, "and putting it in the form of a shell script, so that users that want to try it out can simply edit out the Usenet header and run it to get the files created.

This would generate a larger posting, but it would be readable by human eyes."

An alternative which Metcalfe is exploring would make the critical source code available in a file that could be accessed via FTP (file transfer protocol). He spent much of 1996 considering this option, weighing the pros and cons between the added informational advantages of supplying source code via FTP vs. a perceived fear that obligating an FTP transfer just to come in under 64K would create an atmosphere of user-unfriendliness.

Russ Hersch, author of "The FAQs about FAQs" treatise carried by several Web sites and newsgroups, deals with this touchy subject in his document. "FAQs have no size limit, although sometimes a system may impose certain restrictions—64K is always a magic number," he writes. "I've also seen 100K used as a limit. In addition to system limits, FAQs that are very large (over 64K) might be difficult to handle. You might consider splitting your FAQ up into pieces, with each piece having its own theme."

Some sites run on older servers that can't efficiently process large gulps of text at once. "Many old Usenet sites will not accept articles over 64K," Hersch notes. "Some on-line services have smaller limits (32K for America Online). FAQ maintainers have to make a trade-off between the universality that they wish their FAQ to achieve, and the convenience of one large article as opposed to several smaller articles."

Not all FAQ writers and maintainers are put off by size, though. Such a view holds that continuity and consistency are sacrificed when a FAQ is divided. Jan Hardenbergh, maintainer of the "VRML FAQ" on the "Oki Advanced Products" Web site, as well as being a FAQ writer for several newsgroups, is an ardent proponent of "united we stand," in both the Usenet and Web FAQ kingdoms. See Figure 5.4.

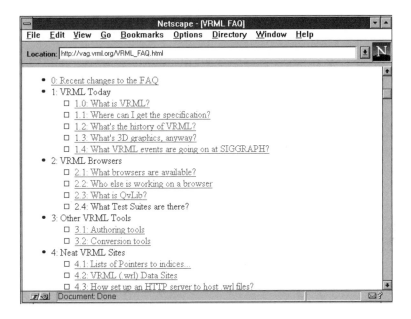

FIGURE 5.4 THE OKI ADVANCED PRODUCTS VMRL FAQ.

"The trend seems to be towards keeping FAQs in one piece, no matter how large they get," she says. "I recently asked the readers of my microcontroller FAQs if they wanted the FAQs split into multiple parts or kept in one piece. Even though two of the FAQs are over 100K, and the third is approaching 100K, the results were unanimously for keeping each of the FAQs intact and in one piece." According to Hardenbergh, "the convenience of not having to juggle different pieces of the document (both for the author/maintainer and for the reader) outweighs the inconvenience of an occasional newsreader program that can't handle large articles. Also, most on-line services are in the process of removing size restrictions, making the size of the FAQ more dependent on personal taste, and less on "technology" (or the lack thereof).

Finding a Good Web Site FAQ Administrator

Anyone can administer a FAQ. Titles and duties run the gamut. Here are some alternatives for the administration of Web site FAQs and occasions when each choice works the best:

- A technical services support person. This would probably be a good choice for FAQs on sites that are run by companies with a strong gizmo-oriented product base, and/or have lots of technological wizardry on the site itself. If you're running Java, RealAudio, Shockwave, and Quicktime applications, technical support will be getting a lot of questions. On the front lines—for Web sites in all domains—they should be the logical ones to write and administer the FAQ. John Dhabolt, manager of technical support for Natural Intelligence and the writer for the Roaster FAQs, is one such person.

- The Webmaster. At smaller companies and organizations, this person handles just about every Web-related event. Sometimes FAQ administration falls to him or her because there is no one else to do it. At many larger companies, the Webmaster has the ultimate responsibility for the FAQ but doesn't run or write it himself.

- The marketing department. FAQs in the corporate world are most often tools to make commercial sites work more effectively. If the function of the FAQ is to explain the benefits of a given product rather than to explain how to get around the site, someone in marketing would be good for the task.

- Outsourcing might work, whether to the public relations department or an outside p.r. firm. On *.com* Web sites, this would probably work for many of the same reasons that giving FAQ administration to the marketing department will. Because public relations people are supposed to have communications and writing skills, this may be another good reason to hand it off to them.

  The mere presence of such skills doesn't insure a good FAQ, however. A marketing or public relations person should at least have some basic knowledge about what the Internet and the Web are. Nothing could be more embarrassing than a dumb fluff of basic information, such as misdefining a term that most people know. I once had a self-defined "Web marketer" call me to pitch a story, but he didn't know what "URL" meant. Find the most Web-savvy person in your firm and have him or her "test" the prospective FAQ writer on Internet/Web 101 subject areas should work. This may sound like it has the potential for confrontation, but if the marketing person gets too defensive, it may cause you to question your entire business relationship with them.

- An advertising agency. The growth of the Web in mid-decade saw an explosion of Web-specialist advertising agencies that now offer many subset skills, such as FAQ writing and maintenance. To meet the mounting threat of competition, full-service ad agencies have been adding Web services departments. Also, if you already have a working relationship with your agency, they are probably involved in devising the message you want presented to the world and will be in the position to tailor the content on your Web site to conform to that message.

- Your hosting service. Some of the larger ones host hundreds of sites. There are those hosting operations that simply rent space to you on their server and don't provide any content counsel; others provide turnkey facilities, which include the full suite of site management functions, including content creation.

- Outside experts. Maybe someone has written a book or article on the same topic your Web site addresses, or is a recognized authority in the field. One approach would be for someone inside the company to write the policy part of the FAQ, and for the expert to compose the section where specific expertise is needed. Whether it is meeting them at trade shows, seminars or perhaps through your association or even your sales department, you probably already know several such individuals. Maybe you run the Web site for a pharmaceutical manufacturer and there's a professor at the local university who specializes in a similar subject. Ask around. Or, you can go on one of the

Web search services and look for such people by keying in a search string conforming to your topic. Lycos, (*http://www.lycos.com*), and Alta Vista (*http://www.altavista.digital.com*), are two of the best. You should get several "hits," which will probably include the author of the cited pieces and their electronic mail addresses.

The larger companies that perform such services will also be in the position to give you the benefit of their experience. With 300 or so sites under their care, the odds are good that they've run sites and FAQs for companies in businesses related to yours.

- A freelance FAQ maintainer. Most members of this subculture are Usenet newsgroup FAQ administrators, not Web FAQ writers. Yet hundreds of newsgroups are topically connected with governmental or corporate counterparts. These folks have a depth of knowledge and experience about how to run FAQs. Since they are probably not paid for their Usenet contributions but obviously enjoy this work, they would be likely to jump for joy should you contact them with an offer to administer your FAQ on a freelance basis.

There are several good ways to look for this talent. Use your newsreader to see if there are any Usenet newsgroups that relate to what your company makes or your governmental bureau does. Go to the newsgroup and look for the FAQ. The name and contact information for the FAQ writer should be contained in the message header. If you like what you see, boot up your Email utility and initiate contact.

Two other good ways to find FAQ maintainers are by reading the posted Usenet FAQs in the *.answers* archives. Each of the major Usenet hierarchies maintains its own archives of FAQ postings, as found in *news.answers*, *sci.answers*, *rec.answers*, and so forth. Or, you can join the *FAQ-Maintainers@consensus.com Listserv*, a mailing list that doesn't restrict talk about FAQs just to the maintainer community.

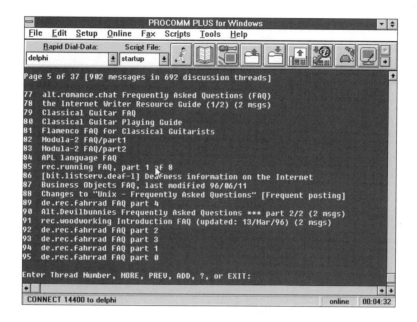

FIGURE 5.5 USENET FAQS LISTED IN THE *NEWS.ANSWERS* ARCHIVES.

LOOKING FOR NEWSGROUP FAQ MAINTAINERS

A newsgroup FAQ maintainer is often the same person who administers the overall group. He or she may be the best authority on what the group stands for, as well as an expert on the field it covers.

When McDermott split up his FAQ, he did what many in the newsgroup world do—asked for knowledgeable volunteers. His guiding principle was that when a newsgroup's topical thrust and threads broaden past a certain point, the knowledge, even of a rocketry buff like himself, simply can't be authoritative enough to originate, compose, and post FAQ questions about every single topic. This is an exercise in humility that FAQ writers everywhere would do well to follow. "The choice of FAQ section editors was made by a simple request for volunteers. You generally get little enough response so that there is not any problem of several people all wanting to do the same thing. I also solicited help from a number of 'experts' in the hobby who were regular contributors to the newsgroup," McDermott says. The outreach worked wonders. "A simple, polite request to the current world scale-space-modeling champion got me a complete rewrite of the section on scale modeling," he says proudly.

As in many other types of business relationships, it is best to sculpt an agreement about how the FAQ will be set up and administered *before* it goes up. People get promoted, transferred or leave. You don't want to leave your Web FAQ a neglected stepchild, with the next person left clueless about how it was formulated or how it should be handled.

Regardless of who administers your FAQ and how many FAQs you offer, you'll have to decide on a general tone for this tutorial. We'll explore the "basic vs. detailed" issue in the next chapter.

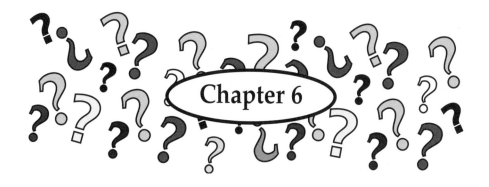

How Basic or Detailed Should My FAQ Be?

In this chapter, you'll learn:

- "Basic" and "detailed" are subjective definitions
- How to set a tone appropriate to your readership or clientele
- How to define the knowledge level of your readership
- If your FAQ readers are different from your site visitors
- Offsite places for your detailed FAQ Answers
- Offsite links for detailed questions: good or bad

I remember my early elementary school years all too well. Diagnosed a "borderline genius," whatever that means, I could find any country on the globe, name all the planets, and do complex arithmetic calculations by the time I was seven.

That served well for my proud parents, but it made me a restless pupil. While I was thinking about the moons of Neptune or doing multiplication drills in my head, the teachers were explaining how, when you add two plus two, you get four. I was interpreting National Weather Service maps while the rest of the class was into the adventures of Dick, Jane, and Spot.

The result: although I wouldn't have used the vernacular at the time, I got bored and thought that school really sucked. So the boy borderline genius became a teenager slacker before slacker was cool.

What does this have to do with FAQs? A lot. Properly done, Frequently Asked Questions lists can function as a lesson plan for your newsgroup or World Wide Web site. Think about it. On the lead FAQ page, there's usually a table of contents. You then proceed with an introduction in the form of your first question. Then, each subsequent question or section of your FAQ functions like a chapter in a textbook. The site-search engine you employ on your FAQ to enable word searches is like the index of the book, and the links you insert are like a bibliography of "further reading."

The only problem is that while all men and women may be "created equal," we learn at different rates to a site visit. Some of us will bring more preparatory understanding and background than others. There will be those reading your FAQ who may be unfamiliar with jargon that just about everyone in your occupational and social circle uses dozens of times a day. Some will have short attention spans, and not absorb lengthy descriptions of concepts well. Perhaps English won't be the first language of some of your visitors, and they will have trouble understanding idiomatic or overly arcane phrases. Hey, this is the **World Wide Web** we're talking about!

Conversely, "dumbing down" your FAQ can have deleterious effects. Because they've come to your site, you must assume that at least some of your visitors have a bit of grounding in whatever it is you are dealing with—hotel reservation how-tos, what is a Java application, what actress played Deanna Troi on "Star Trek: The Next Generation."

STRIKE A BALANCE

So, a balance must be struck. There's nothing wrong with a "What is..." as your first FAQ question, but unless you are creating different levels of FAQs on the same subject for varying knowledge levels, don't let too many of your initial questions dwell on the remedial stuff.

That's a general guideline. In deciding how basic or detailed a FAQ should be, though, there are numerous intricacies the FAQ writer has to keep in mind. "Basic" and "detailed," after all, are amorphous, abstract concepts, often specifically defined by a community of users or the individual FAQ writer or reader. When it comes time to write the FAQ, the writer will bring his or her notions to the computer screen. In deliberating what kinds of questions to put in as well as how to answer them, there needs to be some pre-planning. Here are some of the factors that you should consider and solutions to guide you on how to tilt the "basic" vs. "detailed" scale.

Define Your Audience

Who is your audience? Silicon Valley programmers? Newbies? Movie cultists? If your readership is narrowly-based, with a specific interest, it's likely that with the exception of a few lurking curiosity-seekers, your community will be quite knowledgeable about the basics of your product or topic. No reason to insult their intelligence by simplifying too many of the questions down to an elementary level.

Notice we said "too many of the questions." That doesn't mean it would be wrong to start with the basics and advance from there. Beginners should be find the first questions helpful, and more advanced users can go straight to the later questions which will answer their needs more appropriately.

There's a philosophical argument for this multi-tier approach. Some will look for a FAQ, and like the mountain climber who scaled the peak "because it's there," click to the FAQ for the same essential reason. This argument contends that FAQs, by their very nature, are going to attract the more curious browsers. If FAQs are well-written, they won't necessarily produce closure of inquiry, but will stimulate more curiosity and questions.

Start with the Basics

Even if you're absolutely convinced your Web site or newsgroup is only hit by the knowledgeable, there's still a powerful justification for some basic FAQ questions. Every month, millions of people around the world are gaining the ability to access the Internet. Given the staggering numbers involved, you're likely to get visits from a few newbies by virtue of random chance alone. Energized by what for them is a new experience, ("hey, look, I'm on the Web!!") you have the opportunity to make friends or new customers if the FAQs for your site do not present too daunting an experience. So start your questions simply, and go forward from there. "I first have some basic stuff and then delve into details. Starters will read only the first parts and more experienced users will skip to later parts," says Perry Rovers, maintainer of the "Anonymous FTP" FAQ, shown in Figure 6.1.

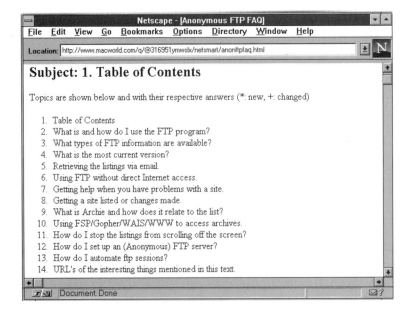

FIGURE 6.1 THE "ANONYMOUS FTP" FAQ.

"I believe in answering the question as simply as possible, at least in the first two sentences. Then hit them with detail. My attitude is that this FAQ will be picked up, downloaded, and printed, to be read at one's leisure," agrees Leslie Basel, FAQ maintainer for the *rec.food.preserving* newsgroup.

Fine-Tuning Your Audience(s)

Assuming you already have a Web FAQ, do you find that the people who read it are a different audience from your existing customer base? If your FAQ has a Webmaster or customer service mail-to, you can easily figure this out. Walk over to customer service or Email them and ask what kinds of questions they get over the phone and through Email links, if they have them.

If customer support operates a Help Desk with an automated series of push-button selections, they should have software that will enable them to tell what questions on the Help Menu are asked the most. Especially if you are a FAQ writer for a Web site that promotes technological products or even household appliances, this will give you a good sense of the skill level your customer base has, and how to tailor FAQ questions to the skill level of the most petitioners for help. "Look at tech support mail to see what questions are being asked. Phrase them in that way," says Jamie Holmes, FAQ writer for Progressive Networks' *RealAudio* Web site.

If you write FAQs for newsgroups, go through each thread microscopically and analyze the relative knowledge levels of the various respondents. Are some of the threads—and messages within these threads—overly simplistic, while others imply substantial knowledge of the subject? If this is the case, your newsgroup probably appeals to a wide audience and your FAQ should be balanced between introductory, intermediate, and sophisticated questions.

"The questions should be as nearly identical to what people are writing in the newsgroup as possible so that they can identify that their questions are being addressed," says Jordan Lund, FAQ maintainer for the "Stephen King Dark Tower" FAQ.

"I include articles that are basic ("what is stock") as well as advanced ("tax complications of shorting stock"). I guess I'm trying to be all things to all people. The basic questions are the true *raison d'etre* of a FAQ, because they help newbies get started," adds Christopher Lott, who writes a common FAQ for the *misc.invest* and *misc.invest.stocks* newsgroups, shown in Figure 6.2.

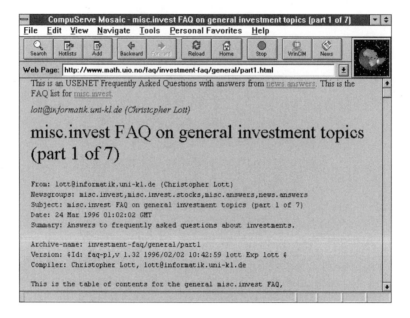

FIGURE 6.2 THE *"MISC.INVEST"* NEWSGROUP FAQ.

Simple Questions, Tricky Answers

Can the candidate questions be answered simply? Sometimes a question might be simple but the answer cannot be accurately phrased in anything but complex language. On other occasions, the answer, while not complicated in and of itself, would require 4K to cover all the ground it needs to. Getting by with just the basics, and then putting in a "for more information" link to an outside source or publishing it in a specialized document could be the solution for you.

Sometimes a FAQ writer will also stay away from complicated questions because the answer is over his or her head: it's a wise person who knows his or her limitations. Then, Madame Fortune calls, and the maintainer happens on a source that answers the question so succinctly that bells go off. "The advanced questions were put in when I found an article that explained the issue particularly well and it seemed like a shame not to include it," adds Lott, who got permission to use the quotes he excerpted.

Links May Help

Do you include the answers to detailed questions in your FAQ or do you link to sites where they can be answered more completely? This is one of the hottest topics of debate in "maintainerdom." The CNN Web site, which uses just about every multimedia application in existence, has very brief definitions of some of these programs, but provides links to the Web sites of companies who make the products discussed, as can be seen in Figure 6.3.

The flip side of this argument is the feeling by some that the failure of a FAQ writer to adequately explain a concept within the FAQ itself is a sign either of laziness or lack of knowledge. Buzz McDermott, FAQ maintainer for the *rec.models.rockets* newsgroup, has been down this road. "I started with simple questions with general answers. I tried to point to other books, archive sites, etc., as much as possible rather than answer questions directly," he says. "When I received multiple 'suggestions' that an answer was incomplete or a question too simplistic, I then updated and expanded that question and/or answer."

We'll discuss this issue more thoroughly in Chapter 10, but there's also a fear on the part of some Webmasters that if you "send them away," they (site visitors) won't come back.

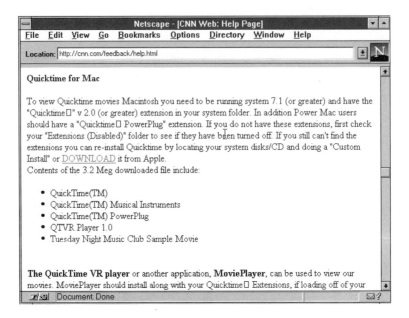

FIGURE 6.3 CNN's WEB SITE FAQ STICKS TO BASICS, BUT LINKS TO FAQS ON
OTHER SITES FOR MORE DETAILS.

How Much Detail?

If your FAQ is to have some "detailed" questions, what kind of "detail"
are we talking about? Software companies face this problem frequently.
Most software comes with README documentation files that act as an
onscreen tutorial for the user. Some READMEs are constructed in a
menu-driven format, while others essentially serve as bundled FAQs.
Some software companies solve the basic vs. detailed dilemma by
putting less-complicated questions on their Web site FAQ and using the
README for more specific, operational command-related topics.

This is the approach taken by Natural Intelligence, Inc., which makes the
multimedia-enabling, Java-compliant family of Roaster software products.
Roaster (*http://www.natural.com*), is a development tool that designers of
multimedia-offering Web sites use to compile Java applets. "We usually
write our Web FAQ to the least common denominator," says John Dhabolt,

manager of technical support for Natural Intelligence and the writer for the Roaster FAQs. "The new user needs to be able to understand the basics first. Once you get into the power users, though, the issues they care about are going to be of a different type than would normally be put in a FAQ." Because Roaster is a specialized application that assumes a degree of professional knowledge and acumen on the part of its users, Dhabolt assigns higher-level topics to the README file. It isn't a strict system of hierarchical separation, though: the Web FAQ links to the README file so that prospective buyers have a better idea of what awaits them.

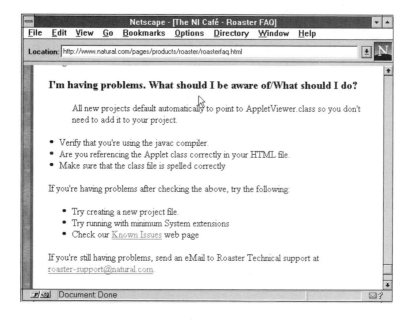

FIGURE 6.4 ROASTER'S WEB FAQ QUOTES FROM ITS README FILE.

DON'T LIMIT FAQ PLACEMENT TO THE FAQ PAGE

As many other skilled FAQ writers do, Dhabolt realizes that FAQs can spark other types of dialog than more questions. The answers can also lead to tangential but useful discussions about related technologies. For this purpose, he has started a Known Issues page on the site. The tone most frequently taken on this page is the explanation of technical bugs that the company knows about and intends to fix in forthcoming versions of its software. These matters presumably could be explored in a questions-and-answers format on the FAQ itself, but the existence of the Known Issues page allows Dhabolt to migrate all these topics to one central location. Known Issues is linked from the FAQ, but this way the FAQ itself is freed up for broader exploration. See Figure 6.5.

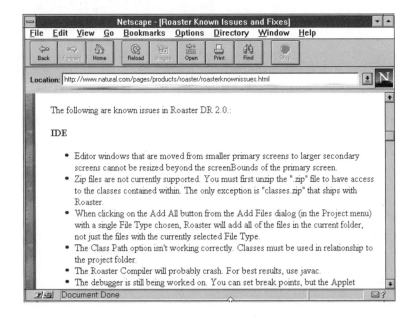

FIGURE 6.5 ROASTER'S KNOWN ISSUES PAGE IS LINKED FROM THE ROASTER FAQ.

A related, useful approach some software FAQ writers take is to put a wide-ranging series of subjects on their Web site FAQ and put meatier FAQs on floppies.

RSA Data Security, Inc., a leading Internet cryptography company, does this. Their Web FAQ (*http://www.rsa.com/rsalabs/FAQ*) kicks off with basic questions, like "What is encryption?" "What is authentication?" and "What is a digital signature?" See Figure 6.6.

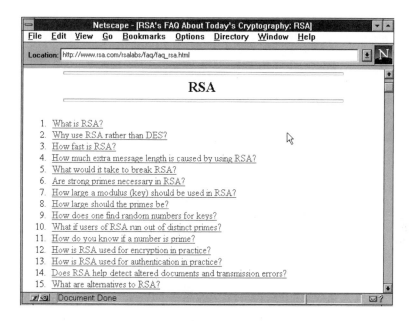

FIGURE 6.6 THE "RSA DATA SECURITY" FAQ.

Meatier specifics are put on disk in the form of "Answers to Frequently Asked Questions About Today's Cryptography." The disk, which contains more than 900K of data, is readable through the Adobe Acrobat PDF format. See Figure 6.7. The disk label includes Adobe's Web site address (*http://www.adobe.com*), from which a free Acrobat reader can be downloaded.

There are at least three additional practical reasons for using disks to house "graduate-level" versions of your Web FAQ. A disk like the one used for RSA's Cryptography FAQ can hold several hundred thousand bytes of data, but a FAQ that long on a single subject would be unwieldy on a Web site. There's also the issue of transfer time. It will be near the end of the decade until relatively slow 28.8K baud modems are ready for the museum, so for the time being, downloading massive amounts of FAQ text and GIFs from the Web can be timely (and costly) for many.

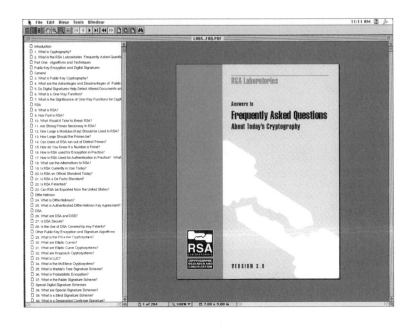

FIGURE 6.7 A MORE-EXTENSIVE RSA FAQ IS ON DISK, READABLE THROUGH THE ADOBE ACROBAT FORMAT.

Also, by their very nature, floppies or CD-ROMs are far better media to walk the FAQ reader through tutorial demonstrations of particular software attributes. These demonstrations, which can be appended to specific FAQ questions, would be more difficult to execute in the point-and-click environment of the Web, when just about all the computing power of the application would be on the remote server. Some Web sites also attempt to address this challenge by offering demo or tutorial software for download.

You've done all you can to identify the target audience—or audiences—for your FAQ. Perhaps you've done this before you've even written a FAQ. Your site has been up for months now, but you haven't felt you've needed a FAQ until now, because you weren't exactly sure what tone to set. Now that we've given you the information you need to decide what type of balance between basic and detailed content you should strive for, we'll talk about the timing and placement issues involved in getting a FAQ page up on the Internet.

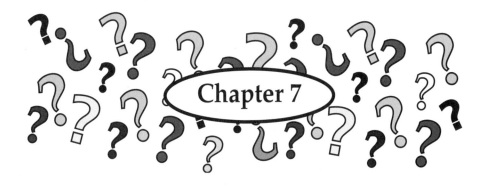

FAQ Rollout, Timing, and Placement

In this chapter, you'll learn:

- When you should post a FAQ before your site is up
- Planning for a FAQ with site rollout
- Timing your first newsgroup FAQ
- How to promote your FAQ
- How to list your FAQ on the search engines
- Where on your site your FAQ page link should be

Thousands of new Web sites go up every day, and hundreds of newsgroups are born each month. FAQ maintainers for these entities must be concerned with several timing and placement issues. Two of the more critical ones include, when you do your first FAQ, and where do you announce it.

Like so many things in this world, and perhaps other worlds as well, deciding when to do your first FAQ is a philosophical issue. Do you believe that a FAQ should be comprised of questions that are actually asked, or do you wait for the questions to start coming in before you inaugurate your first FAQ? Should you in fact put up an FAQ on rollout, or wait till you actually get questions? What did you do, and why? The issue is similar for Web and newsgroup FAQ writers, but because the two realms are so different in terms of organization and presentation, some of the logistical variables will differ greatly.

Let's first take a look at some FAQ rollout variables for Web sites. To decide when within the gestation, birthing, or maturation process your first FAQ should be posted, there are several things to think about.

THE SITE GESTATION PERIOD

Human beings, of course, take an average of nine months between conception and birth to be formed. Different mammals take shorter and a few, like the elephant, can take up to 11 months to come out of the womb. An almost identical model exists for Web sites. It takes time for that first gleam in the eye from a cyber-aware junior exec in the marketing department to work up the chain of command, until the decision about whether to put up a Web site reaches the desk of someone who can actually say yes.

After the initial approval, there will be the endless cost- benefit analyses, casting the (no pun intended) net out to find veteran employees or new who know HTML—or a worthy site-building service that can provide these skills. Within an effort to get other parts of the company excited enough to participate from a content-planning standpoint, there will be even more meetings. Your ad agency will likely want to be called in for input and perhaps more. After three or four stabs at it, you have a crude, alpha version of your site put up on your Local Area Network or company Intranet. Doubtless you've taken the time to register your site name as well.

Parts of the site are still being built, but on a rainy, manic Monday, you find out that three of your competitors' are rolling out new Web sites this week. You hurry up and put skeletal concept up on the Web, with the disclaimer that the full site is "Under Construction." To their credit, such sites rarely advertise. They frequently put up only one page "outside the firewall," with some message that the site is being built and to come back soon. Inside the company there may be battalions of Starbucksswilling worker bees racing to bring the site to the world in three weeks; from a current click, you wouldn't know it, though.

Is It Time Yet for a FAQ? Quite Likely, It Is

An important disclaimer first: at this stage, the FAQ you may want to put up will be substantially different from the one you'll administer as your site matures. The reason for this has to do with the typical state of a Web site that has gone up with an "Under Construction" sign. Such sites are not going to have the customer navigation or content-explanation issues that sites that have reached puberty often have to deal with. First of all, an "Under Construction" Web site is just that. It's real early. The site may only be a page or two. Its entire text might read something like, "Welcome to our site. It's under construction. Come back in a month for some exciting content!"

Hopefully your creative juices will enable a less generic introduction than that, but the FAQ writer is faced with a Catch-22 dilemma here. If the site has been put up prematurely just to secure the domain name and beat a competitor to the Web, that means that the site's features have not been specified in detail. Regardless of the domain, many Web FAQs devote a significant proportion of their questions to how-tos dealt with on the site: "How Do I Order?," "What hours is the law library open?," or "Where can I find a General Widgets service center in my area?"

It may not be time to write a FAQ until ambiguities in the overall site are cleared up. Providing cogent and clear answers is difficult if what the site visitor gets pointed to will only produce more confusion and frustration. Careful planning and design of the site can eliminate many questions from being asked in the first place. Clearly understandable, easy-to-find headers and links can enable the Web site to "support" the FAQ rather than the other way around.

If you haven't yet perfected the type of electronic commerce-facilitating Common Gateway Interface (an electronic mail utility included in most Web browsers) your site will use, nor completely worked out how you are going to migrate the names and addresses of your 534 authorized service agents from your internal database to a Zip Code-searchable content area on your site, it seems that it's too early to announce these specifics on a FAQ. You haven't identified the content, its presentation, or worked out all the bugs with regard to the technical aspects of your site.

Since so much of a Web FAQ will be content-explanation or technical tutorial, there won't be any questions to put up yet, because you won't even know the answers yourselves. But didn't I say earlier in the chapter that you should probably put up a FAQ anyway during gestation? Yes, I did. Let me explain what I mean.

During the "Under Construction" period for a Web site, there's nothing wrong with a FAQ being "Under Construction" too! This FAQ will substantially morph itself when the actual site debuts and grows, but even in the womb, a nascent Web FAQ can be useful. A good bit of promotional buzz can be put into the FAQ, such as in this hypothetical example of a FAQ that can be linked directly from the "Under Construction Home Page."

Q. What is GameGate?

A. GameGate is a brand-new company in Los Gatos, Calif. that will design and distribute CD-ROM games and Multi-User Dungeon platforms through retail channels as well as through direct order over this Web site.

Q. What are some titles you'll be offering?

A. Our first title, Neptune Man, will ship in about two months. We're working on several other exciting games we'll let you know about soon.

Q. Will your Web site offer Web-based games?

A. A bunch of us were discussing that over cappuccino last night. Web games are a strong possibility. Keep checking this space for news.

Q. Will you offer downloadable betas of your games?

A. We're thinking about it.

Q. Can I place an order for Neptune Man through this Web site?

A. Not yet, but we plan to build a Common Gateway Interface to let you do this sometime in the future.

Q. When will this site be fully operational?

A. In about a month. Bookmark us now. Come back then, and be sure to reload.

Q. I have an idea for a way cool game. How do I contact GameGate?

A. Email us at *fmulder@gamegate.com*, or call 408-555-0869.

Get the idea? This mythical company is so new, they only have one product and haven't exactly figured out mission-critical issues like marketing and electronic security. Their Web site is just two screens—an "Under Construction" announcement on the Home Page and a FAQ. But see how useful the FAQ is even at this early stage? It has served many purposes. A new company has been announced. However inexact, an exciting future has been articulated. Promotion has been presented under the forgivable guise of inquiry. Because feedback and game-development suggestions have been invited, a sense of community is already being formed. You've given visitors the incentive to bookmark your site and come back when your site is finally ready.

Such an approach works in other parts of the Web as well. In a skeletal form, the Web site for "Language: The Journal of the Linguistic Society of America," was brought to life while most of the content was under construction, but a FAQ was put up on rollout with the express purpose of touting what was to come, see Figure 7.1.

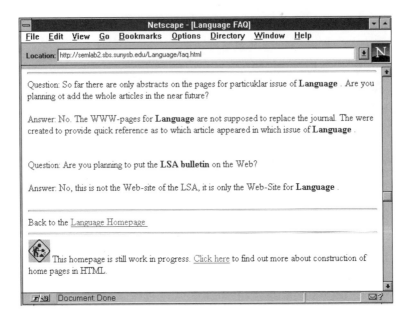

FIGURE 7.1 "LANGUAGE: JOURNAL OF THE LINGUISTIC SOCIETY OF AMERICA" PUT UP AN FAQ EVEN WHILE IT WAS UNDER CONSTRUCTION.

In summary, a FAQ might be worth your time—even in the Under Construction time period—if you want to convey a marketing or future content message.

CONGRATULATIONS, IT'S A SITE!

It's a month later and your site has finally gone up. There will be so much more information to impart. The nature of this information will depend on exactly how fully formed your site is. Even though you might not consider your site still Under Construction, all vibrant Web sites, in a sense, still are: new material keeps getting added as products are released, additional departments come on line, new multimedia applications come to your URL.

Maybe your site is going "live" tomorrow. Perhaps you haven't had time to think about putting up a FAQ. Now might be the right time to start but it depends on you. This would be a good occasion for you to log on to a search engine and look for Web sites put up by companies in the same industry as yours. If you are looking for a specific site, the simplest index is Yahoo! (*http://www.yahoo.com*). Once there, go to the search form box and type in either your industry segment or the name of a company or two that you compete with. Because Yahoo! is a basic index of Web sites, rather than the individual pages within them, such a strategy won't be the best way of routing you to FAQs. For that, I suggest any one of three more conclusive Web indexes: Lycos (*http://www.lycos.com*); Excite (*http://www.lycos.com*), or Open Text (*http://www.opentext.com*). In the search field, put in a company name, and then the word FAQ. You'll find hyperlinks to such resources, if they exist.

We discussed this some in Chapter 4, but at this point in time a FAQ decision will largely rest on what sources you derive your content from. If your company has been in business for awhile, there probably is an archive of questions that have frequently been asked of your sales staff, your customer support people, even you! You may want to take this opportunity to promote your new Web site by direct-mailing your customers and saying something like: "Thanks for doing business with us. We'd like to tell you about our new Web site, at *http://www.ournewsite.com*. This will be a source of information about our company and products. Do you have any questions about what we offer and who we are? Drop us a note or call us and we'll add your question to our Frequently Asked Questions (FAQ) page."

Once again, the Goddess of promotion has been well-served. You've managed to promote your brand new Web site as a place for appreciated customers to go, and justified the timing of your new FAQ as well.

"Put up a FAQ on rollout, if you can anticipate questions, which we usually can," says Jamie Holmes, FAQ maintainer for Progressive Network's RealAudio Web site. There are those "fundamentalists," however, who would reject such an approach. They would scorn this manufacture of questions as artifice. Far better to start the FAQ when enough "actual" questions come in. Such a methodology might take a few months before a FAQ comes to your site, but it stems from a basic belief that a FAQ should not be started until enough questions have been posed to justify its existence. "A FAQ isn't a FAQ unless you got questions. Otherwise, it's called a README file or a User's Guide," says Jim Dumoulin, maintainer of the Kennedy Space Center Web FAQ for the National Aeronautics and Space Administration (NASA).

Stimulatingly, comprehensively, and authoritatively written, a FAQ also attracts or inspires questions.

NEWSGROUP FAQ ROLLOUT ISSUES

Usenet FAQs are significantly different from most Web FAQs in several ways. While some newsgroups welcome posts from businesses, the newsgroup in and of itself won't be a mercantile entity, so the promotional potential inherent in FAQ rollout timing is normally absent. Unless you count postings within an existing newsgroup, proposing a new spin-off of that group, there is no real parallel with a Web site's Under Construction announcement.

Still, there's plenty of justification for newsgroup FAQs when the Group first goes up on the Internet. A FAQ can be a great place to state the Group's purpose, say what types of postings will be allowed and which ones will be discouraged, and give some basic information about the subject area the newsgroup has been formed to discuss.

The biggest difference between Web and Usenet FAQs, however, has to do with the difference between these two entities. Newsgroups are by their nature, communal entities, while Web sites are often the central concern of a small group, not likely to inspire company or organization-wide input. Because of this communality, many newsgroup FAQ maintainers feel a tug toward getting members involved in FAQ construction. Inviting such "community" participation at rollout can justify putting a FAQ up even during the very early stages of a newsgroup's existence.

Such a course was taken by Jordan Lund, FAQ maintainer for the "Stephen King Dark Tower" FAQ. "I made the members of the group at that time part of the creative process," Lund says. "I took the snippets of text that I had written, posted them and told everyone 'I'm making a FAQ; please let me know what you think.' From there the floodgates were open and about two or three weeks later the FAQ reached its alpha release (as opposed to the beta transcripts). So what did I consider a beta and an alpha? Well, since the FAQ is about three different books at its core, until I covered all three of them I considered the text to be a beta release. Once I finished talking about the third (novel) then I figured FAQ was done," he adds.

Dave Mordor, who has written several automotive-related FAQs, agrees with the FAQ-on-rollout approach. "I'd say put it up on rollout, based on what you've seen in relevant newsgroups and mailing lists. First see if there is already a relevant FAQ; if so, contact the maintainer and start working on it together, or adapt relevant parts as you need to," he suggests. "But be sure to provide credit to the original maintainer." See Figure 7.2.

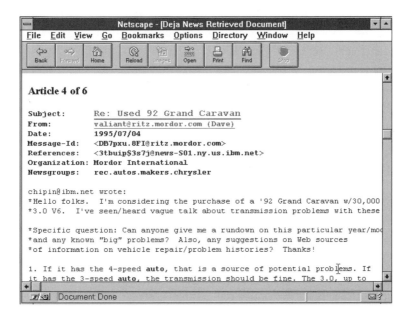

FIGURE 7.2 THE "REC.AUTOS.MAKERS.CHRYSLER" FAQ.

Other Usenet FAQ maintainers take a more purist approach, preferring to start a FAQ thread only when enough of a critical mass has been reached to justify it. "I waited until posters started begging for answers and no one else volunteered to coordinate the effort. Again, I've found Usenet readers/posters to be very responsive in answering specific questions, often taking a great deal of time in making their responses," says Buzz McDermott, FAQ maintainer for *rec.model.rockets*.

If McDermott had taken the lazy way out and not written a FAQ, lurkers wouldn't have become posters. On Web sites, lack of a FAQ can be as cardinal a sin as a mediocre one. Such a critical content-omission can leave the rest of the site unguided, often driving away visitors in confusion. And guess what? Unlike Arnold Schwarzenegger in "Terminator," they won't be back.

ANNOUNCING YOUR FAQ

Especially for Web sites, people won't be able to find your FAQ until they can find your site. This means letting people know that your site exists. The three best ways to get the word out are by:

- Looking for Usenet newsgroups with a similar topical focus to your Web site, and where permitted, putting your "come visit our new Web site" posting there, or;

- Tapping the search engines. Capital markets have invested hundreds of millions of dollars in these startup companies, for the precise reason that these companies provide the best and most timely guides to what is on the exploding World Wide Web.

- Using the "add URL" feature in search engines to announce your URL. If your FAQ has a separate URL, you can add it individually. The larger search engines like Alta Vista, Infoseek, Open Text, Excite, Hotbot, and Lycos all reference "deep enough" onto a site to locate and hotlink to FAQ pages, should they be sought in a user-initiated keyword (or in the case of Excite, in a concept) search.

No matter what type of site you have on the Web, there are probably several Usenet newsgroups devoted to the topic as well; because of the commonality of interests, the synergies are evident. If the message is overly "shilly"—especially in newsgroups that look down upon overt commerciality—any perceived marketing benefit can quickly become a negative; still several newsgroups, including the "*.marketplace*" ones, welcome such cross-postings. You can even cross-post your FAQ there as an inducement for people to visit your Web site.

"The energy required to properly 'market' one's presence on the Internet has to be one of the most underestimated tasks for those venturing onto the Web," says Rick Gutlon, president of Air Cruise America, a San Clemente (CA) company that offers aerial tours of Southern California in vintage aircraft. His company regularly posts its Web site announcements on such newsgroups as *rec.travel.marketplace, rec.travel.usa-canada*, *rec.travel.air*, *rec.aviation.misc.*, and *rec.aviation.military*. "Most believe that 'if you build it—they will come,' and that registering with the various search engines/indexes is all that it takes to attract visitors," he continues. "There is nothing further from the truth! To be successful, marketing a commercial site on the Web must be treated with no less effort than a traditional brochure. Newsgroup participation, when done properly, can be an effective way to make others aware of your site. "Since the inception of the World Wide Web. one of the primary methods to announce the existence of new Web sites was through appropriate Usenet newsgroups," he says. "While it is true that the NCSA 'what's new' list was the 'official' method of announcement, many more people would find a particular web site via Usenet postings than from 'what's new'."

The key issues here are:

- The newsgroup must be appropriate for the announcement. Spam is very, very bad and soon may result in caning for the perpetrator.
- The announcement must be useful to most of the readers. If the site provides a service or information useful to the readers of the newsgroup, post away. Remember that Usenet is a cooperative effort paid for by the recipient, not by the sender. You wouldn't make telemarketing cold-calls collect, would you? You must provide value in exchange for sending these people your announcement 'collect.'

- It must not be posted too often. If it's really that useful, try to get it into the newsgroup's FAQ. If you can't get the FAQ keeper to put it in the FAQ, people probably don't want to see it getting posted every week either.

Obviously, a lot of people are doing this. When writing this book I went to Deja News and launched a search for Usenet documents with the terms "FAQ" and "Web site." I thought this useful because if asked for a search string in this manner, Deja News will look in individual postings and not pull up extraneous FAQs within the newsgroups themselves. By the way, I found more than 11,000 citations. See Figure 7.3.

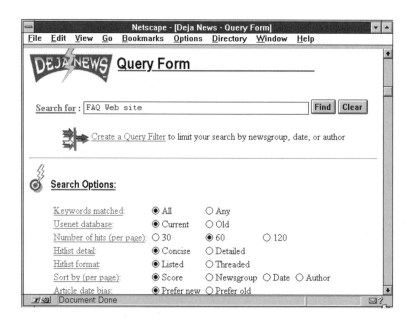

FIGURE 7.3 DEJA NEWS' SEARCH ENGINE IS A GOOD PLACE TO LOOK FOR FAQ CROSS-PASTING AND PROMOTIONAL OPPORTUNITIES.

Posting the URL of your FAQ, and your site, on the search engines and Web indexes is also critical. The engines all like to say they will index your new URL within a day or two after it first goes up, but with my own Web pages I've found that it can take several weeks. So take the time out, visit the search engines, and register "manually." It sounds far more primitive than being discovered by a powerful "spider" or "crawler," but this method actually helps to hotwire the process. See Figure 7.4.

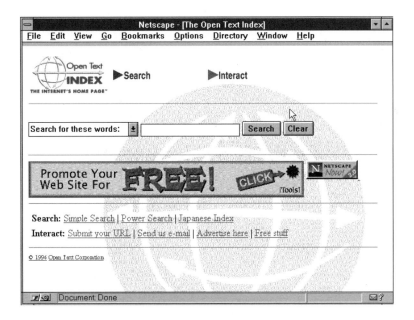

FIGURE 7.4 LIKE MOST OTHER SEARCH ENGINES, OPEN/TEXT ALLOWS YOU TO REGISTER YOUR FAQ PAGE AS A URL.

Search engines use "spiders and "crawlers" to comb the Web on a daily or weekly basis. When they find new sites that aren't in their existing database, or sites that may have added or eliminated content since the last check, they build it into their index. Some services like Lycos and Yahoo! will also highlight new sites in their sub-directories. These are not necessarily, but are likely to be, the result of paid advertising that can cost upwards of $10,000 a pop.

LEADING SITE VISITORS TO YOUR FAQ

There are two approaches Web sites take to do this. For me, actually having a FAQ page icon and/or link on your Home Page is the best. You've taken the trouble to compose your FAQ, so why not let your visitors know its there if they need it? See Figure 7.5.

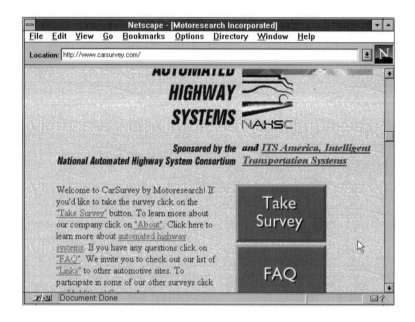

FIGURE 7.5 THIS SITE HAS A CLICKABLE FAQ ICON ON ITS HOME PAGE.

The other basic tack is to tout your FAQ on the front page of a helper-application section. Typically, this means putting up some indicator of available assistance on the Home Page, like "Technical Support," "Customer Support," or just good old "Help." Then, when that link is clicked and the main page is accessed, the FAQ icon or link will be identified and clickable from there. To me, the only time this makes sense is if the Home Page is already so cluttered with icons that putting a FAQ graphic up there would just add to the congestion. Otherwise, it's self-defeating. If someone is looking for the tech support area on your site, odds are strong they have a question, right? And what's the best place to archive these questions into a user- friendly format? Why, Frequently Asked Questions lists, of course!

After you've worked out the timing issues and launched your FAQ, you need to keep it vibrant and relevant. We discuss how to do so in the next chapter.

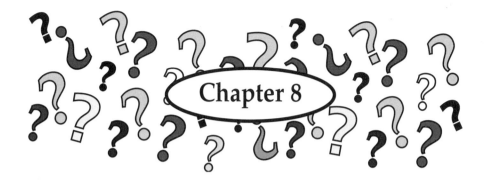

How do I Keep My FAQ Relevant?

In this chapter, you'll learn:

- Why a FAQ must be relevant
- Ways to keep your FAQ relevant if it is and make it so if not
- How to "open channels" to mine for relevant information
- When to add questions to your FAQ
- When to delete or modify questions
- How to get around the "expiration of relevancy" problem

A FAQ is unlike a set of instructions in a computer manual, a README file on a software program, or a passage in a textbook. The reason is that these sources of information are, in essence, facts frozen in time. The instructions and data they contain were meant to have permanence, lasting as long as the software or hardware is usable or the knowledge imparted hasn't been rendered obsolete by newer findings. A FAQ is more like a plant that needs to be "fed" and watered. Think about it. Doubtlessly, you perceive your Web site or newsgroup as a breathing entity, subject to the liveliness of discourse, the experiences and viewpoints of its participants or customers, influenced by new developments, products and research within the overall field in which it covers.

For these, and other reasons, a FAQ must remain relevant. Why is relevancy a key criterion for most Frequently Asked Questions lists? Regardless of where in cyberspace the FAQ is posted, it must remain flexible enough to be responsive to the world outside.

IS YOUR **FAQ** RELEVANT?

Here are several operational issues with accompanying solutions that you, the FAQ writer or FAQ maintainer, need to keep in mind in your quest for relevancy. Think of the following as both a self-diagnostic checklist and as a prescription pad for the "creeping irrelevancy" symptoms you're able to identify from the following questions.

Q. Do you monitor your site's feedback channels (electronic mail, threadings, customer support, snail-mail, phone calls) to ensure that once they are asked often enough, questions posed by outside sources become candidates to be added to your FAQ page?

A. This is a critical issue, especially for FAQ writers in the corporate world. Much of the communications traffic routed through these channels originates either from confusion or frustration about a product. Unanswered, these sentiments can soon be transformed into the kind of hostility which results in dissatisfied customers, canceled orders, and requests for refunds.

Sure sounds good in principle, doesn't it? Of course, but especially in the *.com*/Web FAQ world, this self-evident must-do is not often done. The reasons for this are many; the most glaring of these is both organizational and cultural. The *.com* FAQ writer is likely not to have direct dialog with customers.

Unless care is taken to make sure that he or she does, the writer is likely to be in a different part of the building, a different department, and possibly in a city different from the one where the question-bearing calls are being taken.

Know the Company You Work For

Unless the FAQ writer cares enough about the marketing goals of the Web site to occasionally immerse himself in these issues, an ivory-tower syndrome is likely to result.

There's an even more insidious element at work here: the trend at many companies to outsource customer support functions. From a managerial perspective, this makes sense because businesses won't have to pay for rapidly increasing health-care premiums and related employee benefits if they can farm this work out to third parties; yet, too many firms—including some of the largest software companies—grant these outsource contracts without any provision for occasional repartee with supervisory personnel at these service organizations. With minimal training, the staff at these third parties are placed at a desk and given a headset and a basic series of instructions on what to say if a customer asks a certain question. They are likely not to have the motivation, knowledge, or power to give creative solutions to even simple questions.

This can affect you, the FAQ writer in a number of ways. None of them are good. In too many cases, contracted staff are likely to be unfamiliar with issues such as how a product works, the shortcuts a user can try to jury-rig their way around difficulties, or the fact that (perhaps) a newer version of the software that will solve these questions is being planned for release in two months. If these people are low-paid, part-time, twice-removed chattel, they are not going to be able to answer some key questions. Heck, they may not even know that the company they are allegedly "representing" has a Web site with FAQs that answer these questions. They might not even be able to tell you what a FAQ is. Putting something like "for more detailed documents, refer the caller to the site FAQ" on the Q-A answer sheets the reps get might be helpful.

This mindless outsourcing trend means that the manure truck of customer dissatisfaction may back straight up to the company that made the product; don't think of this as an "uh-oh," but an opportunity to make things better. How? Get to know the people you work with. Send an Email note to the person at your company where the customer-feedback buck stops. This is a good way to make an influential friend. Why? Because when your company decided to spend hundreds of thousands of dollars to put up its Web site, this person was probably involved in the decision. If she gave her assent, this means that the smooth operation of this Web site will only serve to validate her approval. As the FAQ writer, you are in position not only to improve your FAQ's relevancy, but to boost site hits and perhaps even your company's profits.

Here's a possible model for your internal Email note to the right person:

```
To:   Lisa Morrison, Vice-President, Customer Service
From: Dave Frazier, Web Services Team
Re:   Suggestion to improve our Web site

Dear Ms. Morrison:

     I'm a member of our Web Services Team.  First, I'd like to thank you
and the other members of our executive staff for initiating and supporting
our Web site.  We're getting more than 20,000 hits a day, lots of favor-
able reviews, and as you know, are considering some enhancements that will
make our site even more of an attractive pit stop for our customers.

     Despite the success of our site, we here in Web Services don't want
to rest on our laurels.  We have some ideas for making the site even more
of a dynamic Customer Services tool than it is now.  Since customer satis-
faction falls under your department's bailiwick, I'm writing with a spe-
cific suggestion as well as a request for the input of your wise counsel.

     My particular site-management role is as the maintainer of our
Frequently Asked Questions (FAQ) pages.  We have five FAQs, one a general
company information FAQ and four pertaining to specific product lines.
We know that FAQs can be a great tool for managing customer feedback,
simplifying their interface with our products, and perhaps lightening the
load of our contracted back-office customer support team in Sioux Falls.

     Unfortunately, there has never been a dialog between those folks and
us worker bees in Web Services.  Based on a few pieces of customer
inquiry Email that have found their way to our department, our gut feel-
ing tells us that there are questions the support team is fielding that
should be migrated to the FAQ page.

     If, in fact you agree, would there be a way for your office to ini-
tiate channels of, and a schedule for, communication between my depart-
ment and Sioux Falls, so that we could enhance our FAQ and make it even
more of a useful tool for our customers?

     Thanks for taking the time from your busy schedule to read this
note.  Your feedback and advice would be both welcomed and graciously
appreciated.

     Sincerely,
     Dave Frazier
```

Get the idea? If you emphasize that you are not a "gearhead" but a team player, you'll win friends and influence people. Powerful people.

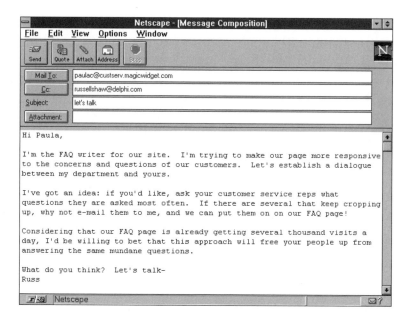

FIGURE 8.1 WEB SITE FAQ MAINTAINERS MIGHT WISH TO COMMUNICATE WITH CUSTOMER SERVICE MANAGERS, AS IN THE ABOVE EXAMPLE.

USE YOUR HEAD, READ YOUR THREADS

In the newsgroup FAQ world, effective feedback-FAQ migration patterns won't be driven by dollars, but will be equally as important to you. Dependent on the newsgroup, there may be threadings after your posted FAQ that re-pose the questions that you sought to answer. Other members of your newsgroup may join in on the thread to answer these questions, but unless your group is moderated, there is no assurance that their replies will be accurate. This is potentially an endemic problem, especially in newsgroups where members post FAQs gleaned from outside sources. Such FAQ writers may use automated re-posting routines, and spend little if any time either "lurking" or mixing it up on the given newsgroup. So, they have little sense of the questions being asked and how often they are presented.

Don't overlook postal mail as a possible FAQ source. "We are currently trying to get coordinated enough to update the FAQ once a month…or at least post it once a month," says Jeff Wayman, a member of the FAQ-writing team at The Mentos FAQ (*http://www.mentos.com*). "The FAQ has also spawned some Mentos Fan-fiction and classic letters and papers that we now put out monthly in the Mentos Journal…a distant cousin of the FAQ." Mentos is a flavored mint candy with a large customer base and a subculture of devotees. See Figure 8.2.

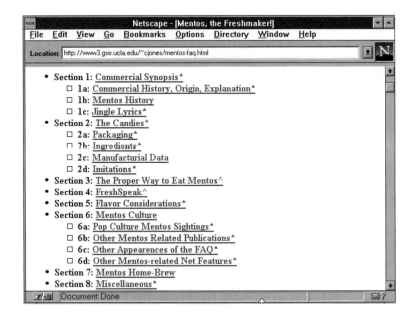

FIGURE 8.2 THE MENTOS FAQ.

ADDING QUESTIONS TO YOUR FAQ

Q. Whether informal or empirically based on the number of times a question is asked, do you have a self-alerting mechanism that will set bells off in your head with the message that yes, it's time to add this question to your FAQ list?

A. This is perhaps the most subjective issue a FAQ writer will have to deal with. It's a matter of "knowing when," a judgment call based almost entirely on instinct and experience.

For most maintainers, the "when to add" decision is not formally set, but represents the frequency with which a new question is asked within a given time frame. Standards vary widely, depending on how closely the "unanswered" question is to one that is already posted in the FAQ. If the new query poses the same question but with different words, it might only be necessary to add a sentence or two to the "Answer" field for the posted version of the question.

If the issue can't be solved this way, it might be time to incorporate the new question into your FAQ. Again, a pattern should have been established. What constitutes a "pattern?" Most FAQ writers like to see the "candidate" question posed three or four times within two to four weeks before they'll consider adding it to their FAQ. "A good FAQ is a living, breathing document," says Kevin Savetz, whose mostly Internet-related FAQs are posted to several newsgroups as well as to the Web site *http://www.northcoast.com/savetz/faqs/html*. Savetz identifies potential new questions through Email links and threaded postings. "The FAQ writer needs to listen to the community of people who read the FAQ, taking their comments, suggestions, and further questions into consideration." Savetz adheres to the "three or four times" rule. See Figure 8.3.

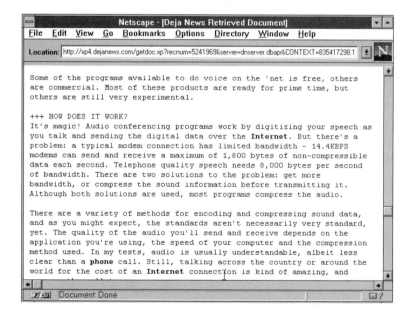

FIGURE 8.3 THE "INTERNET PHONE" FAQ.

An important note: if you follow the "three or four times" rule, make sure that the petitioners are not the same person. Do you really think its worth it to add a question just because one poor soul "doesn't get it?"

Q. Do you keep up with new developments not only in your field, but in allied disciplines or trades that might engender either new questions or the rewording of older ones?

A. This is an issue where "worldliness" is a priceless asset and tunnel-blindness is a curse.

You might think you know everything about a piece of software, a musician's discography, or your hobby. Heck, you're not only the newsgroup FAQ maintainer, but you converse often with your given community of *cognoscenti* and perhaps even work in the field or profession. Sorry to burst your bubble, but that's not enough. Potential difficulties are especially possible in Usenet, that 20,000-colony mass of subcultures. The enlightened FAQ writers for newsgroups dealing with commercial entities tackle this several ways. One hard and fast rule is to cultivate sources *within* the organization your group is about.

As a result, many FAQ writers are well-known by the press departments of companies their newsgroups discuss. Savetz, for instance, has regular contact with the public relations departments of several Internet-phone companies. "I try to get on their press list. By doing so, they keep me updated," says Savetz, who writes the "Internet Phone" FAQ. See Figure 8.4.

Companies will occasionally like you so much they will link to your FAQ from their Web site or incorporate some of your FAQ into their corporate FAQ. You are helping them out and helping to stem the flow of misinformation, or stop it before it starts. Who knows, you might be rewarded with free product or even a job offer someday.

Cultivating sources, or even contributors, within the companies is another way to keep your FAQ relevant. Floyd Maxwell, FAQ maintainer for the Novell FAQ, has several formal and informal sources in the company.

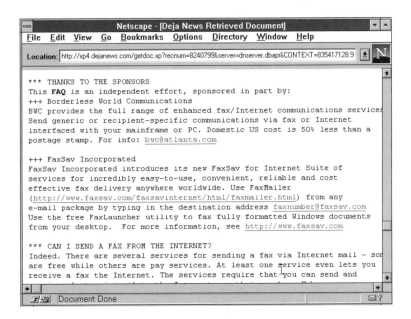

FIGURE 8.4 SAVETZ' "INTERNET PHONE" FAQ IS COMPILED WITH INFORMATION FROM INDUSTRY SOURCES.

If you're a writer for a FAQ discussing a product with a customer base, don't ignore that resource as well. Tom Baltis, whose NetTEK consultancy helps companies integrate Windows NT applications into their systems, has regular contacts at Microsoft as well as within the large Windows NT customer base. Baltis writes the "Windows NT" Internet FAQ. "Being a consultant in a company that provides Internet consulting services, I have to deal with various FAQ-related issues almost daily," he says. See Figure 8.5.

You don't have to be a computer-industry FAQ writer to benefit from staying in the loop. "When you are dealing with an author, as I do, it's easy. Whenever they put out a new book it's going to change the dynamic of the group for about 3 to 6 weeks as everyone discusses the merit (or lack thereof) of the new material," says Jordan Lund, FAQ maintainer for the Stephen King Dark Tower FAQ on *http://ph`tay10.ucsd.edu/ed/sk/dt/faq.html.*

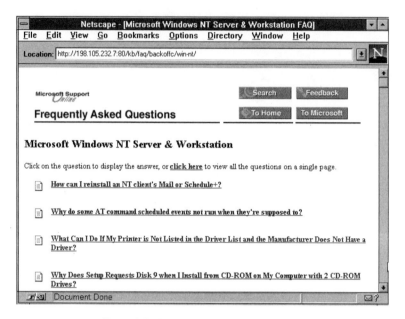

FIGURE 8.5 THE "WINDOWS NT" INTERNET FAQ.

Lund also stays current by watching the media for announcements of that rare Stephen King interview. Authors use media appearances and press tours to announce new projects. If you are a FAQ writer dealing with his or her works, you ignore this potential source of new, breaking news, and FAQs, at your peril. He remembers one instance back in 1994 when the horrormeister told a talk show host that he was going to write four more Dark Tower books in addition to the three already published at the time. A question about how many more Dark Tower books Stephen King would author was added to the FAQ within a few hours after the interview aired. See Figure 8.6.

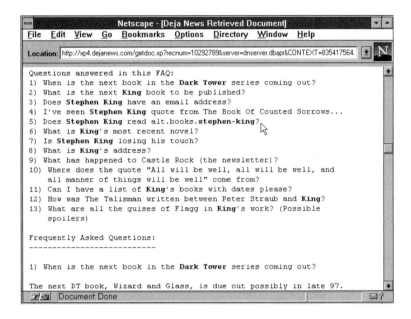

Figure 8.6 The Stephen King Dark Tower FAQ.

Some FAQs Should Have Short Lives

Q. If a FAQ has a future chronological element to it, are you cognizant enough of the dates or time ranges it specifies to take the question off once it becomes obsolete?

A. This can be a dilemma. The two main reasons why are interrelated.

In the *.com* world, hundreds of high-profile Web sites are running contests or promotions at any one time. Putting up related information on your FAQ (or even writing a special FAQ for the promotion) is always a useful strategy, but there is a hitch: any such event, of course, will by its very nature have a cutoff date. If you don't change your FAQ after the expiration of the event, you'll give the wrong impression. Maybe people won't intentionally visit your FAQ any more, but the powerful unabridged search engines like Open Text and Alta Vista are sure to find it. FAQ writers for software companies have to be especially aware of this. As I'm sure you know, any software company worth its salt issues a series of beta releases of forthcoming products. Sometimes, a bug will be discovered and a FAQ question added to address the problem; yet if the techies fix it and don't bother to tell you, then you can be caught with your pants down. "We remove outdated information all the time. Any recurring problem in beta releases that gets fixed is removed from the FAQ," says Jamie Holmes, who writes the FAQ for "Progressive Networks' RealAudio," a program that delivers sound over the Web. See Figure 8.7.

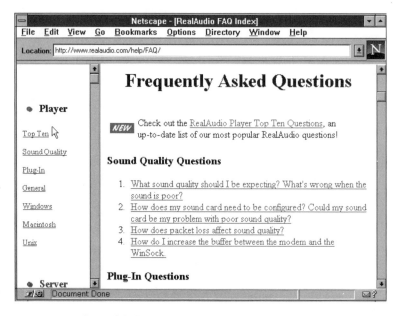

FIGURE 8.7 THE PROGRESSIVE NETWORKS REALAUDIO FAQ.

The expiration-of-relevancy issue can also arise with FAQs that are timed to specific, anticipated, one-time events in the future. Jim Dumoulin, maintainer of the Kennedy Space Center FAQ (*http:// www.ksc.nasa.gov/*) for the National Aeronautics and Space Administration, (NASA), deals with this issue all the time. He also has insight into another problem, the tendency of some Webmasters to maintain some content on "old" URLs months or years after the old address has been switched. Elimination of confusion is a worthy goal, but Dumoulin says that if you are going to do this, then by all means don't ignore the FAQ you've left back there on your "old" URL. See Figure 8.8.

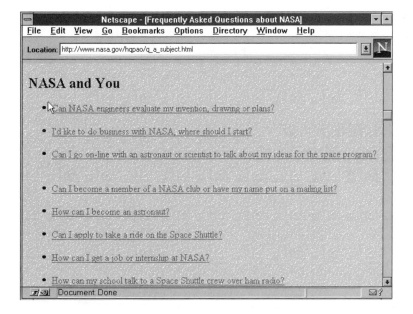

FIGURE 8.8 THE NASA KENNEDY SPACE CENTER FAQ

"It's usually best and easiest to update a FAQ if it is out of date," he says. Due to the long latency of search engines on the Net, it's usually a bad idea to remove anything without putting a forwarding pointer to some-place else. If you are going to do that anyway, then it's best to just update the page. As an example, a few years ago we changed our host to a new machine. We moved the alias but continued to run a WWW server on the old IP number. A year later, we were sill getting hits to that server to the page that says the server has moved."

DEALING WITH "DUMB" QUESTIONS

Q. Are you finding that, despite your belief that your answers are cogent explanations, you are still being besieged by a persistent barrage of questions that, for all intents and purposes, require the same answer in your FAQ as a similar question?

A. It would be very easy to let your ego get in the way here. You might wonder why some people "just don't get it." Not everyone is a genius, but perhaps you can help the learning curve along.

"The FAQ is updated every few weeks. The update includes explanations of issues that people might have found confusing, whether it's a guideline, or a question," says Rachel Zemser, the FAQ writer for the *sci.bio.food-science* newsgroup.

The wisest approach is to swallow your pride. You're not perfect. Maybe you can rephrase the question, your answer, or both; as Spock's father Sarek said in the movie "Star Trek IV, The Voyage Home," "It is difficult to know the answer when one does not know the question."

Q. This sounds like a question your mother would ask, but do you ever get so buried in other tasks (like higher-priority corporate duties or a 60-hour-a-week "real job," for instance) that you don't give your FAQ a periodic relevancy checkup?

A. If you're like me, you tend to gloss over details when you are tired. You're working 60 hours a week too, huh?

Two causes, but the same result. In companies with limited resources, one person is responsible for everything having to do with the Web site—the client-server software, relationship with the host, discussions about building an Intranet, HTML coding, Java programming, design, Email—and, oh, yes, the FAQ. Your mind gets cluttered by all this, and so FAQ updating either doesn't occur to you or FAQ maintenance is about 34th on your priority list. I know it's tough, but try to steal a few more minutes a week and deal with this key issue.

The time problem is also a crunch in the Usenet universe. Few FAQ maintainers get paid, so they have to tend to this housekeeping whenever they can. No disrespect is intended, but you can't take a print-out of your highly-rated FAQ list to the electric company in lieu of your check for payment. Do what you can, but be aware of the problem.

Like a tune-up for your car, a periodic FAQ relevancy check is necessary. Just don't do it at four A.M. when you've been working for 16 hours straight and are about ready to crash.

But why are you putting in such long hours? Maybe you are spending more and more time on FAQ maintenance because your newsgroup or company has grown—more products, more issues to discuss. Hey, that's good. Nevertheless, it presents you with some formidable FAQ management challenges that we'll discuss in the next chapter.

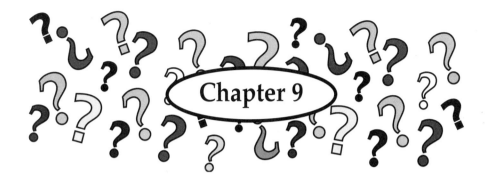

CHANGING TIMES, CHANGING FAQS

In this chapter, you'll learn:

- How trends in the business world influence FAQs
- Changing your FAQ if your company is merging
- Spinoffs and FAQs
- New Tech: new FAQs
- How to augment your FAQ with tech notes and patches
- How FAQs can bridge the old and new
- FAQs can explain and promote the future

Regardless of how painstakingly well a commercial Web site Frequently Asked Questions list is assembled, this is the most tenuous existence of all the breeds of FAQs that can be found on the Internet. That's because of the nature of the *.com* world itself. When something major happens to a company with a Web site, the site may have to be moved, combined with another site, expanded, contracted, substantially revised, or perish. And because FAQs both define and are defined by the content they serve as a tutorial for, they should in a real sense be accountable to the Web site as a whole. Such watershed events may be beyond the control of the FAQ writer, the Webmaster, possibly even the company's board of directors. Let's look at some general examples and then explore how some particular FAQs affected by these developments have managed to change but remain viable.

BUSINESS TRENDS AND FAQS

This morning, your newspaper's business section probably carried detailed accounts of a proposed merger, acquisition or spinoff. The trend has been continuing for most of this decade and shows few if any signals of stopping. Driven in large part by partial deregulation of the telecommunications and banking sectors, the urge to merge has been especially prevalent among financial services firms, travel-related enterprises, and telephone companies.

At the same time, corporations have come under increasing pressure by Wall Street to streamline operations and become lean and mean. In some cases, this means divesting poor-performing or non-synergistic divisions or products, and concentrating on core competencies. Having whittled down the product or services inventory to these core competencies, companies also find themselves with an opportunity to cut labor costs by investing in technology. These investments may yield new products, which must be efficiently promoted and distributed to cost-conscious but technologically sophisticated consumers.

What do these seemingly irreversible economic trends have to do with maintaining a Frequently Asked Questions list on a Web site? Plenty.

Here's how the shifting eddies and currents of commerce can affect a Web site FAQ:

Mergers

This is more than just a matter of one company buying another, and Web sites combining. Most corporate mergers have complicated life cycles, the passages of which must be important to the FAQ writer. Here are some strategies for the FAQ writer to use during the various points in the merger process:

1. The merger might first start out as a rumor in the media. The FAQ writer should be concerned because after such rumors hit, customers will gravitate to the Web site in search of validation. That's

only a natural result of the site as a whole having performed its appointed duty as a readily-available, up-to-the-minute source of information on the company.

Your FAQ Strategy: Contact a reliable source, such as your Chief Financial Officer, Investor Relations director, or public relations counsel. Mention that rumors about a merger have hit the airwaves and the newsstands, and ask how this should be played on the FAQ page.

If you're told that it's just a rumor, you might want to add this question to your FAQ:

Q. I've read news reports that First Amalgamated Bank may merge with Great Sunbelt Bank. How will this affect my credit cards and auto loan I have with First Amalgamated?

A. First Amalgamated's policy is never to comment on rumors. If anything concrete develops, we will announce it in the "News" section of our site (it would be useful to hyperlink to the site's News section here), and if applicable, explain it on our FAQ page as well.

2. What was once rumor is now fact. First Amalgamated and Great Sunbelt have agreed to merge into a new entity, First Sunbelt Bank.

Your FAQ Strategy: Contact your company sources for information on how to proceed. At this stage, they won't know enough about customer service implications of a merger, but should have a rough idea about the parameters for approval as well as the timetable needed. Nervous visitors to your Web site will want to know answers to questions like:

Q. I've read that First Amalgamated and Great Sunbelt will combine. When will the merger take effect?

A. These mergers require regulatory approval from several agencies, and the process normally takes several months.

Follow the process by coming back often to our "News" or "FAQ" page (each should link to the other).

Q. I have Visa credit cards with two different interest amounts at each bank. What will happen? How will my accounts be combined and which interest rate will prevail?

A. That has yet to be decided. You can check back here in a couple of months. By then, you should also have received a packet in the mail describing your account options.

3. The allotted time passes and the merger is slated to be consummated in six weeks. Everything, including what existing branches of both banks will remain open and which will close, has been finalized. It's all over now except for the sign-changing.

Your FAQ Strategy: Hopefully, you still have a job. If you're fortunate enough to have been designated the FAQ writer for the new bank's Web site, you should lean on the decision makers and image-crafters to give you as much information as possible on how things will change for customers. Plus, when banks combine, they usually send out a detailed brochure explaining key implications for their depositors. Get an advance copy, spend a weekend with it and redline the important parts. Then, contact customer service for both pre-existing banks and find out what questions have been asked the most "frequently" over the previous two weeks. There may be too many questions to put in the FAQ. No problem, because you can use links or pointers to other parts of the site, as in the following:

Q. I've been banking at Great Sunbelt's Fernwood Mall branch. Will it stay open as a First Sunbelt branch? Where can I get a list of First Sunbelt branch locations and hours?

A. As a result of the merger, about 40 First Amalgamated and 25 Great Sunbelt branches will close August 9. However, since most of these closings will take place where branches are very close to each other, this shouldn't inconvenience you in any way! Search for a list of First Sunbelt branches near you under "Our Branches." In fact, look for longer hours in select locations, as well as some exciting new services under the First Sunbelt name!

4. Finally, assuming the new First Sunbelt entity is given a new Web address, it might be a good idea to leave "mirror" versions of the new site—and the new FAQ—up at the old URLs for awhile. This works better than a simple: "We're now First Sunbelt. Click to **http://www.firstsunb.com/** and reset your bookmarks." By mirroring the site and its FAQ, you give visitors the content where they are used to getting it but setting a friendly environment for them to come to the new place and explore.

That last answer, by the way, shows that a *.com* Web site FAQ writer is more than a simple courier of information from customer service. He or she is in customer service. People being creatures of habit as they are, customers may be apprehensive when their established banking relationship is torn asunder by events beyond their control. Officers of rival banks know this, and are probably sending marketing literature to your customers. That's why using the FAQ on your Web site as a customer service road map, morale booster, and general assuager of fears can be critical for your company.

How Fleet Bank Did It

After absorbing Boston's Shawmut Bank in a merger completed in 1996, Fleet Bank is now the largest depository institution in New England. On its Web site, Fleet has regularly provided a series of informative and comforting updates to its FAQ, as exemplified in Figure 9.1.

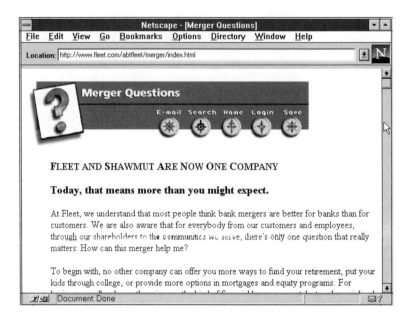

FIGURE 9.1 FLEET BANK'S "MERGER FAQ" EASED THE TRANSITION FOR THE CUSTOMERS ABSORBED AFTER THE BUYOUT OF SHAWMUT BANK.

Using the term "comforting" may seem hokey, but it really isn't. Like many banks that are being absorbed, Shawmut had a long tradition, which spanned several generations in some families. Now that the financial institution which underwrote your parent's first mortgage, helped them with a college loan for you, and gave you your first credit card is going away, it is disquieting to some people. The Fleet FAQ adopted two main messages. These can be described as: establishing a broad comfort zone; and attempting to convey excitement about how the merger will only lead to bigger and better things.

The three subheads on the "Merger Questions FAQ page bear this out. The page head reads, "Fleet and Shawmut Are Now One Company." The sub-heads are "Today, that means more than you might expect;" "Tomorrow, it will mean more than you can imagine," and "What's in it for me?" "Starting today, we are one bank," reads the text under the "Tomorrow" subhead. "Moving ahead, we intend to become one of the best financial service companies in America. We want to be a leader. But we know that to do that, everything we do has to lead to something good for each and every one of our customers."

Specific FAQ questions deal with the logistics of what happens when one bank absorbs another. For this reason, much of the FAQ addresses how former Shawmut customers will find their different types of accounts administered once they become Fleet customers.

Closure of convenient bank branches is both an inevitable and unnerving consequence of these mergers, one which can lead to ill feelings and the loss of business. Fleet deals with this as follows:

> Q. "I recently read about Shawmut divesting its branches? Why is this being done? Does divesting take the place of branch closings?"
>
> A. "As part of the merger of Fleet Financial Group and Shawmut National Corporation, we are required by the government to sell or 'divest' some branches. These branches are not closing, but will be sold to another bank. However, even after the merger, we will be committed to serving every community in which we are now located. And we will be taking every measure possible to provide a network of convenient and efficient services."

Here again is the use of a FAQ to calm fears and instill customer confidence. These goals are once again dealt with at the end of the FAQ, where a customer service phone number is given. The fact that Fleet ends this vital FAQ on such a note should not be underestimated. In times of company sea change, a FAQ can be a superb source of information, but it can't take the place of a reassuring tone communicated by live, human beings. In times of major change, your last FAQ answer should contain info on how to contact a human.

The banking example I cited can apply to almost any industry. Superregional telephone companies, chemical firms, airlines, newspapers, software providers: merger mania will continue unabated for the foreseeable future.

A Case Study of Spinoffs

Along with catching merger fever, companies throughout the last several decades have been shedding or selling divisions while acquiring others. Some divested divisions become companies on their own, like the multi-billion dollar divestiture by AT&T of its computer and telephone-equipment businesses. These became publicly traded giants of their own, now known respectively as NCR and Lucent Technologies. In such cases, the AT&T Web site changes, and two new ones—each with several newborn Frequently Asked Questions lists of their own—are created. Let's take a look at some of what was done, and the lessons that can be learned of interest to all .*com* Webmasters and FAQ writers who might be in the same position one day. Refer to Figure 9.2.

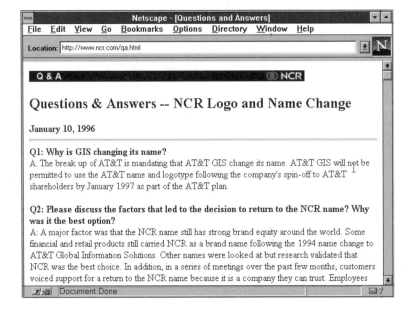

FIGURE 9.2 AT&T CREATED THIS FAQ AFTER THE SPINOFF OF NCR.

Shortly after the NCR spinoff was announced in early 1996, AT&T added a new FAQ to its Web site, "Questions & Answers—NCR Logo and Name Change." The divestiture, which brought back the time-honored NCR name to what was known for two years as AT&T Global Information Solutions, was discussed in a short, to-the-point FAQ that dealt with the reasons why this action was being taken, the timetable for its implementation, and the fact that despite the fact that NCR would be a separate entity, pre-existing alliances with certain other units of AT&T would be continued. The final question was a perfect example of how a well-written FAQ can communicate a marketing message without trying too hard to be overly commercial. It read:

Q. "Tell me some things that would surprise me about NCR."

A. "NCR is the leader in the commercial massively parallel processing market with a 50-percent market share. NCR installed and maintains the single largest commercial data processing system in the world. NCR is the world's leading provider of retail point-of-sale slot scanners with an estimated 40-percent market share. NCR is the world leader in automated teller machines with a 33-percent market share."

Just like they say about real estate, "location, location, location." If that last question were the first or second on the critical NCR spinoff FAQ, a strutting-stuff tone would be set. Yet the placement of this question occurred at the end, accomplishing two things. It was the electronic equivalent of a handshake. The previous question, alluding to some problems Global Information Systems had been experiencing at the time the decision was reached to convert it to an independent NCR, was frankly answered: "NCR realizes that its return to profitability depends on its ability to deliver in the marketplace." Thus, the rah-rah of the last question leaves the FAQ reader with a positive, almost unstated "well, they have some problems but they have a firm foundation" impression. Here, once again, is the role of a *.com* FAQ as an assuager, a digital Prozac if you will.

As 1996 wore on and NCR started its own Web site, (*http://www.ncr.com*) the FAQ went up there as well. To assure continuity during an amicable separation, AT&T kept links within its own site to the NCR and Lucent sites, and thus to the new family of FAQs each one spawned.

During the same period that AT&T was re-establishing itself as primarily a telecommunications company, it was taking a hard look at its suite of services, adding some, cutting others. The phase-out of AT&T's ill-thought-out, poorly performing Interchange online service in 1996 was reflected in a series of questions posted to its "Frequently Asked Questions about AT&T New Media Services FAQ." You might think that the elimination of an online offering could be accomplished in the blink of an eye. Given the complexities of billing adjustments, negotiation of escape clauses with content providers and an understanding willingness to avoid corporate embarrassment at what had clearly been a bad concept, it was inevitable that the process of discontinuance wouldn't be easy.

Enter, then, the concept of a FAQ as a damage control device.

The effect on the FAQ was profound. When the company was still trying to make a go of Interchange, one of the FAQ answers explained the sign-up procedure. After the discontinuance was publicized, the phraseology was changed to read, "Unfortunately, we are no longer accepting software orders or distributing software electronically for AT&T Business Network on Interchange, because Interchange is being phased out. So, unfortunately, you can no longer sign-up to the service."

But AT&T is too skilled a marketer to leave their customers lost at sea. The next sentence provided a solution: "You can access the first Web-based service from AT&T Business Network, Lead Story, through the URL *http://www.leadstory.com.*"

Since the suspension of Interchange would doubtlessly result in a temporary billing morass, the last question on this FAQ was, once again, in the assuage mode:

Q. "I have a question about my AT&T Business Network on (my) AT&T Interchange bill. Who can I call?"

A. "Please call Customer Care at 1-800-299-9699."

Its all in the semantics, folks. "Care" is warm and fuzzy. It's no answer that the last answer to the concluding FAQ question about a subject with the potential for chaos had the comforting word "care" in it!

New Tech, New FAQs

Sometimes, particularly in technology-related companies, a corporate acquisition or a research and development initiative spawns a new product line or a new series of services. In these cases, FAQ writers have several choices, including:

1. Creating an entirely new FAQ.
2. Adding a series of new FAQ questions to an existing FAQ.
3. Not changing the FAQs but providing a link from the FAQ to some other portion of the site where the concept can be explained in greater detail.

There are numerous examples of each. Let's take a look at a few.

AT&T's Toll Free-888 FAQ

In March, 1996, a new three-digit toll-free call prefix, "888," made its debut. It was started because the growth in 800 numbers was about to exhaust all vacancies and thus make the wait for new numbers long and intolerable. Almost everyone welcomed the change, but there was still the potential for customer confusion. Some people without much familiarity about how the phone system works, assumed that "888" was a toll-call option similar to "900." Given the rampant cynicism in the U.S., an out-of-the-starting-blocks explanation was necessary. Here we see another role for the FAQ, as a heralder and interpreter of major technological change. Thus, this particular ten-question FAQ was hatched. See Figure 9.3.

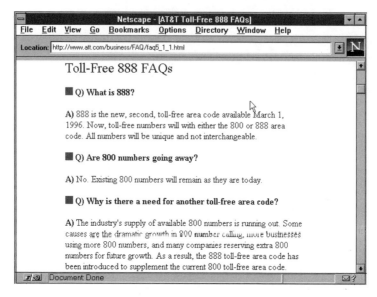

FIGURE 9.3 WHEN TOLL-FREE "888" NUMBERS WERE INTRODUCED IN 1996, AT&T CREATED
THIS SEPARATE FAQ TO EXPLAIN THE PROCESS.

The first question is a standard "What is" (888) query. If there is a boilerplate kickoff item for a FAQ page, that's it. As a matter of fact, a mid-1996 search of the Open Text search engine for the terms "What is" and "FAQ" yielded nearly 65,000 joint citations. With the growth of the Internet, there are surely more by now.

The answer to this particular "what is" is cogent, pointed, but distinctly non-threatening:

A. "888 is the new, second, toll-free area code available March 1, 1996. Now, toll-free numbers will work with either the 800 or 888 area code. All numbers will be unique and not interchangeable."

In the answer to its last question, AT&T managed, in only 35 words, to soothe and sell. That's not easy to do without artifice, but they pulled it off:

Q. "Can I still get toll-free directory assistance through 1-800-555-1212?"

A. "You can call Toll-Free Directory Assistance at 1-800-555-1212 to get an 800 number listing or a new 888 number listing. And now, the Toll-Free Internet Directory gives you Internet access to the directory."

A link was provided to the Internet Directory from this answer. We'll discuss more about links in Chapter 10.

Apple Computers' "Cyberdog" FAQ

After nearly a decade of mostly flagging fortunes, Apple Computer announced a major new Internet-centered business strategy in 1996. Deemed one of the major initiatives in Apple's mercurial corporate history, the components and features of this product set were originally named Cyberdog. Within a few hours of Cyberdog's inauguration in the spring of 1996, it had its own Web site, (*http://cyberdog.apple.com*), and its own FAQ as well. The FAQ had a direct link from the Cyberdog Home Page, which was, in turn, reachable from Apple's home page. The high-quality "Cyberdog FAQ" had a content-organization quality seldom seen in Web FAQs. The points it made were well-presented and cogent explanations, largely dealing with Cyberdog's Web browsing capabilities as part of an open platform-enabling technology called OpenDoc. See Figure 9.4.

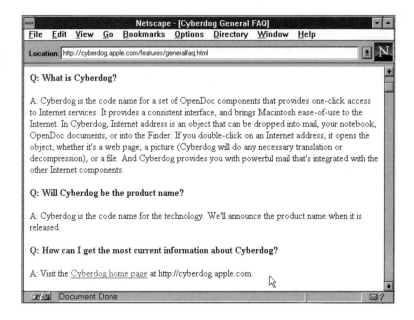

FIGURE 9.4 APPLE'S "CYBERDOG" FAQ WENT LIVE THE SAME DAY THE COMPANY ANNOUNCED A NEW STRATEGY FOR THE INTERNET.

After the obligatory "what is" kick-off question, Apple furnished a "most current information" back from the FAQ to Cyberdog's Home Page. A few questions down came Apple's "shot across the bow," if you will, against the prevailing trend toward using dedicated World Wide Web browsers for all Internet access. Plainly, they did this because if Cyberdog was to be a successful Internet strategy—one that perhaps would restore the company to its former 1970s luster—the FAQ had to play a vital role as an informational storefront and brochure for this major enterprise.

Apple's Cyberdog FAQ handled this critical issue in the following manner:

Q. "Why should I use Cyberdog instead of an all-purpose Web browser?"

A. "Cyberdog gives you integrated access to all services on the Internet (including FTP, Gopher, Telnet, World Wide Web, Netnews and EMail) with the ability to display the full richness of each service. If you try use (*sic*) a browser optimized for the World Wide Web, you're forcing other services and data types to be displayed in a way that's not optimal for them. Cyberdog avoids this compromise. In addition, with customized Internet documents, Cyberdog allows you to fully integrate the Internet more fully into your daily activities and to share your Internet explorations with friends and colleagues."

Just one quibble here, though: the grammatical fluff indicated above doesn't detract from the relevance of this FAQ, but it does indicate that all FAQ writers might do well to either use a spelling or grammar checker, or run their copy by an in-house wordsmith before they post it.

On its Apple Webmaster FAQ, the Cupertino, Cal.-based company pursues another strategy for major events. Question five, "I've heard that Apple is working on a new product called…," is a boilerplate that is answered with a plea that the company can't talk about stuff that hasn't been released. Still, the function of FAQs as answering resources and problem solvers is found by a link from this question to the company's press release library, "Apple Directions newsletter developers," as well as to the archive of "Things to Come" posted on the Mac OS Web site Home Page.

Bridging the Old and New: The Lotus FAQ Approach

Whether it is digital video disks instead of VHS tapes, an improved version of a microwave oven, or a new edition of software, basic laws of consumer economics create some important decisions for the *.com* FAQ writer. Unless a company is foolish enough to stop supporting an older version of a product, it will take months or years for a new edition to gain enough penetration in the market to totally consign the ancient product to the scrap heap. Think about it; music CDs first hit the stores in 1983, but it took at least a decade for LP albums to virtually disappear. Similarly, it took nearly two decades for typewriters, rotary dial phones and black and white television sets to vanish, even after personal computers, touch-tone phones, and color TVs started rolling off the assembly lines. In the computer world, there are still people running 2400-baud modems.

The challenge this reality presents for the FAQ writer is how to ensure that the right type of informational balance between new and old exists on the FAQ page as well as on the Web site in total. There is a dilemma here. Marketing may want you to emphasize the new and forget about the old, but can you really afford to do so? It's a tough walk. I think the best approach is one taken on the "Lotus Notes Support" Web site (*http://www.lotus.com*). Let us look at how Lotus solved the "bridging" problem on their FAQ pages. The Home Page of Lotus Notes has five icons, each of which points to an area where more information is available. There is a keyword-search function for answers in the Notes knowledge base, a Notes file library, a link to additional Lotus Notes information in newsgroups, and, of course, a Frequently Asked Questions section (refer to Figure 9.5).

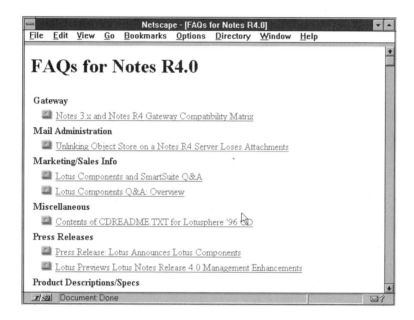

FIGURE 9.5 LOTUS NOTES CREATED AN ENTIRELY NEW FAQ FOR ITS 4.0 RELEASE.

The Lotus Notes FAQ is not structured around a long list of questions and answers, but is instead, organized as a list of individual answers to reported problems and performance notes about particular Lotus Notes applications. Problems such as "'You Have Insufficient System Memory' Running OS2/ Scheduling Agent" each have their own hyperlinks that route the user to the answer.

As is true in any new version, Lotus Notes Release 4.0 in 1995 presented another whole list of problems to be solved and questions to be answered. Lotus did not drop support references for earlier Notes versions in its FAQ; instead, it took a two-pronged approach, integrating the most common R4.0 questions in its main Notes FAQ, while creating a new FAQ for Notes R4.0 that addresses a greater number of issues in closer detail. This way, R4.0 users can find answers in both places.

Netscape and Quarterdeck: Tech Notes and Patches

There's no law that dictates that every new product or application needs a new FAQ; in fact, some companies won't even admit that a new product even needs a new FAQ question. Netscape, the browser kings, and Quarterdeck, which also makes a number of Internet-enabling software tools, both rely on technical support notes, and from time to time, product patches, to answer questions and remedy problems.

Netscape's Navigator and Server FAQ's don't have a surfeit of content, but do offer links to a "Technical Notes" page which at any moment can have more than 50 posted notes. Updated frequently, these notes are classified in two ways—by nature of the note and by application platform. The Navigator Tech Notes menu, which is actually an extension of the FAQ, has a section called "Glitches, Errors, Freezes and Crashes." The page menu lists these assumed problems, like 'unable to launch external viewer! error code 16' on downloading" and "FTP transfers stop after a specific number of bytes on a SLIP connection." Clicking on the hyperlink gets you to a two-paragraph explanation and solution to the problem, along with the date the Technical Note was created and who at Netscape wrote it. We discuss the Netscape FAQs in greater detail within Chapter 12.

TOO MANY FAQ QUESTIONS? THEN CHANGE YOUR SOFTWARE

If Webmasters migrate Emailed or phoned-in questions to their FAQ but the problem and confusion just get worse, the only cure might be surgery: fixing the difficulty in the product itself. A full upgrade or revision may not be necessary; sometimes enough can be done through a patch to fix and overwrite the faulty parts of an application.

At other times, you've issued an upgrade and want your customers to migrate to it without jumping through hoops. Assuming the upgrade is an improvement over the older version, they should be willing to do so if the overwrite process isn't too much of a pain and you let them know the option is available. A FAQ page is a good place to let your customers know you've done this. See Figure 9.6; Quarterdeck's FAQ page, for example, links to a "Product patches and updates" menu where you can upgrade to later versions of software you already have installed.

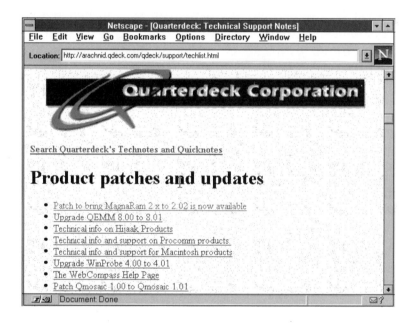

FIGURE 9.6 QUARTERDECK'S PRODUCT PATCHES AND UPDATES MENU.

Games Web sites, which use a huge amount of processing power, are also good places to push an upgrade on your FAQ. This is a strategy followed by the Web FAQs maintained by game developer Spectrum Holobyte (*http://www.holobyte.com*). On its "Terror From The Deep" FAQ, for example, a nagging problem in an earlier version of the product is explained this way:

Q. In two-part missions (i.e., Ship Missions), I cannot keep the artifacts from the first part of the mission.

A. The version 2.0 update for the game changes this and allows you to keep items in the two-part missions. Click here to download the update.

SOON TO COME

Web FAQs can also be ideal forums for announcing new product features which, because of ongoing research or regulatory hurdles, aren't quite ready yet. These announcements can be couched within FAQ answers as remedies to a problem while also serving as an unstated sales pitch for coming attractions. In this way, the FAQ answer, in a manner of speaking, "writes" the question.

One Web site that has perfected this to a high art is the Fidelity Investments site (*http://www.fidelity.com*). Because the world of electronic commerce, and the things you can do with it, is still in its relative infancy, Fidelity, the largest mutual funds company in the world, adopted this strategy as a kind of fallback position.

Here's an example of a "soon to come" FAQ question, from Fidelity's main FAQ:

Q. Can I view my Fidelity account balances, and buy and sell mutual fund shares and individual securities from this site?

A. Currently, we do not offer the ability to view account balances, or place transactions for either mutual fund shares or individual securities, primarily because of concern over the security of transactions over the Internet. We have been making a careful study of ways in which to ensure the security of the system in order to protect customer accounts and transactions, as well as Fidelity's back-end computer systems, from being compromised by 'hackers.'

Exciting developments are happening every day in the field of encryption technology, however, and we look forward to providing customers with these functionalities as soon as we are able to implement a satisfactory, secure communications mode.

In the meantime, we do offer online account views and trading and transactions through Fidelity Online Xpress (FOX) which you can install on your PC. This DOS-based software will eventually be available in a Windows version.

Most of the Fidelity FAQ answers, even the routine ones, end on an upbeat note rather than letting the user hang in limbo waiting for a better future. That's a sound approach, don't you think?

WHAT ABOUT OTHER KINDS OF FAQS?

The *.com* section of the Web is the most subject to sea changes. Its very nature dictates this. It's more likely for a version of updated software to correct an old glitch, or a new product to be released than a scientific shibboleth to be overturned and thus create havoc on a research-oriented Web site FAQ.

The only other type of Web FAQs subject to rapid revisions and changes are found on governmental or political Web sites. A Senator may take a position on a flareup in another part of the world and might want to post his views on the conflict on his Web site FAQ. A Presidential candidate might drop out, causing both the FAQ and the Web site to vanish. Or, the party in power might change, causing a significant shift in policy within a Cabinet-level department. Such changes will migrate down to the Webmaster, and then to the FAQ writer.

Bombshells can also happen in the newsgroup community. If a television show is canceled, the *alt.* or *rec.* domain newsgroup won't necessarily disappear immediately, but the FAQ will almost certainly have to be rewritten. One way to avoid redoing a FAQ and keeping it simple is to link to outside sources of information rather than housing the data on the site. In the case of software FAQs, links to client programs that can make the software perform better are *de rigeur*. In Chapter 10, we explore how links from your FAQ page can improve not only the quality of your FAQ, but your entire Web site.

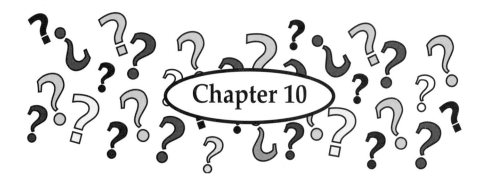

LEARNING FROM LINKS

In this chapter, you'll learn:

- When links are appropriate for a FAQ
- How to avoid linking pitfalls
- How FAQ links can calm customer doubts and fears
- How FAQ links can reinforce a marketing strategy
- When to link your FAQ to your archived material
- How to link for updates and upgrades

John Donne once wrote that "no man is an island." To that, add that "no FAQ should be an island." Frequently Asked Questions lists exist as a highly useful, but small, part of the bigger world of the Internet, where multimedia-equipped, 800-page Web sites and newsgroups with hundreds of threads make a road map necessary. The more complex the site, the more cumbersome it may be to crowd all the information that absolutely needs to be there onto the FAQ.

That's where links may help.

WHEN SHOULD YOU CONSIDER LINKS?

Webmasters might think about links from the FAQ to other places when:

1. A FAQ answer, or series of answers, introduces subject matter that isn't directly connected to your site's mission—but is of enough interest to your visitors to merit a hyperlink to a site or newsgroup where the issue or concept can be discussed in greater detail.

2. Executing an on-site technical application which is explained on your FAQ requires software that the site visitor isn't likely to have loaded on his or her machine. This need could be for a new product, or a new version of an existing client program that is an improvement over the old edition. It could well be that the site visitor has come to your FAQ page for the exact reason that something isn't working as well as it should.

   At times, this visitor need can even lead to revenue for the linking Web site. If you've been linking from your FAQ page to a software-provider's site for a month and can document a few thousand downloads, that is proof of a synergy between your site's visitors and their customers. That's the kind of connection that may convince the provider to expand the relationship from a link to an iconed, clickable ad. A good example of this is the clickable Netcom ad on "Getting Online with Windows 95" page on the "TWIG" Internet magazine Web site (*http://mass.thunderstone*).

   We explore this approach more fully in the next chapter. Clearly, linking to a Web site that makes the product available for either download or order is an attractive option.

3. A company or an organization has several Web sites, with FAQs on each of them. I favor linking to other FAQs directly from that page, rather than simply furnishing an icon back to the Home Page and then asking the visitor to click to another URL. Think about it. If your customer or constituent is looking for information, he or she is in a service-seeking mode. Routing her back to the Home Page, then linking from there to another site, making her parse down through three sub-menus until she finds the FAQ on a site she has never been to seems silly. Do the math: you're asking someone who already has a frustrated mindset and a short fuse to go through five stages until she reaches a related FAQ put up by another branch of the government or division of the company.

Local Links

Not all links need to be from FAQs to other sites or newsgroups. Some FAQ links can be "local," i.e., to other places on the site.

Depending on the particular answer you link from, here are some common-sense places within your site you can link to your FAQ page:

1. Depending on what kind of Web site you have, a page that contains a search form for company branch offices, satellite campuses, field representatives. A typical example:

    Q. How can I find a life insurance agent near me?

    A. Click here (you should put in code to hyperlink click here) for a list of our more than 200 nationwide offices. From there, you'll be able to search for the agent nearest you.

2. A link to get more company information. A typical example:

    Q. You're a new company. How do I know I'm dealing with reputable people?

    A. Our three managing partners have more than fifty combined years of industry experience working with major multinational clients. Click here (insert hyperlink) to learn more about them.

3. A link to a site-wide text search. An icon on either the first or last FAQ page should be enough. Such capability, by the way, should be a mandatory feature in almost any Web site, especially one with more than one FAQ. Several vendors, like Excite! and Personal Library Software, provide this service.

4. A link to the Webmaster or customer service where, through a Common Gateway Interface electronic mail form, more questions can be asked.

5. A link to on-site data repositories. In the last chapter, we learned how Netscape uses Technical Notes to embellish issues more gen-

erally discussed on their FAQ pages. Even sites that aren't technocentric can link back to archives, for example.

6.   Newsgroups might want to put up links from their FAQ to other newsgroups with similar missions.

7.   This sounds obvious, but simple advice rings true sometimes. Always put a link from your FAQ back to your Home Page! For your guest, that's so much easier than asking them to scroll up a browser's session menu until they find your site's Home Page cache.

In short, just about anywhere is a fair destination for a FAQ page link.

POSSIBLE PITFALL

There's a negative school of thought about links. It's a conundrum, really. FAQs well endowed with links are places with rich informational resources. Where appropriate, links to helper applications and vendor partners can push the marketing ball forward; but what happens if a visitor follows a link off your site and doesn't come back? That's a real concern. Two ways you can address this problem:

1.   The FAQ should have an invitation to "Bookmark This Page." If it's a FAQ that changes frequently, add "Reload Often."

2.   Have links back to your FAQ (or at least to your site's Home Page) **from** the offsite link. Folks' attention spans are short. What happens if, in the middle of a followed link, your three-year old walks up to you at the computer and says "Daddy, look!" Then your wife walks in, the phone rings…you get the picture. You'll make it easier for people to get back to your pages if you let the link door swing both ways.

Let's examine how some Web site and newsgroup FAQs have used the link process to enhance the helpfulness of their pages.

Wells Fargo Help

When San Francisco-based Wells Fargo Bank (*http:wellsfargo.com*) picked up millions of Los Angeles-based First Interstate Bank customers in 11 states after it bought the institution in 1996, it was faced with the existing challenge of providing a non-threatening Web presence to customers who had been used to a far less detailed First Interstate Bank Web site. Wells Fargo kept the shell of First Interstate Bank's site up for several months. The only content was a "change your bookmarks" referral to the Wells Fargo pages (see Figure 10.1).

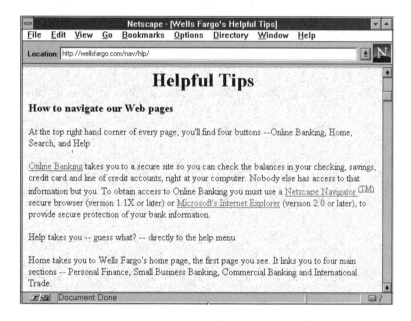

FIGURE 10.1 WELLS FARGO BANK'S "HELPFUL TIPS" PAGE.

Wells Fargo doesn't have a FAQ page in the traditional sense. Instead, it chooses to incorporate most of this information in a "Helpful Tips" page. A not-too-uncommon "links rationale" is evident here. Wells Fargo is one of the largest, most technologically sophisticated banks in the world, and was one of the first to allow more-or-less true online banking on its Web site. Obviously, such offerings present security and processing power issues—both for the server (Wells Fargo) and the clients (depositors).

These issues, in turn, endorse creation of a site with helper pages that explain and facilitate the several types of technical applications that online banking requires. That's why the "Helpful Tips" pages of the Wells Fargo Help area are chock full of informational access and software download links. The second paragraph of "Helpful Tips" contains links to Netscape and Microsoft, where, respectively, the latest versions of Netscape Navigator and Microsoft's Internet Explorer can be downloaded. Rather than just providing an icon from which a download access link can be launched, Wells Fargo does something important: it not only explains the link but tells you why you should go there: "Online Banking [another section of the Wells Fargo site linked from the "Helpful Tips" page] takes you to a secure site so you can check the balances in your checking, savings, credit card, and line of credit accounts, right at your computer. No one else has access to that information but you. To obtain access to Online Banking you must use a Netscape Navigator secure browser of Microsoft's Internet Explorer to provide secure protection of your bank information." If I were a new user, I'd want to know why I should take 15 or 20 minutes out of a busy day and link to a site for an application that will crowd my hard drive even more than it is. Using several trigger words, Wells Fargo tells me why.

In the following section, "How to Jump from One Site to the Next," the bank describes what a jump is, and does it in an enjoyable way. Rather than using a hypothetical example, a link is actually provided to "Holmenkollen," the official Web site for the Holmenkollen Ski Jump in Oslo, Norway. There is no relation between ski jumps and online banking, but obviously, this has been done to lessen the intimidation factor for new users.

Online Banking also requires processing and display power that not every computer user has. To its considerable credit, Wells Fargo avoids such pronouncements as "you must" in favor of far more user-friendly language: "Let us recommend software for you that can make your system as fast, robust and enjoyable as possible." Isn't that nicer than some Web sites which act like digital drill sergeants and literally order you to download some software? If I don't have that software, I am likely to be a new user. I may already be feeling much dread from this whole new Web experience I am undergoing. The last thing I need is to be ordered around!

But just how do you download from a Web link? It sounds easy, but isn't, for newbies. The mechanics of capturing and then bringing to life a self-compressing file can be frustrating not only for new users, but for experienced ones. Fargo's Help Page realizes this and takes a page from the "this won't hurt a bit" school of customer counsel: "The following section has hyperlinks to software that you can download to (your) computer from the Internet. To do this, you need to set your software to 'save to disk' before clicking on one of the following links." Netscape Navigator and Microsoft Internet Explorer links are again provided here, as well as a series of "helper" programs that facilitate experiencing sound, graphics and movie watching.

There may not be moving pictures on the Wells Fargo site, so why link to such programs from the Wells Fargo Help page? One word: marketing. If you take advantage of the Fargo link to a program like Player (for watching Quicktime movies) maybe, just maybe, you'll remember what site turned you on to this way cool experience in the first place. It's sort of like getting a cool tie from your cousin for your birthday. Every time you're complimented on your tie, you think of your cousin and what a nice gift she bought you. Do you suppose that spirit of beneficence on the Wells Fargo Help page will help them get more customers? Maybe not a lot of them, but I'll wager it gets them at least a few more.

The "Games Domain" FAQ

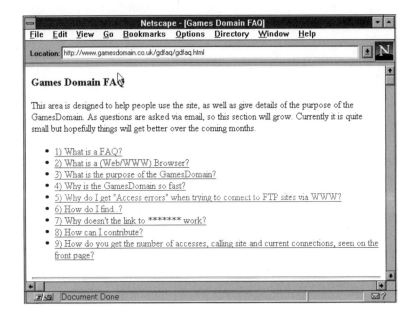

FIGURE 10.2 GAMESDOMAIN WEB FAQ.

An interesting FAQ on the highly popular "GamesDomain" Web site (*http://www.gamesdomain.co.uk*), exists for a special purpose—one that will only increase in popularity. Until recently, playing games on the Web was not a fulfilling experience. The Web was a static, point-and-click medium. This meant that playing games on the Web was mostly a matter of choosing a series of actions from a multiple-choice menu. B-O-R-I-N-G.

Yet with the explosion of multimedia applications like Shockwave, RealAudio and Quicktime, true interactivity has come to Web game sites. There are new versions of these programs, and accompanying helpful utilities every few months. For game developers, this means that regular updates of existing games are mandatory. And when you put out a new version of your Web site, you need a FAQ to explain how the new edition differs from the old.

Since you will likely bring some of your older users along for the enhanced, thrilling new ride, linking to facilitating utilities libraries is important knowledge for users. Here's an example of how the eight-question "Direct Download" FAQ deals with this issue:

Q. "What do I do with a file that has a ZIP extension?"

A. "You need to expand the archive using a program such as PKUNZIP. If you do not have a copy it can be found at *wcl-l.bham.ac.uk*. Once you have a copy of PKUNZIP and the game archive file (.ZIP) do the following:

- "Create a new directory for the game.
- "Place the file in the directory.
- "Type: **pkunzip -d file.zip** (where `file.zip` is the name of the down-loaded file).
- "Play the game."

In its link, this file performed an important service that just about every Web FAQ download link needs to. Remember this advice well: **Don't only provide the link, but tell your FAQ page visitors how to download and activate it!** This will save you quite a bit of ill will and make you new friends.

LINKING FOR ELECTRONIC COMMERCE COMFORT

The torrid growth of electronic commerce on the Web has at least two implications for FAQ writers.

1. For many, customers it is a poorly understood, intimidating concept. On Web sites where electronic commerce is used, the FAQ writer must be, in a sense, a missionary to the heathens, explaining how electronic commerce works and why it's safe.

2. Electronic commerce uses and requires sophisticated client-server tools. Linking to the Web sites of companies that provide such tools is a sound approach.

In 1996, Pineville, KY-based Security First Network Bank (*http://www.sfnb.com/*) became the first Internet-only financial institution. Within a few months of its opening, SFNB became a site where you could do virtually any financial transaction online that heretofore had been limited to branch office visits or "press 1" telephone banking. This complicated suite of services now offered in an unfamiliar environment naturally spawned a FAQ. SFNB calls theirs "Commonly Asked Questions," but a "rose is a rose…" (see Figure 10.3).

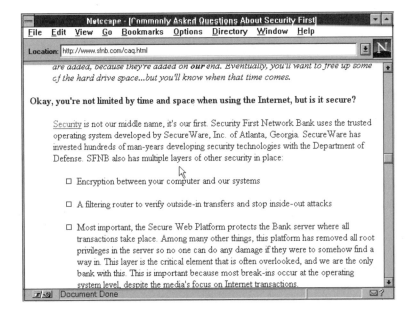

FIGURE 10.3 SECURITY FIRST NETWORK BANK'S FAQ TAKES THE FEAR OUT OF ELECTRONIC COMMERCE.

Twenty-seven questions went up on the SFNB "CAQ." There's only one link, but its placement is innovative. Several "Further Information" Q-A's follow the main CAQ. The second of these is:

Q. "Is my money insured by the FDIC?

A. "Yes. Subject to applicable limits, deposits in Security First are insured by the FDIC. For more information, see What is the FDIC?"

This link doesn't take you to the Federal Deposit Insurance Corporation— at least not right away; you're whisked first to an information page within the SFNB site. Once you're there, you see links to the FDIC Home Page and the FDIC Gopher.

The link instructions carry an understated, but vital, confidence-building marketing message. The particular location on the FDIC site where the certification information on SFNB resides is given. Thus, the link from the "CAQ" to an organization with as much confidence-building ability as the FDIC is no accident. The bank is based in Pineville, KY, which few people have heard of. It also is an Internet-only institution, so some sort of legitimizing inprimateur is mission-critical.

SFNB's CAQ, incidentally, also has a link to "the President's Office." Putting a human face on a bank with no branches once again uses a link from a FAQ (OK, CAQ) page to convey a marketing-driven message of confidence and friendliness.

The SPRYNET FAQ: An Onsite Link Bonanza

The SPRYNET site, (*http://www.sprynet.com/*) the Web presence for the CompuServe-provided beginners-level online service that went online in 1996, has more links from its main FAQ pages than almost any other site I've been to. Just about all these links are internal but SPRYNET isn't being isolationist, it is just being resourceful. The number of these links from their FAQ pages testify to the comprehensiveness of the site in general. Refer to Figure 10.4.

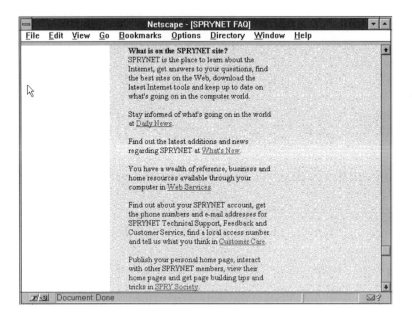

FIGURE 10.4 SPRYNET FAQ LINKS TO OTHER PARTS OF THE WEB SITE ENRICH ITS INFORMATIONAL CONTENT.

There are at least eight links from the SPRYNET FAQ to other places on its Web site. Each link has a clear purpose, one which FAQ writers for almost any well-endowed *.com* site would do well to emulate. Some of these links are to:

- SPRY Online Support;
- A download for SPRYNET's SPRY CHAT program;
- SPRYNET's Internet Support Forum;
- An electronic mail link to SPRYNET customer support;
- A searchable list of local access numbers for SPRYNET;

- The "What's New" Page, where, it is explained, future news may involve such enhancements as allowing multiple Email addresses for each SPRYNET account.

- A place where you can download a version of the SPRY Mosaic browser that will work with 32-bit systems.

- A direct download of SPRYNET. This, perhaps, is the most important link, establishing the SPRYNET FAQ as an effective storefront not only for ordering the product, but for receiving it.

- Last, and certainly not least, a link to CompuServe, SPRYNET's "bigger brother" service. This link is introduced with the disclaimer that some users may want the greater collection of online content on the corporate parent's online offering.

CHECKFREE'S FAQ LINKS: SAVE YOUR WALLET, SAVE THE EARTH

CheckFree (*http://www.mc2-csr.com/vmail/checkfree*) is an Atlanta-based company that enables subscribers to pay utility, credit card, and other bills over the Internet using the customers' checking account. In essence, the company's CheckFree Manager service functions as a cyberspace paymaster, cutting all checks that a customer requests and mailing them out to creditors on a pre-scheduled basis.

Their 16-question FAQ sticks to the basics, but with a few salient points thrown in. Most of the early questions deal with how to sign up, what kinds of electronic and hard-copy check plans are available, and CheckFree's method of disbursement to the accounts that you specify. Yet the tone of the FAQ, as well as its links, tackles two key issues and turns them into a solid marketing advantage.

Electronic commerce companies all have the challenge of convincing prospective customers that the comparatively new field is safe. Security break-ins by hackers are liable to make the Business section of the morning paper—and have been referred to in prime-time news shows. The majority of Americans get their news from these vehicles. Appealing to a general interest audience, the editors and news directors of these operations realize that a sensational security violation at a major bank is "sexier" news than a detailed description of security-enhancing encryption technology. Add to that a public already in a red-alert mode about crime, and you get a healthy dose of skepticism about seemingly vulnerable technologies like electronic funds transfer.

CheckFree tackles the subject head-on in its link from the FAQ to an "Is CheckFree Safe?" page. On this page, the company could have responded in pious tones. It didn't, choosing instead to promote the image of safety with a user-friendly game replete with symbolism. With a GIF of a nine-compartment, CheckFree Safe, the game pages consist of five multiple-choice questions about site security. See Figure 10.5.

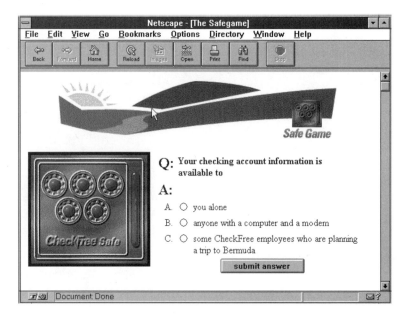

FIGURE 10.5 CHECKFREE'S FAQ HAS A SPECIAL SECTION DEVOTED TO SECURITY.

When I was a part-time college instructor, I learned a couple of neat tricks about how to phrase multiple-choice questions: always put at least one non-plausible choice in the answer field, as well as an answer that makes a key point. Then, include the correct answer as well. Taking this approach, one of CheckFree's game questions asks how someone can tell the technology is secure. Proving the old adage that if you are standing in the middle while being attacked from both sides, you are probably right, the two wrong answers are both ridiculous, while the correct choice is a non-intimidating mention of encryption technology.

CheckFree's "Eco-Links"

We've mentioned several times that a FAQ, and the links to and from it, are great marketing tools. CheckFree has taken this advice as gospel. Its FAQ question, "Does CheckFree Help the Environment?" has an answer with a link to a page of environmental sites called Green Days. On this page are hyperlinks to more than 25 "ecologically minded organizations," including the Rainforest Action Network, the Planet Earth Home Page, and the Biodiversity and Ecosystems Network (see Figure 10.6).

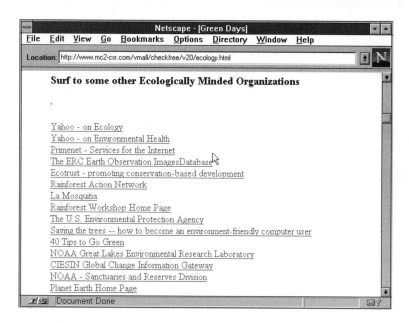

FIGURE 10.6 BY LINKING TO SEVERAL ENVIRONMENTAL WEB SITES, CHECKFREE'S FAQ REINFORCES A COMPANY MARKETING MESSAGE.

What does this possibly have to do with paying your bills through CheckFree? The implication is obvious: electronic funds transfers reduce the demand for paper checks, saving a few trees. Plus you might even be able to cut down on your trips to the post office to mail your bill payments, and thus use a few less gallons of gasoline per month. By linking from the FAQ page to organizations that are looking to save the air and the forest, CheckFree is positioning themselves as a friend of the environment. The people at CheckFree realize, though, that positions taken by some of these linked environmental groups might not be wildly popular with some of their more conservative customers. There are those people who think "left-wing tree hugger" every time they see an environmentalist. That's an important reason for a disclaimer.

By the way, every Web FAQ that carries offsite links needs a disclaimer. It's a contentious world out there and a disclaimer lets you cover your tail. This is an emerging aspect of Internet law on several fronts, not the least of which are copyright, libel, and negligence. If you provide a link to a site that gives bad financial advice (without its own disclaimer), people may remember just how they found that accursed URL: you directed them there. Similarly, if you point your visitors to software that crashes their system, you'll be blamed for creating the problem.

CheckFree's is one of the most cogent link disclaimers, and might make a good boilerplate for you:

"The preceding sites are not under the control of CheckFree Corporation. We make no representation regarding the content of these sites, or the quality, safety or suitability of any software found on these sites. CheckFree Corporation does not endorse any of these sites, but provides them as a convenience to you. There are dangers inherent in the use of any software found on the Internet. Make sure that you completely understand the risks before retrieving any software on the Internet."

At the bottom of the "Green Days" link page, you can click right back to the FAQ. It's good to know that unlike in real life, you can go home again.

THE FAQ-TO-ARCHIVES LINK

There are several thousand Web sites run by newspapers, magazines, and book publishers. Most of these entities have something in common: they've been around for awhile, and have terabytes of legacy content. It's possible that they've been digitizing this content for several years, either for their own internal use or for sale to for-profit online data repositories like Dialog or Lexis-Nexis.

Another paradox is put into play here. The editorial or research content the publication has assembled over the years has been done for the purpose of attracting readers. Now that some of these readers have Web browsers, they are going to come to the publication's site and may want to execute keyword searches for archival or newly published material.

And just where on the site will they go for directions? To the FAQ page!

The Right Connections: The "TechWeb" FAQ

Since data searching can be a fairly complicated topic, you may not only want to explain the process in your FAQ, but you might want to provide a direct link to the archive from your FAQ. A good example of how to do this right is the TechWeb FAQ assembled by CMP Publications Inc., publishers of such titles as *NetGuide*, *Communications Week* and *Information Week*.

"TechWeb" is an organically flowing site, carrying daily editions of several CMP titles. There's a link from CMP's main FAQ both to the main CMP archive and to its Newsroom central news directory, which contains a list of current stories. Another Q-A sequence directs visitors how to do a search, also taking them there (see Figure 10.7).

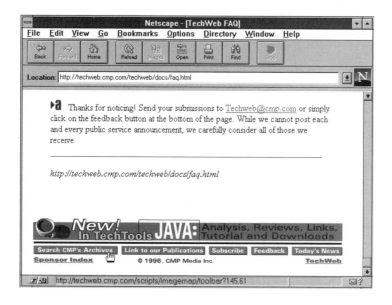

FIGURE 10.7 CMP's "TECHWEB" FAQ LINKS TO ITS ARCHIVE.

Q. I use *TechSearch* quite a bit and I've noticed that when I search on terms like Windows 95 the results page sometimes brings up stories that include 'Windows' and '95' but not necessarily 'Windows 95.' How can I improve the results?

A. The Search Tips link on our main TechSearch page explains how to best complete searches on multiple words and phrases using Boolean connectors. What's a Boolean connector? We're glad you asked! [the sentiment is placed here in an attempt to make the user feel less intimidated] They work this way: For best results on a phrase such as windows 95 enter 'windows AND 95' or 'windows ADJ 95' (ADJ stands for adjacent). Note that the connectors are uppercase and the search terms are lowercase.

The Search Tips page also has an electronic mail-back link for further questions. That's a good idea.

Like a growing number of news-related Web sites, CMP also has "information agent" capabilities. Such "agents" electronically filter news stories containing certain keywords the subscriber designates, and then delivers these via Email every business morning. These revenue-producing services often work best with specialized software. You can download a copy of CMP's TechWeb Direct information agent software directly from their FAQ page.

Medical Site Links: the "Typing Injury" FAQ

Most health-related Web sites don't have FAQ pages, preferring fact sheets instead. Maybe that's because they view the FAQ format as a bit too gimmicky for their solemn missions. That's their choice. Still, medical topics, with their trove of published literature, are the right type of site to provide links to libraries. Links to disease-prevention sites are another valid approach for medical FAQs.

Maybe it's because I've been at the keyboard for days, but one of the best FAQs for medical links is the "Usenet Typing Injury" FAQ, which is mirrored on the Web at (*http://ww.cs.princeton.edu/grad/dwallach*). This

FAQ was assembled not by a team of medical experts, but by Dan Wallach of the Computer Sciences Department at Princeton University. People who work with computers know what typing injuries like carpal tunnel syndrome can be like. They "feel your pain." See Figure 10.8.

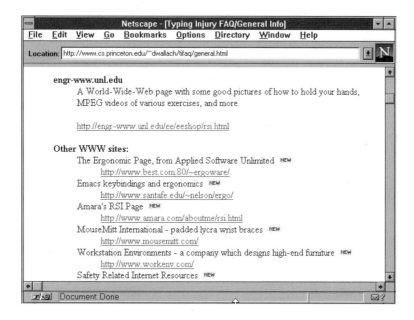

FIGURE 10.8 THE USENET "TYPING INJURY" FAQ HAS PHOTOS AND LINKS TO WEB SITES OF COMPANIES WHICH MAKE ERGONOMICALLY FRIENDLY KEYBOARDS.

In his 58KB FAQ, Wallach has taken a different approach than might be expected. He hasn't loaded it up with medical links, but with listings, reviews of, and contact information for, manufacturers of ergonomically correct keyboards and peripherals.

With its Home Page graphic featuring a photograph of a pair of hands on an old manual typewriter, this location looks much more like a Web site than a standard, text-only newsgroup.

One noteworthy link is to the anonymous FTP (File Transfer Protocol) of Matias Corporation (*explorer.dgp.toronto.edu:/pub/Half-QUERTY*). Based in Rexdale, Ontario, Canada, this company makes a cleverly named product called Half-QUERTY. Wallach describes this as "software (that will) mirror the keyboard when you hold down the space bar, allowing you to type one-handed." As one who has suffered from tendonitis, this sure sounds great to me. The only problem is, Half-QUERTY only runs under Mac OS and DOS, as we learn from the "Supports" sector included with each review in this FAQ.

Another section of the "Typing Injury" FAQ contains a link to the University of Nebraska-Lincoln's RSI (Repetitive Stress Injury) Page. Once there, you can see exercise videos as well as a searchable locator for physicians who treat RSI.

Another powerhouse on the "Typing Industry" FAQ is the "Keyboard Alternatives" section. "Answers To Frequently Asked Questions" contains links to more than 40 Web sites maintained by manufacturers of wrist-friendly keyboards and speech recognition software. Several GIFs are included as well, swelling the size of this portion to more than 700K. Speech-recognition links are included because these devices will cut down on your keystrokes and save your beleaguered wrists and hands.

I've saved the best for last. Wallach's "Answers to Frequently Asked Questions about Typing Injuries" is part of the "Typing Injury" FAQ— but isn't phrased like a FAQ. Instead, the "Answers" are divided into seven sections, with links everywhere you click. You could have fooled me. The quality of informational and graphical presentation resembles a high-dollar Web site, not a low-cost newsgroup. The links have a lot to do with that quality. Most of the links are in the first portion, "Publications, mailing lists, newsgroups, WWW pointers, etc." In turn, this trove of links is divided into seven sections, most of which are graced with links. Webmasters and FAQ maintainers, you'd have a lot to learn by visiting his FAQ. Here's how Wallach has divided this section of his FAQ and what links are provided from where (refer to Figure 10.9).

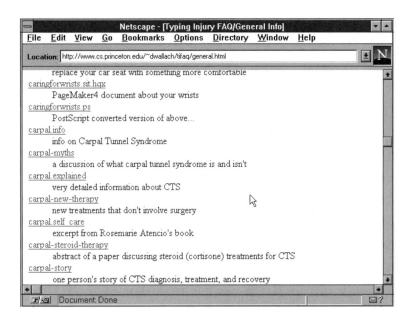

FIGURE 10.9 THE "TYPING INJURY" FAQ ALSO LINKS TO SEVERAL MEDICAL LITERATURE SOURCES.

1. Publications: links to CTDNews, a publication that covers related pain and trauma issues.

2. FTP, Gopher and WWW Sites: links to the Boston RSI Archive and Electronic Rehabilitation Resource Center Gopher, as well as to more than 20 appropriate Web sites. Some of these include "Safety Related Internet Resources," "A Patient's Guide to Carpal Tunnel Syndrome," and the U.S. Occupational Safety and Health Administration (OSHA). There's also a link to the FAQs for "a2x," "a program to interface an external keyboard or speech synthesizer to an X-window system," and "DragonDictate," not a Multi-user Dungeon, but a speech recognition system.

3. Listserv Mailing Lists: you can't actually link to Listserv's; however, Wallach has done the next best thing, describing several, giving their URLs and instructions on how to subscribe to each.

4. Usenet newsgroups: several are linked, including the self-explanatory *misc.health, therapy.occupational, sci.med.occupational*, and *alt.support.arthritis*.

5. Real-Time Chatting: Mentions online service forums that occasionally deal with typing industry issues.

6. Books/Literature: links to bibliographies of medical literature about the typing industry, as well as to the Email addresses of several authors who have written books about the topic.

7. Societies/Support Groups: Wallach intends to have several links here soon. He says he was too busy to put connections there when his newsgroup first went up. No apology needed: plainly he burnt the 3 A.M. oil putting this exhaustively intricate offering together. Hopefully, he didn't get carpal tunnel in the process.

FAQ LINKS FOR TOOLS: JAVASOFT

We detail site-software information exchanges via Frequently Asked Questions lists in the next chapter, but links from the FAQ page are a natural for this type of application. Why? Because in its common role as a problem-solving resource, a software-related FAQ is likely to contain questions about why such and such an application or applet doesn't work—and tips about how to make the given application function properly. At times, the application is faulty because a few bits inside the software code are causing problems. In this competitive environment, it is incumbent upon either the software company or its partners to fix the problem. The dilemma is most often solved by either rewriting a few bits of code, or coming up with a subsequent version of the software. The Internet is a logical platform for dissemination of these fixes. What better place to post the availability of these transferable fixes than on a FAQ page—a gathering point for solution-seeking software bug victims?

The JavaSoft site (*http://www.javasoft.com*) has a five-part, 27-section "Frequently Asked Questions about Java" FAQ that addresses these problems. Most of its links follow one of two general models: onsite or offsite informational and operational tips; and places to get updates. Here are some of the sections and questions of the JavaSoft FAQ that contain links. The specific connections are mentioned after each question (refer to Figure 10.10).

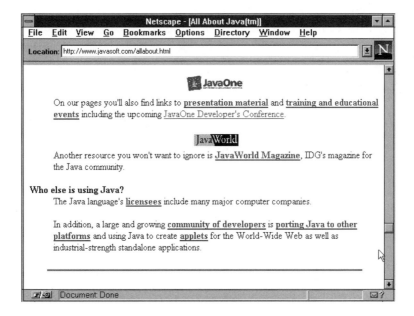

FIGURE 10.10 THE JAVASOFT FAQ IS LADEN WITH USEFUL LINKS.

Getting Started With Java: availability, latest releases, ports, downloading, installing, JavaScript.

> Q: What platforms is the 1.02 JDK (a recent Java release) available on?

> Links To: *http://java.sun.com/devcorner.html*, an URL within the parent Sun Microsystems site that details how to configure 1.02 JDK with various Windows, Mac, and other platforms.

Q: What about a version for my favorite platform 'XYZ?'? (a hypothetical platform). When can I get it?

Links To: *http//java.sun.com/Mail/external lists.html*, Java's archive of third-party platform-specific mailing lists.

Q: How can I get started with programming in Java?

Links To: *http//java.sun.com/starter.html*, a guide to material helpful to beginners.

Getting Information and Staying in Touch: the Java name, documentation of all sorts, newsgroups, mailing lists, Java courses, bug reports.

Q: Can the Java team keep me informed of latest developments?

Links To: *http://java.sun/com/*, the Sun Web site Home Page, and *http://java.sun.com/new.html*.

Q: What newsgroups carry information about Java?

It isn't hyperlinked, but the *comp.lang.java* newsgroup, which covers Java language and programming, is mentioned.

Q: What documentation is available? In what formats? How can I get it?

Links To: *http://java.sun.com/doc.programmer.html*, where White Papers and other data about Java are stored.

Q: Are Java programming courses available? Where? At what price?

Links To: *http://www.sun.com/sunservice/suned/*, a regularly updated online schedule of in-person Java programming courses held around the world. This answer and link, like so many others on well-executed FAQs, moves the marketing ball forward.

Q: How do I file bug reports or feature suggestions?

Links To: *http://java.sun.com/GettingInTouch/Bug Report.html*, a site for user feedback.

The next section of the JavaSoft FAQ acknowledges the need to link to specific sites on the Web pages of vendor partners.

Java-Enabled Netscape: which versions, alpha/beta applets.

Q: Can all Netscape 2.0 versions run Java applets?

Links To: *http://home.netscape.com/eng/mozilla/2.0/relnotes/*, which contains Netscape platform-release notes.

Q: Can you help me with using Java in Netscape?

Links To: *http://home/mcom/com/assist/support/client/*, a site that contains specific advice on how to work with applets in Netscape browsers.

Marketing, Licensing and Planning: licensing, logos, plans.

Q: Is Java free? Where can I get information about licensing?

Links To: *http://java.sun.com/license.html*, a Web page that lists guidelines for using and licensing Java technology.

Troubleshooting doesn't have any links but does provide brief tutorials on specific problems Java users may face.

NEWSGROUP LINKS FOR TOOLS: THE "INDEPENDENT JPEG" FAQ

With few exceptions, you won't find software links within newsgroups. One worthy exception is the "Independent JPEG Group," which can also be found on the Web at: *http://www.cis.ohio-state.edu/hypertext/faq/usenet/jpeg~faq/top.html*. There are several links, for tools or additional instructions. Refer to Figure 10.11.

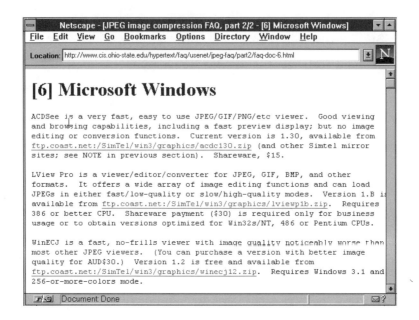

FIGURE 10.11 THE "INDEPENDENT JPEG" FAQ LINKS FOR ADDITIONAL TOOLS AND INSTRUCTIONS.

There's only a few links here, but they are quite useful. The answer may seem overly obtuse, but keep in mind that earlier sections of this FAQ described what JPEG (the Joint Photographic Experts Group 256-color Web graphics format) is. I'm including a significant portion of this answer not only to illustrate the one link's roles and how it is introduced, but to give an example of a well-answered FAQ.

> Q. How do I recognize which file format I have, and what do I do about it?
>
> A. If you have an alleged JPEG file that your software won't read, it's likely to be HSI format or some other proprietary JPEG-based format. You can tell what you have by inspecting the first few bytes of the file.

Section 4 of this answer shows how FAQ writer Tom Lane prepared for the introduction of the link:

A. Macintosh PICT file, if JPEG-compressed, will have several hundred bytes of header (often 726 bytes, but not always) followed by JPEG data. Look for the 3-byte sequence (hex) FF D8 FF. The text 'Photo-JPEG' will usually appear shortly before this header, and 'AppleMark' or 'JFIF' will usually appear shortly after it. Strip off everything before the FF D8 FF and you will usually be able to decode the file (This will fail if the PICT image is divided into multiple 'bands'; fortunately, banded PICTs aren't very common).

A banded PICT contains multiple JPEG datastreams whose heights add up to the total image height. These need to be stitched back together into one image. Bailey Brown has some simple tools for this purpose on a Web page at *http://www.blarg./net~bailey/photo-jpeg/photo~jpeg.html*.

Brown also posts on the Independent JPEG Group, and is known to FAQ maintainer Lane. Such familiarity isn't a necessity, though. Web and newsgroup FAQ writers should use search utilities like Alta-Vista to look for Web pages and Listservs where answers to questions about their FAQ are stored (often without their knowledge). Then, send an Email to the site's Webmaster or moderator and ask if a mutual link might be feasible. Odds are strong that he or she will be flattered.

Your customers will be happy, too. In the next chapter, we'll discuss how a FAQ can be both a money-maker and money-saver.

MAKING MONEY, SAVING MONEY

In this chapter, you'll learn:

- How to make money through links to subscription ordering pages
- Making money by selling advertising on your FAQ page
- Making money by announcing products on your FAQ page
- Using your FAQ to sell products you no longer market
- How FAQs can save you printing costs
- FAQs of the future will be proactive money-savers

A well-designed Frequently Asked Questions list can generate revenue for you. It can help the commercially-minded Web site directly or indirectly sell products and services the company is offering.

At the same time, a comprehensive FAQ can save you money. By answering most of the simple-to-intermediate questions customers have, it can lighten the load of simplistic inquiries that plague many help desks. Since bits and bytes of helper application information stored on your server won't need health insurance or flex time, payroll savings may result if you are able to migrate some of the problem-solving apparatus from human beings to silicon. By using a few commands to update your Web site content and announcing the new information on your FAQ, you may also save a bundle on printing and postage costs by not scheduling a special production run for new, hard-copy brochures.

MAKING MONEY DIRECTLY

There are no exact, foolproof formulas out there that will tell you to the dollar how much money a FAQ can make you. There are, however, three basic models for how a FAQ can make money for you:

1. The most direct connection can be seen in FAQs that provide direct access to a revenue-producing mechanism, like subscriptions, or an electronic mail link where your site visitors can order your products. Parts of your FAQ that make it possible for customers to order or subscribe become real, front-end information generators.

2. A FAQ can carry advertising on its Home Page. The popular search engines find that such a strategy can earn them several thousand dollars a month per ad. These color ads, which allow links to more information about the advertisers' product, can appear either at the top or the bottom of the FAQ cover page.

3. A FAQ can solicit advertising for the site. We'll explore a couple of specific models later in this chapter, but a typical sequence might involve placing the following Q-A near the end of a series of marketing-driven answers that have explained the Web site's intent.

Here's a typical revenue-generating FAQ Q-A template you might wish to use:

Q. How can I advertise on your Web site, and how much will it cost me?

A. Listings in our directory start at only $300 a month. Our servers say our directory gets 5,000 hits a day. That means that over the course of a month, 150,000 people will see your ad. If your ad costs $300, that means that you'll be paying only two cents each time a prospective customer sees it.

   An attention-getting ad on our site's Home Page costs in the $800-a-month range. About 20,000 people will see your ad every month. If, on average, only one-tenth of one percent (20 people) click on your ad and buy your product, the ad will have paid for itself and you'll be yet another of our satisfied marketing partners. Click here for a list of companies who advertise with us, and how they say it helps them.

Why did this particular Q-A work?

1. It sold a financial transaction directly, rather than simply offering a link to another part of the Web site. If the FAQ writer had responded with "How can I advertise…?" with a dispassionate statement along the lines of "click here to go to our Marketing Opportunities page," she'd run the risk of losing sales. Time-pressed people sometimes don't follow every link you give them, but you know that if the answer is in the FAQ they will read it. They are "there" anyway!

2. The least-expensive option is mentioned first. This is a timeless sales tool. A salesperson will try to convince you about the basic viability of a product before he or she mentions an enhanced version.

3. A quantifiable relationship is laid out between the money you are asking them to spend and results they should expect. Media buyers like to see not only how much an ad will cost them, but how many readers their ad will get. Two cents per reader impression is actually very little.

4. Your FAQ fosters a sense of community. Both sides know you want their money, but for their check, your ad prospect gets a seat at the table.

MAKING MONEY INDIRECTLY

Obviously the connection is less demonstrable, but when a FAQ on a *.com* Web site does a good job as a road map to other parts of the site that allow for revenue-producing mechanisms, the FAQ's money-making value is as a cohesive part of a greater whole.

Here's a template you might wish to use. Let's say your company makes four basic product lines. Several preceding Q-A's have been devoted to an explanation of the product's characteristics and assets.

Q. How can I order these products directly?

A. You can dial 1-800-555-3825 between the hours of 9 A.M. to 6 P.M. Monday–Saturday, Pacific Time, and a courteous representative can help you. Or, you can click *here* for a state-by-state listing of authorized dealers. We're also working on a secure, electronic ordering program where you'll be able to purchase our products directly from your computer. Watch this space for updates.

You've used the FAQ to sell the product and point to places where your site visitors can buy your merchandise. You've also sketched out the possibility of an exciting future when ordering your goods will be even more convenient. This way, they will repeatedly come back to your FAQ—setting the income-generation phenomenon of your FAQ and your Web site back into cycle time and time again.

Let's now look at how some companies have turned their FAQs into money-makers.

THE "USA TODAY" FAQ: SELLING SUBS ONLINE

Early in 1996, the full-content "USA Today" Web site added a live link from its FAQ to a subscription form for its newspaper and sister publication, "Baseball Weekly."

"In the first month alone our FAQ generated 58 subscriptions," says Larry Sanders, business manager of the USA Today Information

Network, the newspaper department that runs the highly-trafficked Web site. For much of its first year, the FAQ-to-subscription-page link has generated more than 200 new subscribers a month. In its first year, this resulted in more than $200,000 in estimated revenue. There's no practical way to tell how many people would have subscribed even if the link weren't there. Still, $200,000 has a nice ring to it. That pays the salaries of three or four experienced reporters for the print side—journalists whose skills presumably enhance the value of the core product.

Enhanced value, in turn, makes the product that much more appealing. You don't have to run a newspaper to tell that incremental FAQ revenue can add cash to your coffers. If you develop the FAQ-writing skills within your organization, adding a FAQ to your site will cost almost nothing. At the same time, improvements you can make as a result having this "extra" cash can enhance your product's worthiness, which should bring in even more customers.

Direct FAQ-to-sub links should be placed after you've already conveyed your marketing message. Placing the link before you've delivered your pitch wastes a valuable opportunity. As any salesperson will tell you, it's almost always better to close the deal before you ask for money. By the time your visitors notice the subscription questions, they will either have tuned out or will still be on the hook. This is the time to get them to your subscription mechanism. USA Today does this with a direct link from the FAQ to the circulation department. A server there retrieves the Emailed sub requests, and processes them according to the information the applicant submits. This approach will also work well for FAQs on *.edu* or *.gov* sites with back-issue documents for sale.

It also isn't a good idea to overload your subscription Q-A with a lot of hyperbole. Link it, and they will click, as USA Today does in Figure 11.1.

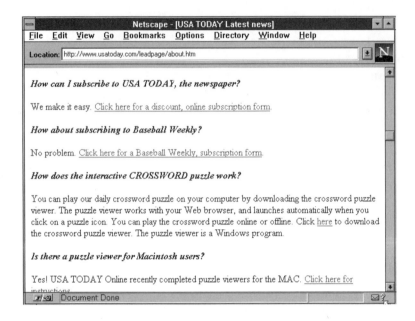

FIGURE 11.1 THE "USA TODAY" FAQ GENERATES INCOME BY LINKING TO THE CIRCULATION DEPARTMENT.

Q. How can I subscribe to USA Today, the newspaper?

A. We make it easy. Click here for a discount, online subscription form.

Advertisers call these "copy points." Just in the one-sentence question and the two-sentence answer, there are three:

1. "How can I" uses the first person and thus establishes a personal connection. The question's phrasing goes inside the mind of the reader. Too many "how" questions are phrased "How do you?" which just isn't as personable.

2. "We make it easy" plays Devil's advocate. Since some visitors to the USA Today site may be time-pressed or confused about how electronic ordering works, the phrase is reassuring. It's the FAQ writers' version of "this won't hurt a bit." Usually, it doesn't hurt.

3.   The pricing benefits of the subscription link are clearly positioned. The magic mantra is "discount." Someone might be prone to think, "yes, they say it's easy, but I've got to turn over the roast in five minutes." Plus, some people have a natural aversion to filling out forms. You've got to take some of the anticipated pain away or else people won't play your game.

The following Q-A asks "How about subscribing to Baseball Weekly?" The answer also communicates the no-hassle message: "No problem. Click here for a Baseball Weekly subscription form."

New Sales for Old Issues

In another revenue generator for content providers, the "USA Today" FAQ asks an on-purpose leading question about obtaining back issues. Thousands of publications, most of whom keep some back issues around, might do well with adapting this particular Q-A:

Q. How can I find a past article or BACK ISSUE of the USA Today newspaper?

   [Note that by putting "BACK ISSUE" in all-caps, USA Today highlights the bigger income-generating of the two retrieval services.]

A. You can find many articles by clicking on the SEARCH button on USA TODAY Online's front page. Archives of past stories are not yet available on-line to the public. To track down an article that appeared in a past issue of USA TODAY, Baseball Weekly, Gannett News Service or USA Weekend, call Research Line at 703-276-5864. Hours are Monday through Friday, 9 A.M. to 5 P.M.

   Research Line is a fee-based service. If you need a specific back issue of USA TODAY and you know the date, call the USA TODAY Customer Service Center at 800-872-0001. The cost is $2.00 for each back issue, plus shipping & handling. Each order must be prepaid either with an American Express,

Visa or Master Card. If you would prefer to mail a check or money order, please call for the total cost.

This highly serviceable answer mentions the services rendered, phone number, available hours, price, and transactional alternatives for the service. Each is important for the following, reasons:

1. Give your customers an idea of what's available should they take the time to call. It will make them more willing to do so, as well as shorten the time spent online. They won't have to ask the poor customer service rep the same tiring questions. Calls will be handled quicker, reducing hold time and enabling more income-generating questions to be handled quicker

2. A phone number is vital. Your customers have to know the best way to reach you. I've read many FAQs that put in the wrong number, like a main switchboard number instead of a direct line. Some list no phone number at all. Sounds comical, but it is really a bit sad. Customer-relations, like love, can easily wind up on the rocks because of poor lines of communication.

3. Nothing is wrong with running your operation from 9 to 5, but let your customers know about it first. This way, someone sitting down to order at 8 P.M. won't be disappointed. If they are, they might not come back.

4. The low, $2.00 price quoted in the FAQ is obviously a selling point. If people are interested in a product or service but think it costs too much, they might not pursue it further. Using your FAQ to communicate lots of value for little cost is a sound strategy.

5. Most people have credit cards. Mentioning these three familiar brand names makes the process sound even easier.

THE STARSIGHT FAQ-TO-SUB MODEL

StarSight is an interactive on-screen program guide service with seven-day information grids of programming available to cable television subscribers and satellite-dish owners alike.

StarSight's excellent, 13-question FAQ starts out with the boilerplate "What Is (Starsight)?" Subsequent answers address its main features, how it works, and what type of StarSight products are available. All questions are in capital letters. See Figure 11.2.

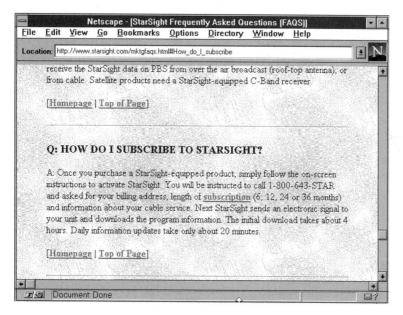

FIGURE 11.2 THE "STARSIGHT" FAQ HAS A LINE FOR SUBSCRIPTION APPLICATIONS.

Then, **after** all this information is conveyed, comes the subscription-link set-up question. This is the ninth of the 13 questions, and reads as follows:

Q. How do I subscribe to StarSight?

[Once again, the firstperson is used here to establish conviviality.]

A. Once you purchase a StarSight-equipped product, simply follow the on-screen instructions to activate StarSight. You will be instructed to call 1-800-643-STAR and asked for your billing address, length of subscription [the word subscription is hyperlinked], (6, 12, 24 or 36 months) and information about your cable service. Next StarSight sends an electronic signal to your unit and downloads the program information. The initial download takes about four hours. Daily information updates take only about 20 minutes.

In this answer, StarSight not only provided a link for subscriptions, but also described the rather futuristic way in which subscriptions are activated. Knowing that their customer base is somewhat more technologically sophisticated than average, this strategy makes sense.

Attention FAQ writers everywhere: if your customer base or readership shares any distinguishing characteristics, don't be afraid to use this as a community-building tool in your FAQ. StarSight didn't get into specific bits-and-bytes schematics, but gives enough teaser information for a mild "Wow" from an audience already somewhat favorably disposed toward the magic of technology.

StarSight's FAQ also has a Subscription icon link under the 13 questions and before the answer field. Two links to where the "money" is make this more visible, increasing the chances that their visitors will go there.

REPRINTS, ADS, AND SUPPLIES: THE "CMP TECHWEB" FAQ

CMP is one of the largest computer-magazine publishers in the world. Some of its titles include *Communications Week, Information Week, Network World* and *NetGuide* magazines. TechWeb is the CMP corporate Web site where the content of these and other CMP publications is archived and updated continuously.

The 17-question FAQ uses multiple approaches to generate revenue:

1. An advertisement is usually included at the bottom of the FAQ. This brings in several thousand dollars a month. Not surprisingly, the ad usually comes from a company that provides a product or service of perceived interest and value to the TechWeb readership.

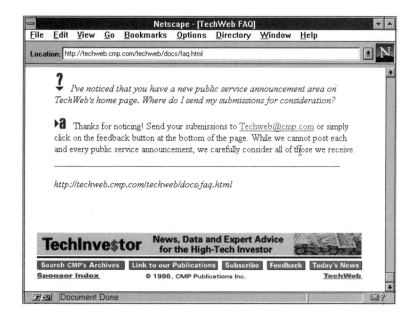

FIGURE 11.3 THE "CMP TECHWEB" FAQ PRODUCES PROFIT BY SELLING SPACE.

Lesson for FAQ writers: if you want your FAQ to earn newfound respect in your company, give your marketing department a call and ask them about possible synergies between the interests of people visiting your Web site and likely advertising partners.

2. Conclusive data is furnished about ways to get reprints. Keep in mind that unlike with back issues, where the per-payback price is small, reprints can generate a fortune for a content provider. Often, a corporation will request a reprint of an article they are mentioned in. Their intention is to use it as a sales tool.

Here's how TechWeb's FAQ positions this lucrative service:

Q. How do I get electronic reprints of articles on TechWeb, including TechSearch articles?

A. We took this question to our overworked Reprints Department. Our sources there say you can easily submit your requests for reprints via Email (address: *brhoden@cmp.com*) or call 1-800-682-4972. The requested article will be put on a diskette and reformatted (including graphics and photos) to look exactly like it appears on CMP's print publications. The cost is $1,500 per article or $3,000 for five articles. If you hyperlink back to TechWeb you receive a $500 discount. Please note: electronic reprints cannot be transferred to paper reprint.

Note the first sentence in this answer, written with a mixture of humor and empathy. A FAQ Q-A sequence also introduces the site's other main money producer, an online "technology catalog" that CMP calls TechMall.

Companies that list in TechMall give CMP a proprietary portion of revenue they derive from this source. When you visit this area, you are likely to see everything from computer memory component testers and Local Area Network switching devices, to companies that conduct seminars in different cities. There is an obvious synergy between a company that makes LAN-related products, and the readership of several CMP magazines that cover networks.

A smart marketer, CMP mentions TechMall on its online sign-up screens. This is a tool for people to register for the free basic TechWeb service. Once there, they are able to read about TechMall within this specific FAQ question:

Q. When I registered, you promised exclusive offers for TechWeb users. Is there a mailing list? Or is there a specific place to go to?

A. Our TechWeb users' exclusive offers can be found in TechMall [the word TechMall is linked].

Lesson for FAQ Writers: using the term "you promised," followed by details of fulfillment of that promise, not only acts as an income-producer; it positions you in your customers' eyes as a company that keeps its promises. Not every company does.

Income through Special Services: the Kodak FAQs

The giant, 71-question, four-section "Kodak Advanced Photo System" FAQ can be reached from the Customer Solutions icon on the Kodak Home Page. It's divided into five sections, the first four pertaining to product uses. These are "Cameras," "Darkroom," "Film," and "Picture Taking." The questions that are answered mostly cover photographic techniques and the use of materials to take pictures. Kodak's income-generating FAQ activities are a natural outgrowth of some of the topics addressed in the first four sections of the FAQ. Through some of its subsidiaries and distributors, Kodak has printed materials available to further explain some of the technical points explored in the main FAQ. Also, since this company is constantly updating its product, it uses the FAQ as a "distribution back channel" for items no longer available at most retailers.

Both of these strategies might work well for you, but first, let's take a detailed look at how Kodak does it.

For those customers needing as many encyclopedic details as possible, Kodak owns a book division that publishes several titles a year. If you're the FAQ writer for a technocentric company with lots of applications for consumer use, you'll know that no FAQ, no matter how comprehensive, will be able to answer everything. Giants like Kodak and Microsoft maintain book divisions for just this purpose. Other companies have archived studies for sale, linking from their FAQ pages.

Keep in mind that the "F" in FAQ stands for "Frequently." But what about the **Infrequently** Asked Questions? You probably don't want an IAQ, but this is a base you may have to cover; "IAQs" might be the questions asked by your most devoted, even cultish, customers. Their fields of interest may be so specialized or so arcane, that the questions they "ask" may be above the heads of your average customer. You don't want to ignore these people.

After most of the other "Frequently Asked" questions have been answered, noting the availability of "more information" is a logical question to put near the end of your FAQ. Since this additional data won't be commonly requested, it may be costly to assemble and maintain. Your FAQ page visitors are, by implication, the most intellectually curious members of your constituency. They may actually prefer separate, more specialized answers not workable in most FAQs.

In the "Misc" section of the Kodak FAQ, the availability of additional information is addressed while a money-making source is pinpointed.

Q. How can I purchase Kodak books?

A. Kodak makes available books and other publications on a wide variety of photographic topics. They can be acquired in a number of ways. For Kodak publications on general picture-taking and professional photography, you may contact a retailer that specializes in photographic equipment and supplies. Kodak commercial books are also available from:

The address, phone and Email address of Kodak's Silver Pixel Press is then given. You might wonder why Silver Pixel was not mentioned **before** the "retailer" option. That was done simply for customer convenience. The FAQ writers didn't want the answer to come across as just a device to sell books, but as part of an answer indicating the type of customer support available.

Another question on the Kodak FAQ has to do with how to obtain a specialized product that is no longer available. This might be the makings of a good question for your FAQ. If you have items that you don't make any more and which are out of stock, perhaps you can point the inquirer toward sources where a given item can be ordered.

I have a bone to pick with some FAQs here. Commercial Web FAQs, especially, tend to be written by marketing people primarily concerned with selling the current product. Nothing wrong with this; that's the way the *.com* world turns. Yet too often, companies forget that there may still be substantial penetration of discontinued products in the user base. Some people still prefer LPs to CDs, electric typewriters to personal computers, Betamax to VHS cassettes.

Kodak knows the iconoclasts may be small in number, but have purchasing power too (see Figure 11.4).

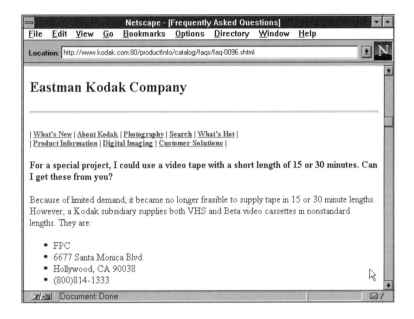

FIGURE 11.4 KODAK'S FAQS PROMOTE SPECIAL SERVICES HANDLED BY OTHER COMPANY DIVISIONS.

Q. For a special project, I could use a video tape with a short length of 15 or 30 minutes. Can I get these from you?

A. Because of limited demand, it became no longer feasible to supply tape in 15- or 30-minute lengths. However, a Kodak subsidiary supplies both VHS and Beta video cassettes in nonstandard lengths.

The FAQ then furnishes the address and phone number of this subsidiary. Lessons for FAQ writers: Kodak may only make a few thousand dollars a year from this FAQ question. That's a drop in the bucket. The key here is noticing the phrasing of this question. Keywords like "special project" crystallize the importance this question has to the loyal customer. "Can I get these from you?" sounds almost plaintive, doesn't it?

Somehow, it resonates more personally than "do you still have these tapes in stock?" Once again, some of the best FAQ writing recognizes customers not as throngs of confused people, but as intelligent individuals with their own needs.

The answer, on the other hand, performs two functions. It posits what seems like a sound business reason why the company no longer stocks such tapes in its primary distribution channels. Anyone with half a lick of business sense will buy that explanation. Yet in the next sentence, an alternative—one owned by Kodak—is mentioned.

Does your company have **any** internal resources from which out-of-stock items can be ordered? Chances are, someone wants them. If your answer is "yes," pointing to such alternatives from the FAQ page lets you, the FAQ writer, be the hero. You are helping your employer cement friendships and make money at the same time. And all from one little FAQ question!

IF YOU LINK IT, THEY WILL BOOK: THE "HOLIDAY INN" FAQ

Holiday Inn Worldwide, one of the largest lodging chains on the planet, brought room reservations capability to its Web site in 1996. The first few months saw only a few dozen room nights booked this way per day, but the chain predicts that by the turn of the millennium, this number will increase: lodging industry analysts project that by the year 2000, as many as 20 percent of available room nights in the U.S. hotel market will be booked directly by customers accessing Internet hotel sites from their home or office. This trend can have major implications. Let's do the math, and then work in how a FAQ can help online booking become a significant revenue generator.

1. A room night simply means one room booked per night, regardless of how many guests stay there. If I own a 200-room hotel, I will have a weekly potential of 1400 room nights (one for every night of the week).

2. Over the last several years, U.S. hotel "occupancy percentages" have hovered around 65 percent. For a 200-room hotel performing to industry norms, this means about 900 room nights in an average week.

3. If even 5 percent of these bookings come through a Web site, that's 45 room nights. Doesn't sound like much, but for a hotel that charges the industry average of about $60 a night, you're looking at more than $2,000 in additional weekly revenue. If a franchised property is floating a mortgage loan and has a payroll to meet, the extra $100,000 a year can come in mighty handy.

Your franchising organization will take off a few percentage points from your gross sales for making such a link possible; but, if this medium takes off like everyone predicts it will, the money-making potential is glaringly obvious.

I cover Internet marketing issues regularly and have also been a contributing editor for a leading hotel trade publication since 1987. Wearing both hats for a moment, I agree with the experts about online booking. The nature of the hospitality industry will demand that more than just booking capabilities are possible through the Web site. Think about it. Booking a room comes at the end of an information-absorption process. The booker has already identified the city and neighborhood he or she needs a room in, and whether or not the lodging chain of choice has a hotel nearby. Next, rates and amenities need to be compared. If you're on a fitness regimen, you may pay $10 more per night for a room in a hotel with a health club.

This need for information in addition to transactional capabilities is not limited to Web sites of hotel chains. It's also a model for the Web sites of individual hotels, restaurants, theme parks and other tourist attractions, rental car companies, etc. If you run such a site and are writing a FAQ for it, you'll recognize that you are talking to an information-hungry audience. Just about every call to a "human" reservations agent starts with a question. Find out what these questions are and put them into your FAQ.

Should the question be answered to the caller or site-visitor's satisfaction, the next obligation is to close the sale. That's where the transactional capability of the site pays off. Remember this advice: curious anyway, your site visitors may come to your FAQ first. Use your FAQ to point them to places on your site that can make you money.

Holiday Inn doesn't flinch from this task. The very first two questions on its hip-toned, 19-question FAQ take care of business right away:

> Q. I don't know exactly where I want to stay. Can I look up where there might be Holiday Inn Hotels?
>
> [Lesson for FAQ writers: maybe there isn't a Holiday Inn in a given community. Maybe your restaurant doesn't have calamari (although every restaurant should). Holiday Inn prepares the questioner-visitor (with "might be") for the remote possibility of disappointment.]
>
> A. **Absolutely Yes!** Holiday Inn offers you two ways to find your hotel of choice:

1. The ability (to) use a graphic World Map [there's a link here to an on-site World Map] to drill down to the country, State/Province and City that interests you. Once you have selected a city, you can further identify the hotels along a given travel route/highway or simply be given popular local attractions.
2, The ability to look up a hotel in our Online Worldwide Directory [site links directly to this from the FAQ here]. You may also check availability and book reservations from this directory.

Next comes a pitch noting the value-added benefits of using the Online Worldwide Directory. Providing these links will make you money, sure, but the customer has to wonder what's in it for him or her. Nothing wrong with creating a little anticipation:

"This search and selection capability will save you lots of time. You can plan your road trips or business trips from your home or office at the touch of a button."

Lessons for FAQ Writers: This simple, two-sentence answer performed two vital functions. It spoke to two core audiences: the leisure and business traveler. If your company has more than just one customer or client base, be sure not to tailor your FAQ only to the largest. Also, the word "you," or variations of it, was mentioned four times in two sentences. Yet again, that's the humanizing aspect of using first-person language. Don't you agree?

Now, with the visitor already excited about being able to look up hotels online, it comes time for the FAQ to do its real revenue-generating work. When the site first went up, online booking was a novelty. Customers had to be convinced not only that it was secure, but that online room reservations were actually possible. Holiday Inn presented this function in a friendly, non-preachy yet non-condescending manner (see Figure 11.5).

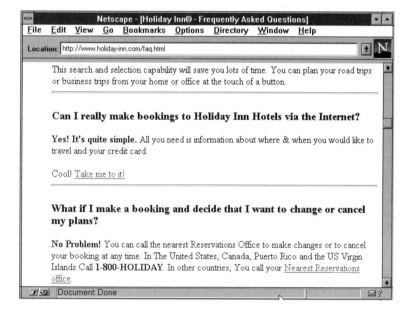

FIGURE 11.5 HOLIDAY INN WORLDWIDE'S FAQ TELLS YOU HOW TO BOOK A ROOM THROUGH THE WEB SITE.

Q. Can I really make bookings to Holiday Inn Hotels via the
Internet?

A. **Yes! It's quite simple**. All you need is information about
where & when you would like to travel and your credit card.

Several following questions describe the flexibility and security of booking online.

Secure Credit-Card Transactions Online—A Major Issue

For companies that want to generate income from secured electronic
transactions like online booking, you MUST address the security issue
in your FAQ. People are still skeptical by nature; if you gloss it over, the
major potential of a FAQ as an income-generating mechanism will not
be fulfilled.

Here's how Holiday Inn handled this delicate issue:

Q. What has Holiday Inn done to protect my credit card number
while I make the bookings using the Internet/WWW?

A. Security is of paramount concern for our guests. Therefore
Holiday Inn has employed state-of-the-art computer software encryption techniques that are presently the *de facto*
industry standards. Holiday Inn's Web site is Netscape/RSA
encryption-enabled.

If you are using the highly popular Netscape WWW browser 1.1 or above, software encryption can be optionally invoked
for all our pages (including the pages that you provide us your
credit card, name, address, etc.) As you are aware this is an
area of the Internet that is improving by leaps and bounds. We
are committed to keep our site up to date with the latest and
greatest in security tools to secure your business transactions
with us.

Holiday Inn also provides a link to Netscape from this question.

Lesson for FAQ Writers: A solid scenario for site security has been projected. The answer ends on an upbeat note, with a tone that new security developments will be adopted when they become available.

If you are doing business from your Web site, few FAQ answers will be as important. "The transactional environment on the Web is still small and the reticence is pretty high. A perception of security needs to be created," notes John Nardone, director of media research for Norwalk, CT-based Modem Media, one of the largest Web-specialist ad agencies in the United States.

It doesn't seem that way from the outset, but talking about site security is a touchy subject for a FAQ answer. It's far more involved than saying what kind of encryption you use. You want to make it clear to customers that you operate in an environment secure enough for them to give you their money. You sincerely wish to instill the notion that electronic commerce security is only going to get better, but you don't want to overemphasize this at the risk of making current encryption technology seem primitive. Like so many other FAQ questions, and yes, like the old Moody Blues song, it's a "Question of Balance." I recommend addressing this subject with the same tone Holiday Inn does.

USING YOUR FAQ TO SELL ADVERTISING: HOW US WEST DOES IT

Numerous sites that rely on advertising for a major portion of their revenue use FAQs to tout the service. One company, Colorado-based regional phone giant US West, even has a special 11-question FAQ devoted entirely to this purpose.

Although each question on the US West Yellow Pages information FAQ concerns advertising, questions three through five are especially instructional; their order tracks the line of the traditional cost-benefits analysis used by executives in most industries. These people come to the FAQ with half a mind to buy an ad in the Yellow Pages. Responsible for their own budgets, they need to be convinced it is worth it. See Figure 11.6.

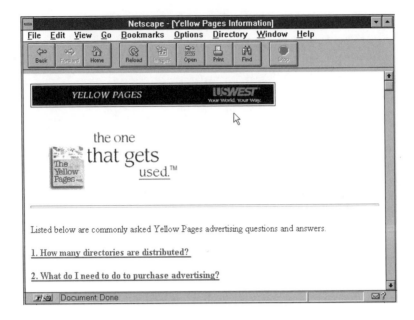

FIGURE 11.6 US WEST'S FAQ TOUTS THE BENEFITS OF ADVERTISING IN ITS 305 LOCAL YELLOW PAGES DIRECTORIES.

Without a direct transactional link, it is hard to quantify how many ads placed in US West's 305 Yellow Page directories were inspired by reading this FAQ. These questions are so usefully phrased, that they bear excerpting and serious consideration as role models for anyone using a FAQ to sell a service. Question Three is the first of three we'll look at:

Q. How much does advertising cost?

A. Advertising costs vary according to the directories (amount of exposure, i.e., more exposure in Seattle metro than Tacoma), and types of advertising purchased.

> Rates are based on your needs, and on the results you want. You can purchase anything from a bold listing to a full page ad.

Lesson for FAQ Writers: Flexibility is always a powerful sales tool.

The next question describes in detail the several types of advertising possible in US West directories. This section is too lengthy to cite in full here, but let us look at the phrasing in the first part of the answer—and how it might work for you:

Q. What kind of special advertising does US West Direct offer?

A. Color: The use of color is an effective advertising tool—it is a way to help your ad stand out and capture attention. Research shows that 80 percent of Yellow Pages users react positively to color and 70 percent say color makes an ad much more likely to be noticed. Color helps organize your copy for readability and allows you to highlight your key points. In addition, color helps portray products realistically, i.e., green—trees, money; blue—water, sky; and red—flowers, fire.

Lessons for FAQ Writers: The Web is a visual medium. Because your visitor has already arrived at your site, you can assume he or she is visually oriented. If there is something visually appealing about your product, describe it and show it. Does your site have some outstanding visual component that would make a good match with a prospective client's ad message? If it does, use the FAQ to flaunt it.

This strategy works. Don't believe me? Reread the last answer from the US West FAQ. If at least a few images didn't appear in your mind's eye, you may have Imagination Deficit Disorder.

After you've dealt with cost issues and fired the imagination, now comes the nitty-gritty. You'll have to use the FAQ to emphasize the value of the service you're trying to sell. Question Five on the US West FAQ does this.

Q. How will I benefit from advertising?

A. People who use the Yellow Pages are not just browsing; they're ready to buy. Four out of five of them will follow up with a visit or a call. According to a 1993 study by the Yellow Pages Publishers Association, 47 percent of purchasers were new to the place of purchase—the Yellow Pages helps businesses attract those customers who don't have a specific firm in mind when they're ready to purchase a product or service.

Lesson for FAQ Writers: Use your FAQ to back up your sales-driven claims with documentable, statistical research from credible, outside sources.

PRODIGY'S CONTACT LIST

A less-intricate but highly serviceable strategy is the Prodigy Web site's approach of listing advertising contact information on its "Who To Contact" FAQ page. Phone numbers are listed for key contacts in several income-producing endeavors, including one "To advertise your company or product on Prodigy." Sometimes, merely reprinting a contact number on your FAQ page works as well as an Email link.

SAVING MONEY—STOP THE PRESSES

Calculating exactly how much money your FAQ can *save* you is a far more inexact science than figuring how much money it will *make* you. Even approaching the subject requires a walk between the quantifiable and the intangible.

Probably the most quantifiable savings benefit is a break on the escalating costs of printing and mailing hard-copy brochures. "In 1996," says Modem Media's Nardone, "printing and design for a four-page, four-color brochure would have cost in the $15,000 range for 10,000 copies. Then, add up to $1.50 in postage for each brochure."

This compares unfavorably to the cost of a Web site. A bottom-line investment figure for a good site is between $3,000 and $4,000, but the growth of Web-enabling self-publishing client packages and the willingness of local Internet Service Providers to "rent" hosting space to your site for only a few dollars a day can bring the costs for a Web site down to less than $1,000 a month.

There's a business reason why you can get a Web site on the cheap. Telecommunications deregulation, which was signed into law in 1996, freed up cable, long-distance, and local phone companies to get into each other's businesses. Many of them launched Web page hosting services. Local Internet Service Providers, who had the entrepreneurial sector pretty much to themselves, were forced to market aggressively to compete with the Big Guys. This means even more price breaks for you, the small business that wants to be on the Web.

How does a FAQ fit into this cost-savings business model? A FAQ, as we've seen throughout this book, is a heralder of the content and services you have on the site.

The main virtues of site-over-brochures are *savings* and *immediacy*. These can work with all kinds of Web sites. Let's examine some prototypical examples.

> Problem: A Colorado ski resort has just converted their country music bar to one with alternative rock. Brochures sent to travel agents refer to the country music feature. The travel agent doesn't know about the change, and guests expecting to hear Shania Twain rather than Oasis become disillusioned and don't return.

> Solution: You could print out 10,000 new brochures. With mailing costs, your tab would be $25,000. Meanwhile, if you have a Web site with a FAQ you can put that change in as follows:

> Q. What type of nightlife choices are there at the Pinnacle Peak Resort?

> A. We've listened to your comments and requests, and have changed our Summit Saloon into an alternative music bar. Come in and dance to the latest in cutting edge!

There. You've typed in two sentences and have saved a whole bunch of money in printing and postage. But not everyone is online yet, so don't forget to call your key accounts.

> Problem: You're a FAQ writer for a university Web site. Due to budget cuts, the intercollegiate rowing program was dropped last month. Unfortunately, your catalog still lists rowing as a team sport. The new edition is on the presses, and it would cost several thousand dollars to replate with the correction.

> Solution: Revise or insert a question in your FAQ, as follows:

Q. What intercollegiate sports programs are offered at Northern Maryland College?

A. Men's and women's basketball, golf and tennis, plus baseball, softball, and lacrosse.

Q. What about rowing? Your squad won the Cumberland Conference meet back in 1991.

A. Due to budget cuts, we've had to suspend our intercollegiate rowing program recently. But plans are being worked on to keep rowing as a club-level sport.

You've avoided a replate of your new catalog, while using your FAQ to keep rowing partisans informed and up-to-date.

SAVING MONEY BY CUTTING PAYROLL

In the era of downsizing, such talk can be coldhearted, but a FAQ might let you cut down a bit on payroll. There are few studies on this subject, but customer-service industry experts estimate that on average, 20 percent of calls to help desks cover very rudimentary, entry-level issues. It might be easy, then, to recommend that a FAQ that addresses these issues might save you 20 percent on payroll. That's seldom the case, especially on *.com* Web sites for technology-based companies. In such cases, there's no guarantee that people in the 20 percent rudimentary question-asking category even have knowledge of the Internet. The cruel paradox is that the more threadbare an individual's capacity is to solve technical problems with a stereo or camera, the less likely they are to be comfortable with something like a Web browser.

Service-industry consultant Dr. Lance Eliot speaks and writes about this issue often. His recommendation: rather than thinking of Web FAQs as tools to cut down on staff, companies should train their Help Desk personnel to be able to point callers to solutions that might be detailed in a FAQ on the company Web site. This strategy should cut down on the number of repeat calls fielded by customer service. Dr. Eliot writes about the topic in a piece entitled "Help desk strategies for the Internet-

Intranet Highway." The piece was published in early 1996 by the Help Desk Institute, a Colorado Springs, CO-based think tank and marketing consultancy concerned with customer-service strategies.

In his article, Dr. Eliot quantifies the Help Desk-FAQ relationship into two "categories." "Help desks venturing into Internet waters must keep these two categories in mind at all times," he writes. In Category 1, help desk agents need to know just enough about the Internet to get into it and search for items or to send and receive Email. Although this capability is definitely a skill, the emerging advances in automated Internet tools make surfing the Net easier with each passing day.

"In Category 2," Dr. Eliot continues, "the help desk staff needs more advanced knowledge of the Internet. Besides understanding the rudiments of the Internet, the staff must know about the intricate aspects of browsers and how they link into the Internet, as well as how to integrate browsers into the customer's equipment. In fact, it's a good idea for help desks that eventually want to reach Category 2 to start in Category 1 so that they can become comfortable using the Internet as a resource to meet customer needs. They can advance their skills to become problem solvers for their customers' Internet-related problems."

FAQS OF THE FUTURE

Just as Web sites are making the transition from static to multimedia-enabled content, FAQs of the future will transform from today's passive Q-A model to one that will use "intelligent agents" to search the site—and the whole Internet—for answers to site visitors' frequent questions.

The savings matrix is hard to project, but if intelligent agents that understand natural language queries become customary on Web sites, the FAQ will not only be a list of posted questions, but will turn into a proactive information search tool as well. "It may be a matter of going to an applet that asks you what the problem is. Then, it [the intelligent agent] will surmise what you want and go out on the Web and come back to you with an answer," says Dennis Privatitera, general manager for technology at the Help Desk Institute. Privatitera suggests that for software-related questions, this technology will stimulate the creation of software support companies dedicated to housing solution-related information from multiple parties.

Intelligent agents wouldn't only be found on Web sites of technology companies. In this model, a user-defined question like "Can you give me some general information on Adjustable Rate Mortgages?" would trigger the intelligent agent to launch a search through a pre-defined series of Web or Usenet newsgroup documents. The agent would be combing for documents containing the phrase "Adjustable Rate Mortgage."

The agent might even find new information the FAQ writer hadn't heard about yet. A minute or two later, the reply would appear on the user's screen. A call to customer service is averted, and the FAQ writer's task is made easier as well.

SITE-TO-SOFTWARE
INFORMATION FAQS

In this chapter, you'll learn:

- Traditional difficulties of providing and getting software help
- How software FAQ writers can fill the breach
- How tech support notes can work with or in place of FAQs
- How to migrate customer questions to your support pages
- How to get around the "jargon trap"
- How to structure your software FAQ
- Using position papers
- Writing FAQs in the "problem-solution" mode
- Seamlessly integrating new questions with old ones
- Listing and describing downloadable product documentation
- Using your FAQ for market combat

The Internet, and FAQs by extension, are natural locations for information about software.

Back in the days before the Web was invented and the advantages of communicating through cyberspace were known only to scientists and academicians, information about software was distributed in one of two ways: Neither of these methods fostered user-friendliness, or what passed for it at the time. Some of these approaches resulted in communications difficulties that persist to this day.

1. New software came with either embedded README.DOC or README.TXT files. These files were helpful if you knew what you were doing, but that degree of understanding often precluded having to use the "READMEs" in the first place. Also, if you couldn't figure out the real basics, like how to install the software on your computer, the README file would become irrelevant because you couldn't get to it in the first place.

2. User manuals would come in the box, but would be virtually indecipherable. Even less than a decade ago, techies used to thinking in non-linear terms wrote most of these things. The result was a non-organized, confusing jumble of instructions. Written non-sequentially with a good dose of jargon, a typical manual might separate two consecutive installation steps by four chapters and 50 pages. Software companies didn't yet have the understanding of the consumer market to hire copy editors who could whip these things into shape. Some firms have figured this out but there is still huge room for improvement.

This led to some major customer-service problems:

1. Then, as now, customer-service help desk people were too ill-prepared and low paid to answer any question not on the "cheat sheets" they kept at their carrels. Low on the totem pole, they were never told that software engineers for the company were working on a given bug and would issue a new release in four weeks to fix the problem. With outsourcing now in vogue, the problem is even worse than it was a few years ago. Very recently one of my Winsock files became slightly corrupted. I got a well-intentioned but inexperienced temporary worker in some service bureau 500 miles from the main office of the company whose software had become problematic. He didn't seem to know what a "WINSOCK.DLL" file is.

2. Long waits for answers to difficult problems. The more complex a new software application is, the more calls to customer service and the longer you have to sit on hold.

3. A related problem: within some high-tech companies, the most knowledgeable help resources only deal with top corporate customers. There's a lack of respect for the small-office, home-office market. Not so long ago, I was having a fax modem problem that was traceable to interference from several satellite dishes less than half a mile from my home. Company reps told me they only made service calls to "offices," not to "homes." Guess what? I'll never buy one of their products again.

4. Sad to say this, but as far back as I can remember, the problem-solving resources available through software retail channels has been rudimentary. The skilled folks don't stick around long: they join companies, start their own, or become consultants. As a result, most of what you get is either inexperience or mediocrity. Lots of wrong advice too—some of which can crash your computer.

Enough commiseration for now. This book is not about venting steam, but pointing you toward solutions. For software, good online documentation—including but not necessarily limited to Frequently Asked Questions lists—is a must.

TYPES OF HELP

There are a number of online approaches leading software vendors take to make the use of their products easier. Let's briefly mention some of them, and then take a look at some successful examples:

1. **FAQs.** This is the most obvious Help strategy of all. Because large software-oriented companies have hundreds of products, you're almost sure to need more than one. I'd recommend a general FAQ, with links to several other FAQs revolving around specific product lines.

2. **Product patches and updates.** We introduced this somewhat in Chapter Ten, "Links," but it bears repeating. People are likely to

come to your FAQ page for one of two reasons: they don't understand how to use your software, or they are frustrated by a bug. If such frustrations have been made known to you, perhaps you've made the patch or update as a response to a techno-quandary.

List these available patches on a separate page. Hyperlink each patch listing to trigger a download when it is clicked on. Last, but not least, remember to link to the patch-update page from your FAQ. Link from there often: perhaps even from each Answer to which an available update or patch applies. Even think of putting a "Fixes" icon on the FAQ Home Page to get attention, and reinforce the comfort level the harried accessor is seeking.

3. **Technical Support Notes.** Some kinds of problems and fixes are so rare, or so obtuse, that they'll only clutter up your FAQ if you put a lengthy explanation in your "Answer" field. There's nothing wrong with including a topical question in your FAQ, but answer it with a link to Technical Support Notes. That's what TSNs are for. They should act as a library for more detailed information. They'll also perform a dual service by not having to update your FAQ every time a new question comes in, or ignoring the question at the risk of user wrath.

4. **OnLine Manuals and Publications.** Maybe a user bought your software three months ago but can't find the confounded hard-copy manual. That's happened to most of us. Make these manuals available online. Link from your FAQ to a page with a hyperlinked menu of these resources. Trust me. You'll become a hero, if not a candidate for beatification. Also, if your company is large enough to have an in-house book division, you might want to excerpt key passages from these volumes online.

5. **Links from your FAQ to Related newsgroup FAQs.** Some user group FAQs contain more seat-of-the-pants information about the bugs in your software, but the dialog may be uncomplimentary. Is it worth pointing to a user's group FAQ with more data than you've had time to put on your own FAQs if a flame-ridden post-

ing about your product is two threads away? This can be a thorny issue, one which you'll have to decide for yourself.

6. **An Email Link.** Putting one on your FAQ is imperative, but don't do so unless you promise to read it. Don't let it become a digital suggestion and gripe box, one never read by your developers or by decision-level management. Your customers may be pointing to a glitch you didn't know existed. A problem-citing Email message in March might be a product patch in April. Open yourself up to the potential from this type of feedback.

There are a number of software-related Web FAQs that have implemented these suggestions. We're going to look at some of them.

QUARTERDECK CORPORATION: VISIBLE MEANS OF SUPPORT

Based in Marina del Rey, CA, Quarterdeck is most familiar to Internet surfers as the developer of Quarterdeck Mosaic, one of the most flexible browsers. It also developed the Web Compass metasearching tool and in 1996, purchased Procomm Plus, a communications software program long used as a straight text, dial-up program for access to some online services and bulletin boards.

Quarterdeck doesn't have a FAQ per se, but includes a significant amount of helpful information in its Technical Support Notes and product patches. The Notes, which are permanently archived and searchable from the Net Search function linked through the Home Page, contain such advice as "Banyan Vines Network Setup," "DESQview: Changing the System Keys," "Disabling Motherbaord Memory," "Mouse Droppings (I'm not making this up) in DESQView," "Quarterdeck Products and OS/2 2.0," "Token Ring Cards and QEMM-386," "Troubleshooting Stealth ROM," and "Windows 3.1 and Quarterdeck Products." See Figure 12.1.

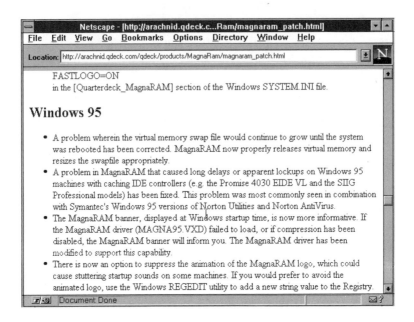

FIGURE 12.1 MOST OF QUARTERDECK'S ON-SITE INFORMATION IS IN TECH SUPPORT NOTES.

This isn't the early 1990s anymore. For good or evil, we are headed toward the millennium, so I'd wager that very few of you use a machine run by Intel 80386 chips and many, if not most IBM-compatible users made the leap from Windows 3.1 to fresher editions some time ago. Sticking tech notes up about Quarterdeck products configured to work with older systems and chips may seem like nothing more than misplaced nostalgia (if not inattentiveness), but Quarterdeck is actually on the right path here. Unlike some companies, they actually realize that the real world of computing is not populated entirely by heatseekers who rush out and buy the newest version of any program as soon as it becomes available. Somewhere in North America, an old pickup truck with an eight-track player is still on the road!

A good lesson learned for FAQ writers: unless a product update totally invalidates an earlier issue, there will be at least a few people that are still interested in the older edition. Maybe these are hand-me down systems donated to impoverished third-world citizens, or ancient devices kept by collectors for sentimental reasons. Archiving a Tech note or putting in one or two FAQ questions about your product's compatibility with rudimentary systems won't produce scorn from right-minded people. It might even win you a few friends.

So as not to be seen as too sentimental, Quarterdeck introduces its Tech Support Notes with the following disclaimer: "these technotes are not kept as up to date as the ones in the above searchable database. For the most current info please use that."

You've guessed what we are going to talk about next! The "above searchable database" refers to Quarterdeck's list of product patches and updates. There are a minimum of five and sometimes in excess of ten patches or updates up at any one time. Representative titles include "Patch to bring MagnaRam 2.x to 2.02 is now available," and "Update Cleansweep '95 to the 1/96 release." Clicking either brings you to a description of the upgrade as well as download and installation instructions.

You can see what Quarterdeck is doing by phrasing these titles carefully. They're using the Product patch menu as a bulletin board for fixes and updates. Like we've said before, such tools are what many who access tech support pages look for.

The Lotus Notes FAQ

In Chapter 10, "Links," we mentioned how Lotus launches new FAQs for each significant upgrade while also inserting some of these upgrade-related questions and answers into the larger, main FAQ. This is a sound strategy, ensuring that the most important questions will be posed, answered, and available in two places. Some, looking for online help, will go to the FAQ less-traveled! See Figure 12.2.

Lotus' main "FAQs-Notes," (*http://www.lotus.com/csswww/faqnotes.htm*) about Lotus Notes, isn't phrased like a customary Q-A FAQ. Instead, it is organized into several general application classifications, like "Workstation/Desktop" and "Server."

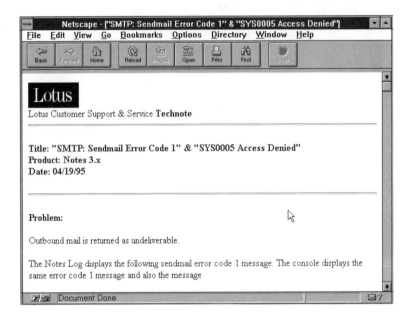

FIGURE 12.2 LOTUS NOTES FAQS INTEGRATE QUESTIONS FIELDED BY CUSTOMER SUPPORT.

The real genius behind the Technotes is the migration of complaints from "human" customer support to the FAQ page Technotes. Unlike in some companies, where the questions customer service gets are logged and then directed to some digital dustbin, Lotus has a process where tech questions the representative can't answer are routed to Technotes. When they are newly arrived, only the question is posted, but a blue-chip crew of techies looks over these on a frequent basis and posts answers as soon as they figure it out. Most of this goes on outside the firewall, so even those of us who are not in "Lotus positions" can observe the process as it unfolds.

On the Technotes section of the Lotus Notes FAQ, "questions" are phrased in one of three ways:

1. As a problem that needs to be solved;
2. As a How to" that will be explained by accessing the hyperlinked answer;
3. As an explanation of a specific product function.

Here are some examples:

Problem: Panic lookup handle is out of range'-UNIX server crashes

Solution: This issue can generally be solved by ensuring that the port buffer on the client is set to the same as the server. In each reported case, the client port buffer and server port buffer did not match.

Problem: Cannot see horizontal scroll bar in Notes R4 document or view.

Solution: By default, Notes R4 on the UNIX and Windows platforms will hide the horizontal scroll bar in order for you to see more of the document or view on the screen. To enable the horizontal scroll bar, select View, Show, Horizontal Scroll Bar. A check mark will then appear next to the Horizontal Scroll Bar setting when you select View, Show, indicating that this feature is enabled. To hide the scroll bar, again select View, Show, Horizontal Scroll Bar, which deselects the horizontal scroll bar feature."

Problem: Option for Textured Workspace is unavailable in Notes R4.

Solution: The Textured Workspace option is available only on systems configured with a display driver capable of 256 colors (or more).

Yes, the "KISS" principle applies here: Keep It Super Simple.

BRIEF BUT POINTED: THE ORACLE POWER BROWSER FAQ

"In simplicity, there is beauty." I may have first heard this phrase on a nature documentary, but it applies here. In 1996, Oracle Corp. introduced its PowerBrowser. More than just a Web browser, it is a server on which you can seamlessly create Web pages as well as read them.

Such an omnipotent product sounds like one with a five-section, 100-question FAQ. Would you believe that Oracle's first PowerBrowser FAQ consisted of only five questions? See Figure 12.3.

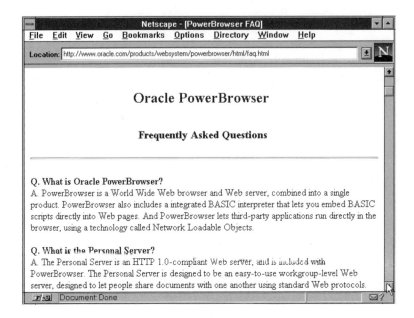

FIGURE 12.3 THE ORACLE POWERBROWSER FAQ STICKS TO THE BASICS.

Verbosity-prone FAQ writers take note. If you've got a complicated product but not a lot of room for your FAQ, Oracle shows you how to do a FAQ "Cliff's Notes" style, without sacrificing key points. The five questions are:

1. "What is Oracle PowerBrowser?
2. "What is the Personal Server?
3. "How does the BASIC interpreter work?
4. "Why would I ever use BASIC scripts in a Web page?
5. "What are Network Loadable Objects?"

The answers to these complex issues are also phrased briefly but thoroughly. So subtly inserted that you'd have to look for it to notice it, a marketing message is there. Here's the answer to Q4: "Conventional browsers have no way of understanding or analyzing the information they display. These browsers typically have to package any information input by a user and send it across the network to a server before any meaningful information processing gets done. With PowerBrowser, a simple BASIC script can perform checks on form-based user input before it gets sent to a server, saving end-user delays and more effectively distributing the processing load. BASIC scripts can also dynamically generate new HTML pages on the fly, using extensions to the BASIC language specifically created for Web-based applications."

Network Loadable Objects are also explained in the context of this new product: "Network Loadable Objects let PowerBrowser execute applications and display documents created by third-party developers. For example, with NLO's, PowerBrowser can insert an inline video player or sound player directly within any Web page. Furthermore, Network Loadable Objects are compatible with Netscape 2.0 plug-ins."

I'll confess. After I read this FAQ, I downloaded the Oracle PowerBrowser. It's now sitting on my nearly full Seagate hard drive. FAQ as sales tool? Hey, it worked with me!

FAQs FOR ISPs

Internet Service Providers (ISPs) do more than allow you unlimited access to the wide, webbed world for $19.95 a month. If their marketing people are doing a good job, they'll have sold you server space so you can put up your own Web page.

MindSpring, (*http://www.mindspring.com*) a large ISP based in Atlanta, gives you 5M of their server space with an account. You need to use your FTP program to access that space. As some of you know, the initial learning curve involved in putting up your first Web page is not easily traversed.

As one of the largest regional ISPs in the U.S., fast-growing MindSpring signs up thousands of newbies a month. Many of these folks don't know HTML from HTTP, but putting up a Web page with pictures of the significant other and the three cats would be way cool. On the other hand, many sophisticated companies seeking a major Web presence rely on ISPs like MindSpring to be their hosting service.

This means that to help customers, ISP FAQs have to appeal to a wide range of readers, while staying away from too much programmer tech-nobabble or dumb-down Internet 101. MindSpring's FAQ solves this dilemma masterfully.

This isn't a FAQ in the standard sense, with a whole bunch of Q-A for Q-A sake. The MindSpring FAQ home page is actually a Help Desk window, routing the visitor to explanations of such Internet and connectiv-ity matters as File Transfer Protocol, Internet Relay Chat, and ISDN (Integrated Systems Digital Network). See Figure 12.4.

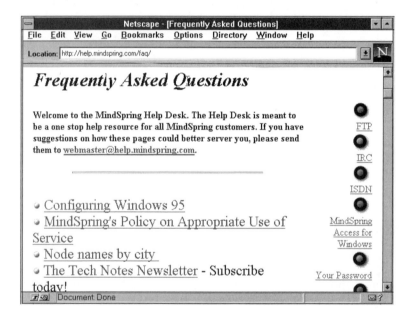

FIGURE 12.4 REGIONAL ISP MINDSPRING'S FAQ ADDRESSES BOTH EXPERIENCED AND NEW USERS.

There's also a link from the FAQ cover page to the meatiest part of the FAQ, a section titled "Using your space on MindSpring's servers." That's where most of the information on the FAQ is, so let's go there.

This Help page is written like a well-organized lesson plan. The first section mentions the space you get with an account, as well as what you can use your space for.

"Getting to Your Space" (something the crew of "Star Trek Voyager" hopes to do one day) comes next. The instructions are positioned and phrased as follows:

1. "FTP to *ftp.mindspring.com*.
2. "Use your username and password rather than anonymous login.
3. "You'll find yourself in a directory named *ul/yournamehere*. For instance, if I logged in with username "cynthia" I'd be in *ul/cynthia*."
4. "There are two subdirectories here, FTP and WWW."

BTW, did you catch the deft "Cynthia" example? Beautiful marketing! Women put up Web pages too.

After the subdirectories passage, the available alternatives are explained in sociable, non-threatening tones:

"What you do from here depends on why you're here. You can:

*   Upload *.plan* and/or *.project* files
*   Upload your web pages
*   Upload files for others to download
*   Make an incoming directory to permit others to upload files to you.

Each of these four choices come with its own point-by-point series of instructions. Arguably, explaining just what in the heck ".*plan*" and ".*project*" files are represented the toughest challenge to the MindSpring FAQ writer. With a few of my own comments inserted, here's how she pulled it off:

"These files provide additional information others can see when they use the 'finger' command. Most people just use the *.plan* file, but some also use a *.project* file. Check any good introductory UNIX book [note the well-placed pointer to a helpful outside source] for more information on what these files are all about. These files are purely optional, but if you want to use them [note the non-commandment, user-empowering tone here]:

1. This step is optional—use the finger program included with your MindSpring software to see what information is displayed when you **finger** yourself (*username@mindspring.com*) now. [I'll assume the phrase in the last sentence was not a wicked double-entendre].

2. Create a file using any text editor you prefer. Save it with a name of *.plan* [nothing before the period] if your operating system allows that, or name it anything you like and you can rename it after uploading it.

3. Go through the Getting to Your Space steps [which were mentioned above].

4. Upload your *.plan* file to the *ul/yournamehere* directory.

5. Use the **Rename** command to change the name to **JUST.plan** if you used another name.

6. Use the **finger** command again to see if the *.plan* information is showing up now."

Why does the MindSpring helper work so well? Two reasons, which all Internet Service Provider FAQ writers should note: superb organization on a hierarchical level, and a friendly enough tone without resorting to superficial "here's what we are gonna do next" hokum.

A final suggestion: if you are a FAQ writer or just someone who might put up your own Web page soon, bookmark this one. It's that good.

THE NETSCAPE NAVIGATOR AND SERVER FAQS

Netscape's (*http://home.netscape.com*) Navigator and Server products are in a constant state of refinement and upgrade. Their FAQ writers have two basic challenges, not uncommon to any FAQ-software author: keeping the FAQ current, while not overloading it with too many complex questions and answers. FAQ writers on tech-oriented Web sites must deal with this. Many prospective new customers will read the FAQ not **after** they've bought the product, but **before**. Write a FAQ that is too intimidating and you'll lose a sale.

Happily for its own sake, Netscape's two main FAQs have solved these obstacles. They are two of the best Web FAQs I've read. Let's see why.

With its sophistication and bulk (the 2.0 version of Netscape Navigator's "netscape.exe" file took up 1,351,552 bytes) you'd expect the Product Information FAQ to be long and possibly convoluted. It's not, because as we learned in Chapter 10, the more complex information is placed in Navigator's Technical notes section. This leaves room for the elementary, including the obligatory "what is" (as in, "What is Netscape Navigator?"). See Figure 12.5.

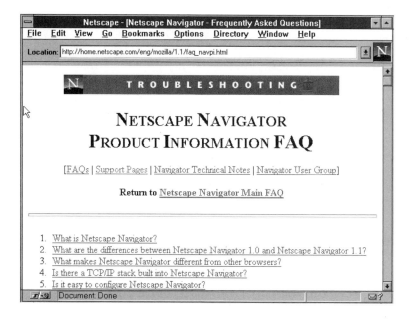

FIGURE 12.5 THE NETSCAPE NAVIGATOR FAQ.

I know I'm repeating myself, but the "What is?" question is a good way to start almost any FAQ page. Netscape knows that many of its prospective customers may have heard of the company but don't know much about the product. Perhaps, at least at the time this FAQ was up, these prospects accessed the Web through a primitive browser provided by an online service. For someone without much Internet experience, it takes a leap of faith to leap from the protective shelter of an online service to a world where you have to download your own choice of browsers and activate a decompressing file.

That's why many of the answers on the main Navigator FAQ are almost as simple as the questions are. Here are three examples:

Q. What makes Netscape Navigator different from other browsers?

A. Netscape Navigator has been built specifically to provide superior performance over other browsers.

A few of the important enhancements:

- You can see and interact with the document as it loads.
- Multiple images and text can all load at the same time.
- JPEG images are supported, to improve performance.
- Document and image caching reduce network traffic.
- The graphical user interface is tuned for ease of use.
- Advanced features include hierarchical bookmarks and a configurable graphical user interface.

Q. Is it easy to configure Netscape Navigator?

[This question is a "gimme." If it were hard to set up, Netscape wouldn't admit it, would they? Still, this question works because it's a fear-reducer.]

A. Yes. Installing Netscape Navigator is very simple, and once installed, personal options and preferences are easily managed by way of the easy-to-use graphical interface.

The last question emulates the end of an effective pitch. It "closes the sale." FAQs can work as sales tools! Many *.com* FAQs would be well-advised to sign off this way:

Q. How can I get a copy of Netscape Navigator?

A. You can download a copy of Netscape Navigator for evaluation or for unlimited use in academic or not-for-profit environments from one of our FTP and mirror sites ["FTP" and "mirror" are hyperlinked].

   If you wish to purchase Netscape Navigator and associated support for ongoing use, you can order it directly from Netscape Communications Corporation. You can purchase it online through the Netscape General Store [linked], contact Netscape Corporate Sales [linked], or call 415/528-2555 to speak with a Netscape sales representative.

   You can also find more information about the various support and training programs we offer under Company and Products [also linked].

Netscape's Server Software FAQ

Netscape's Server Software side takes a more encyclopedic approach to FAQ construction, maintaining separate FAQs on such topics as Product Information, System Requirements, Administration and Security. Because servers are more complicated to set up than a browser is to install, the topic obviously lends to more, and longer, FAQs.

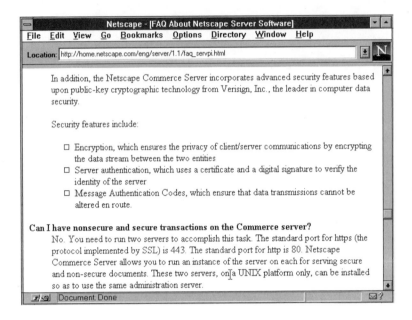

FIGURE 12.6 THE NETSCAPE SERVER FAQ ADDRESSES COMPLEX OPERATING ISSUES.

The Product Information server FAQ acts as an introduction to Netscape servers. As in the Navigator FAQ, detailed information is placed in the tech notes. This leaves a good number of the FAQ questions in the marketing mode. Some of these are:

Q. How can I obtain a Netscape server product?

[Telling your customers how they can acquire your product is a "must" FAQ question for almost any *.com* Web site FAQ.]

Q. Do I get a discount on Netscape Navigator when I buy Netscape Server products?

[A copy of Navigator comes bundled with the Server. This question is obviously sales-driven but it is legitimate and it works here.]

Q. Why should I buy Netscape Server products, when I can get freeware servers?

The answer mentions support for the Secure Sockets Layer (SSL) electronic commerce communications protocol, as well as "five primary reasons," including "high-performance serving, "ease of installation and management, "open standards," "proven security," and "An extensible platform for applications. After this answer, links are provided for more information as well as one to sample the product.

In favor of placement on more detailed FAQs or in the Tech Notes section, operational information transfer is generally avoided here except for the following question:

> Q. Can I have nonsecure and secure transactions on the Commerce server?

> A. No. You need to run two servers to accomplish this task. The standard port for https (the protocol implemented by SSL) is 443. The standard port for http is 80. "Netscape Commerce Server allows you to run an instance of the server on each for serving secure and non-secure documents. These two servers, on a UNIX platform only, can be installed so as to use the same administration server.

An important answer. For the prospective purchaser, it defines how much server he or she will need to buy.

THE FAQ-POSITION PAPER APPROACH

XcelleNet, Inc., a company that builds networking technology for corporate Intranets, has a "Facts & FAQ" section on its Web site (*http://www.xcellenet.com/remote.facts*). With no questions or answers, it's a rather unusual FAQ. The unique approach they've taken involves explaining key applications and operating issues through a series of "position papers" that can be accessed through a link from the XcelleNet FAQ page: See Figure 12.7.

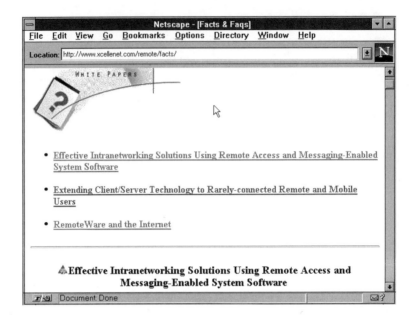

FIGURE 12.7 XCELLENET'S "FAQ" IS REALLY A COLLECTION OF POSITION PAPERS ABOUT ITS
VARIOUS PRODUCTS.

Each of these position papers are explained in 500-750 word overviews
included on the main FAQ page. The three position papers clickable
from the FAQ are:

1. Effective Intranetworking Solutions Using Remote Access and
   Messaging-Enabled System Software

2. Extending Client/Server Technology to Rarely-connected Remote
   and Mobile Users

3. RemoteWare and the Internet

The position paper was co-written by XcelleNet and vendor partner Shiva
Corporation, a company that designs remote enterprise computing software.

If your FAQ is going to point the way to very detailed discussions of
sophisticated topics, it is imperative to detail just what those topics are.

It will take several minutes to download a position paper file. Some of these files might not be in HTML, but in other scripts like Adobe Acrobat. Getting a readable file with a non-HTML or non-ASCII script can be demanding. As the FAQ writer, your job is to convince time-pressed site visitors that once they jump through all these hoops, the information they reach will be indispensable.

I've included XcelleNet's FAQ here not because they are a huge company (they aren't) but because they make the process of going to a link to download a position paper seem like a must. FAQ writers should take note of the balanced, but enthusiastic, phrasing excerpted from the FAQ page:

"Shiva Corporation and XcelleNet, Inc. are leaders in remote enterprise computing. This paper explains cooperative solutions that combine remote access and a messaging-enabled system software foundation to cost-effectively link and provide applications for large numbers of remote and mobile users. The benefits of combining their products include:

- Make remote and mobile users more productive through an application environment that scales throughout a large enterprise;
- Synchronize valuable information resources across an entire enterprise;
- Provide a secure, reliable, manageable, and leverageable infrastructure for both system and application managers;
- Provide users with secure access to LAN (Local Area Network) servers;
- Leverage existing client/server applications and investments in Shiva remote LAN architecture;
- Reduce remote enterprise computing communications costs with deferred processing and connect-time optimization.

Your visitor has a meeting in 30 minutes and is wondering whether or not this download is really worth his time; the message on this FAQ page strongly suggests that it will be.

THE BRODERBUND FAQS

Your software doesn't have to be running on a LAN or on a $4,500 state-of-the-art Pentium notebook for you to include operating instructions on your FAQ. Games, which millions of kids of all ages play on CD-ROMs as well as dedicated cartridges, can have user questions that merit a Web site FAQ or related tutorial. Given the overlapping demographics of game players and Web surfers, the synergistic opportunities to reach your game-playing or lesson-learning customers is obvious.

One of the largest game and educational software firms in the world, Broderbund software (*http://www.broderbund.com*) has a series of especially comprehensive FAQs.

This FAQ, organized not in the traditional "Q-A" mode, but in an alternative "problems-solution" format, might work for you. Each of the FAQ's seven sections is devoted to a particular product. Each sector has several problems listed in boldface, with a solution immediately following. See Figure 12.8.

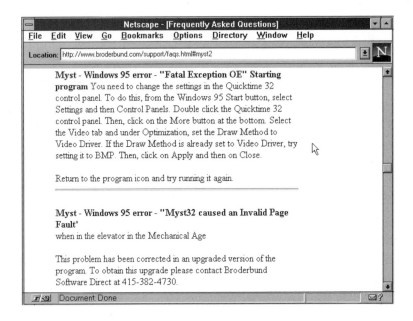

FIGURE 12.8 INSTALLING GAMES SOFTWARE CAN BE PROBLEMATIC, BUT BRODERBUND'S FAQS TRY TO HELP.

Perhaps the most detailed solution field comes in the "Carmen Deluxe DOS CD-ROM, Version 1.2—General Troubleshooting" section. Carmen Deluxe is the enhanced version of Carmen Sandiego USA, a geographically oriented game and teaching tool associated with the popular "Where In The World Is Carmen Sandiego?" PBS series.

Several maladies are briefly posited, including sound glitches, screen freezes, and having to hit the Escape key to enable the game to continue.

There's a 15-step cure. I know it's long, but I've decided to include it here not only as an example of a great FAQ answer, but for its worth as a tutorial on how a very complicated subject can be dealt with via a logically structured FAQ solution. If every FAQ and tech manual writer had Broderbund's ability here, the world would be a better place.

"All of the above problems are due to IRQ conflicts," we learn. "Sound issues like these will occur if the incorrect IRQ address is selected in the Setup of our program. Also if the Sound device is using an IRQ that is already being used by another device. (An example of this would be if your sound card is using IRQ 7. IRQ 7 is often being used by LPT-1, the printer port)."

"Steps to correct sound issues" are then specified. These are:

1. At DOS prompt (C:\>) type SET press **Enter**.
2. You will see Sound Blaster address settings. i.e. BLASTER= A220,I5,D1. The A setting stands for the I/O port address, the I stands for the IRQ setting, and the D stands for the DMA channel, anything that follows the D setting is unnecessary information. Please write down these settings. If you do not have a Set line, you may have to go through the Sound Card Setup again to obtain this information.
3. Change to the directory where the program is installed, i.e., If using Carmen World Deluxe CD: Type: **CD\DELUXE**, press **Enter**.
4. Type: **SETUP** from within the program directory.
5. You're now in the Setup Utility. Move the cursor using the arrows to **Sound Device** press **Enter**.
6. Select **SoundBlaster Pro**, press **Enter**. (or if you do not see your sound card, select **Sound Blaster Pro**).

7. Press **M** to modify hardware address settings.

8. Press **Enter** to accept the "I/O 220" (default).

9. Using the arrow keys move the cursor to IRQ, type **5** and press **Enter** to accept 5.

10. Press **Enter** to accept **DMA 1** (default).

11. Go to **Music Synthesizer [Enter]**.

12. Select **SoundBlaster**, not the SoundBlaster Pro, press **Enter**.

13. Go down to **Save configuration and exit**, press **Enter**. Answer **yes** to the question, "Are you sure you want to..."

14. Hit **Y**, you want to exit to DOS.

15. Type **Run Command** to start the program.

There you have it. A well-ordered FAQ answer has made for a happy game player. Customers are thinking, "Gee, I had some technical problems installing this game on Kaely's computer, but I went to the Web site and got all the information I needed. Now, I can't get her off the computer."

You've made a customer happy. Take a bow. You, dear FAQ writer, are a hero.

Right to the Beef: The "Novell NetWare Client 32 for Windows" FAQ

This networking-tool FAQ is state-of-the-art for its skipping of elementary "what is" questions and cutting-straight-to-the-details-chase. See Figure 12.9.

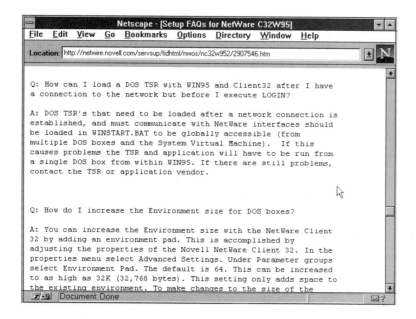

FIGURE 12.9 THE "NOVELL NETWARE" FAQ IS WRITTEN FOR EXPERIENCED USERS.

The 39K FAQ is divided into 11 sections. For FAQ writers, taking a cue from the first section is the most important. This portion is "What's NEW since last update?" The FAQ is updated several times a year. Unlike some software firms, which put updates in the TechNotes, Novell inserts theirs right in the beginning of their FAQ. The "What's NEW can cover anything—fixed bugs, unfixed bugs, updates, tweaks. Placing it at the start of the FAQ gives it the prominence it needs. FAQ writers on almost any kind of Web site or newsgroup should seriously consider this approach for the sake of clarity and of spotlighting key, newsworthy developments.

Take, for instance, what happened after Novell adjusted NetWare Client 32 to more smoothly handle external commands from a log-in script. Soon after the procedure was perfected, a note went up on the Client 32 FAQ as the first Q-A under the "What's NEW" heading.

Here's how the update was handled:

Q. "How do I execute external commands from within a login script? " The question was plainly stated, without technobabble.

A. "External commands can be executed by using the # command or the @ command. Loginw95.exe uses the @ command to spawn a process for the command to run and then will continue with the login script. The # command waits for the process to complete before going on. The NetWare Client 32 for Windows 3.1 will also have the capability to process the @ (at) command. Note: The command line login.exe ignores the @ (at)command in the login script."

This answer clearly and simply spelled out the process.

Other site-software information exchange sections of this FAQ include "Installation Issues," "Provider Issues," "LAN Driver Issues, "Printing Issues," and "Interoperability With Other Novell Products."

Too many FAQs ignore or gloss over nagging interoperability questions. Novell does not underestimate the intelligence and skill level of its customer base. You shouldn't either. FAQ writers might do well to see how Novell explains a specific 16-bit operating difficulty and how the NetWare Client 32 fixes it. The directions are highly technical but have a between-the-lines, "you should really upgrade to this client" message. IPX is Internetwork Packet Exchange, and SPX stands for Sequenced Packet Exchange. These are communications protocols used in Novell Netware networks. Here's how the FAQ managed to tout "32" while at the same time, answering a nagging question about 16-bit IPX/SPX interoperability:

Q: "Why are Rconsole and other 16-bit IPX/SPX applications unable to connect to or display all servers?

A: "Rconsole and other 16-bit IPX/SPX applications will send packets or communicate using the primary board. Client 32 can bind IPX to more than one frame type. By default Client 32 will Auto-detect the IPX frame type to be used for the primary board. If this primary Board Frame type is not the one needed for Rconsole or other 16-bit IPX/SPX applications problems may occur in finding or connecting to servers. These issues can be resolved clicking on the Network Icon in Control Panel and going to the "Novell NetWare 32-bit IPX Protocol Properties" and selecting "Advanced IPX ". Then use 'Primary Logical Board' and change "Frame type:" to the correct one needed for your application. (i.e., Ethernet_803.3 , Ethernet_802.2, Ethernet_II or Ethernet_snap)."

At the beginning of this chapter, I minimized the utility of some README.TXT files. This Novell site is a happy exception. On the first page, it advises users to go to the software's README.TXT and SETUP.HLP files for additional details. A Web site FAQ should not take the place of a README file, and vice-versa. They should compliment each other. Within each text, reference should be made to the problem-answering, lesson-teaching capabilities of the other reference. Keeping that theme intact on its site, several of Novell's FAQs have links to a menu page of online Novell product manuals. From this menu page you can also order Novell Press books.

The ultimate theme here is that the FAQ is a part of a larger entity, one attuned to providing solutions. In Novell, as well as in your company, there shouldn't be any rivalries between the software documentation folks and the FAQ people. If you have a grudge, settle it during the softball game at the company picnic. Your goal should be the same and your aim should be true.

THE "DIGITAL LINKWORKS" FAQ: EXPLAINING THE JARGON

Even for the most skilled FAQ writer, defining a term like "extensible object oriented workgroup" is a challenge. If you try to define it succinctly, you wind up in a trap familiar to virtually all FAQ writers for technology-oriented Web sites: the subject can't be defined without using terms that in themselves, require definition and explanation.

The Digital Equipment Co. "LinkWorks" FAQ (*http://www.digital.com/ info/linkworks/faq.html*) handles this task better than most. It doesn't waste any time getting to the basics:

Q. Describe LinkWorks in one sentence?

A. LinkWorks is an extensible object oriented enterprise workgroup framework built on open, distributed client/server services supporting integration of custom and third party personal, business and groupware applications into a secure and robust heterogeneous, multivendor environment.

   [Whoa, there! You've given me more buzzwords than I can possibly absorb. Help is available in the next Q-A sequence.]

Q. What do these terms mean exactly?

A. A workgroup is a group of people who interact and collaborate regularly to achieve common work goals. An enterprise workgroup is a workgroup that runs across the enterprise.

   A framework is a consistent structure supporting coherent enhancement of functionality. A customizable framework also supports customization and extension of the framework itself.

   An environment is a (logical) space which allows users, tools and objects to interact in an effective way.

   Groupware is software that supports a workgroup in its collaborative activities such as information (document) sharing, conferencing, scheduling and calendaring, electronic mail and workflow.

Truthfully, this FAQ could have done a better job explaining what "objects" are. In case you're wondering, objects are tables, charts, graphics, or other applications created on another platform and then imported into a given document. But the FAQ writers at Digital apparently didn't want to insult the intelligence of their users, so no definition is provided here.

Most of this FAQ is devoted to the benefits of LinkWorks. Like many other companies, Digital has decided to warehouse most of its software specs at another address—the LinkWorks Web server at *http://www.digital.com/info.linkworks*. True to a product with the term "link" as part of its name, a "link" routes the visitor from the answer to the last FAQ Question ("Where do I get more information on LinkWorks?") to the archive.

Here's where the real infomeat is. The LinkWorks InfoCenter, as the page is called, contains a mirrored copy of the FAQ, as well as a rich product documentation library for LinkWorks Version 3.0 products. With nearly 10 megabytes of data, this assemblage has to be as complete a FAQ-InfoCenter software information collection as on any Web site, anywhere.

FAQ writers will do well to not only note the type of documentation provided for download, but the cogent way in which each is described: title, pages, size and function: rat, tat, tat. These are large files, some bigger than a MB. You have to convince your site visitor that downloading these will be a productive use of his or her time.

In terms of the way it is written, as well as the range of its content, The LinkWorks InfoCenter section on documentation is so well written that a detailed excerpt is in order here.

The section is indicated under a listing of "LinkWorks FAQ, Documentation and Presentations" with the heading, "Documentation for LinkWorks V3.0 Products." As you read through the text, you should make mental notes about what publications, helper, and application notes you have at your company that might be migrated to your company's Web sites and explained in the manner Digital has. I've included my own commentary between selected references. So get out your red pens and mark up this excerpt of a guide to the site's downloadable resources as you please:

"Teach Yourself LinkWorks" (66 pages - 823 KB). This manual is intended as a Getting Started manual for the LinkWorks end user. In site-to-software transfer menus, the order in which documentation is listed should always be simple to complex.

[The basic tutorial is listed first, which makes sense.]

"User's Guide" (248 pages - 1780 KB). This guide is targetted at end users and provides introductory information and learning exercises to readers unfamiliar with LinkWorks. The reader is walked through the basic out-of-the-box functions that LinkWorks provides including objects, mail, workflow and default desk top functions.

[I've said it before, and I'll say it again: all online help text should be run through a spellchecker before it goes on the page.]

"Administration Guide" (114 pages - 640 KB). This guide is targeted at LinkWorks administrators and provides information on how to configure user environments (desktops) and profiles, define organizational units, and manage cells and workstations.

[I'm in a charitable mood, so I am going to correct all subsequent misspellings of "targeted" in the rest of this excerpt.]

"System Management Guides." These guides are targeted at system architects, system administrators and technical business consultants. They cover topics such as operating systems, databases, system characterization, upgrading and migration issues, and system reliability issues.

[Three versions available for download are then cited, with page and size information included. The list then picks up with a series of guides and reference works:]

"Configuration Guide" (200 pages, 1250 KB). This guide is targeted at LinkWorks administrators and describes LinkWorks configuration characteristics and LinkWorks configuration tooling. The guide also provides information on software components. Readers should be familiar with the contents of the "User's Guide" and the "Administration Guide."

[The writers have performed a valuable service here. An inexperienced user might be tempted to download this first, but really shouldn't. The knowledge level necessary to understand the "Configuration

Guide" can only be attained with a comprehension of basic concepts contained in the "Teach Yourself LinkWorks" and "User's Guide(s)." The writers make this plain. They've done this because when new users aim for something over their heads, they become frustrated and can easily become non-users or ex-users. I've seen flaming newsgroup postings about allegedly unworkable software. In some cases, the software works fine but the poster didn't take time out to read the basic documentation first. LinkWorks' site advises you to do so.

For our purposes, the next instructive paragraph on the InfoCenter Documentation page refers to:

"Introduction to LinkWorks Solution Development" (100 pages - 640 KB). This guide gives an overview of LinkWorks development techniques, the tools and interfaces available, the programming environments supported and the types of applications/solutions that can be built on/with LinkWorks. It is indispensable for the technical architect or consultant in determining the applicability of LinkWorks for his or her environment.

[This description works because the appropriate users are clearly targeted. Next are downloadable "LinkWorks Installation Guides" for several platforms, including Apple Macintosh, OS/2 and Digital UNIX. The FAQ page also has a link to a LinkWorks Listserv mailing list administered by Ioele/Griggs & Associates, a third-party business partner. This Listserv, an online watering hole for all interested parties, is the type of community-building channel that marketers for other Web sites (both technical and non-technical) might consider starting.]

IBM's SOFTWARE SERVER FAQs

In a textbook case of how to divide your FAQ but keep the newly separated parts cohesive, IBM (*http://www.ibm.com*) has separated its "Software Servers" FAQ into two FAQs: "Frequently asked questions on IBM Software Servers" and "Frequently asked Questions from software developers."

The "software developers" FAQ is much shorter. It basically performs a customer service function, listing application development tools and contact phone numbers for obtaining Developer Connection Cross-Platform Development Kits, or XPDKs.

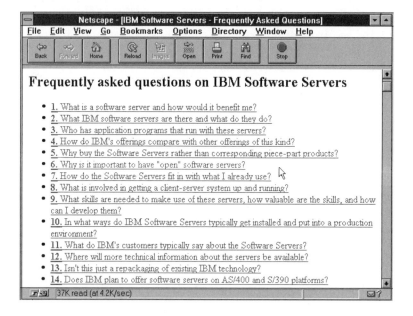

FIGURE 12.11 IBM's FAQ for software developers.

The most technical part of this FAQ lists the "significant" Application Programming Interfaces (APIs) supported by these servers. Under separate "Server" and "Client" headings, specific APIs are mentioned for seven servers, including Communications, Database, Directory and Security, Internet, Notes, SystemView, and Transaction Servers. Curiously, there is no direct Email link from the FAQ.

The "Software Servers" FAQ is much larger. The 35 questions touch on such topics as what services they are capable of, the skill level necessary to run these tools, and how these servers can run in tandem with, and are different from, competing products.

IBM's FAQ writers do not take the easy way out. They don't only use their FAQs for friendly marketing messages, but as weapons of war if the situation warrants.

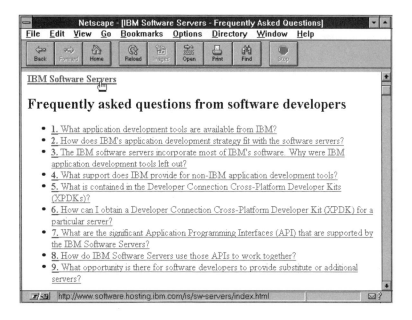

FIGURE 12.12 IBM's "SOFTWARE SERVERS" FAQ.

In this mode, Question 27 lays down the gauntlet diplomatically but firmly:

Q. Is this (a Software Server brand extension) a "me too" response to Microsoft?

A. Definitely not. There are fundamental differences between what IBM is doing and what Microsoft has done. Microsoft BackOffice may be described as proprietary (i.e., works on Windows NT only), closed (i.e., prerequisites between the products require most customers to buy all of the components) and limited to a single computing model (i.e., client/server with "fat clients"). IBM instead intends to address market requirements for open software servers that are versatile, supporting many computing models. They are open because they run on your choice of AIX, OS/2 Warp Server or Windows NT platforms. And they are open because they permit you to add server offerings from independent software developers. Moreover, the computing models they support include the kinds of clients and servers that span enterprise computing needs, and accommodate traditional distributed computing, serving the information needs of "thin clients" who are users on the Internet, collaborative computing, network-centric computing and business process reengineering.

The bottom of this FAQ page has Email, site-search, and product-ordering links. IBM's "Short cuts to IBM software pages" page links to a series of searchable indexes where you can access links to every IBM product by name, platform or keyword.

SO WHAT ABOUT MICROSOFT?

As you might expect, Microsoft has a forest of FAQs, most of which are well done. We needed a few tech site FAQs to examine in our next and last chapter, "How The Pros Do It." That's why we've put the Microsoft Windows 95 FAQ there. In this next chapter, you'll also find "tours" of several other FAQs from the Web, and various other parts of the Internet.

HOW THE PROS DO IT

In this chapter, you'll learn:

- How good Web FAQs talk to customers
- How one FAQ can reach several audiences
- How social and political FAQs can discuss issues clearly
- Writing step-by-step FAQs describing a process
- Issues in writing FAQs for specialized, knowledgeable readers
- How to write sensible government site FAQs—without jargon

In the previous 12 chapters, we've discussed what a Frequently Asked Questions list is, their similarities and differences, how to write one, and how a well-executed FAQ can be a site road map, valuable information tool, and, when appropriate, a profit-generator and money-saver. Our quest for specifics has taken us through dozens of FAQs that excel in one or more of these missions. In this chapter, we'll examine in detail some FAQs that accomplish these goals.

We'll look at how each FAQ works. Not only will we dissect each FAQ on its own merits, but we'll see how each works in the context of its broader position as part of a Web site or newsgroup. Thinking of writing a FAQ or looking for advice on how to improve yours? Let's take a look at how the pros do it.

THE "AMERICAN EXPRESS CARD" FAQ

Formal Name: Frequently Asked Questions About American Express Cards.

URL: *http://www.americanexpress.com/corp/connecting/faq.html*

Location on Site: Reached through a link from the Connecting With Us icon of the American Express Web site Home Page.

Length: 24 Questions, Three Sections, 10KB

What FAQ Writers Can Learn from This FAQ: If you offer it, flaunt it. Talk to your prospective customers in the first person.

This FAQ is strong on positioning the advantage of using the familiar American Express charge card products. As tens of millions know, these brands include the standard American Express "Green" card, Gold Card, Platinum Card, and the Optima Card.

The first question, "What are the benefits of having an American Express card?" is obviously a setup for a pitch for the company's stellar service standards, as well as for the card's flexibility. Key points are made about the fact that no interest is charged, and more than 20,000 service representatives are available to assist with everything from travel logistics to replacing a lost card.

In this answer, American Express has obviously chosen to reemphasize the long-perceived, positive service aspect. I know: a few years ago while on vacation with my girlfriend in the Pacific Northwest I lost my wallet and all my identification. Within about 12 hours, "AMEX" had a replacement card waiting for me at a company-authorized travel agency. That wasn't a plug, just an illustration of a key point every *.com* FAQ writer should be aware of. Through market research, identify what people believe to be your strong service points and then reinforce that in one of your very first FAQ answers.

Still within the first question, American Express then furnishes a phone number for prospective card holders to find out more about benefits.

The next paragraph mentions the American Express annual fee. Even though the fee is less than $5 a month, the FAQ writers took care in where exactly the mention was made:

1. It was at the end of the first answer, but it came *after* the service-positioning text mentioned above.

2. If the fee reference were made toward the end of the FAQ, it might have sabotaged all the well-scripted marketing copy. A few jaded folks would have felt that they were being set up. This early placement achieves credibility while, presumably, screening out people who would object to any fee. Such frugal types might then leave the site, leaving the rest of the questions to appeal to an audience now "on the hook."

Question 2, "What are the benefits of having an American Express Gold Card?," was placed there in part to garner the attention of applicants who might have been excited by the Green card but might be in the market for an enhanced product. This is an old marketing approach: introduce the product line in general, and then go up to the next level of service. See Figure 13.1.

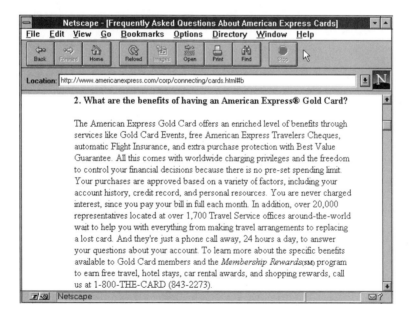

FIGURE 13.1 THE "AMERICAN EXPRESS CARD" FAQ TOUTS THE ADVANTAGES OF SEVERAL OF ITS CHARGE CARDS.

The term "enriched level of benefits" is inserted into the first sentence of the "Gold Card" answer. These benefits, such as the ability to charge tickets for special Gold Card–sponsored events, free travelers checks, and extra purchase protection, are immediately mentioned in the first sentence.

The next paragraph is a boilerplate that repeats the corporate service attributes mentioned in the answer to the first question. Because these service points were mentioned after the amenities, it can be assumed that the company feels special features are more powerful and immediate sales tools than service statistics.

Question 3, "What are the benefits of having an American Express Platinum Card?," discusses the ultimate company offering. The status of carrying such an invitation-only card is directly communicated within the first sentence:

"The American Express Platinum Card expands and amplifies Gold Card advantages by adding a variety of exclusive and personalized benefits like enhanced insurance plans, private airport clubs, and a free Optima Card account, as well as unique Platinum Card services including Platinum Card Concierge, Platinum Card Cruise Privileges, Platinum Card Fine Dining and Hotels & Resorts, and Platinum Card Travel Emergency Assistance."

> NOTE   Lesson for FAQ Writers: The old saying goes, "If you've got it, flaunt it." We can amend that slightly to advise, "If you've got it, flaunt it on your FAQ."

The next several questions elaborate on some other charge cards the company offers. Let's move ahead to Question 8, "What are the benefits of having an American Express Card for Students?"

Many college students are away from home for the first time. This may mean flights home during semester breaks and long weekends—and plenty of long-distance calls back to family and friends they've left behind. It's a confusing time in life, when homesickness is combined with the challenges of managing a newfound sense of freedom.

American Express seems to know this. The Card for Students was structured with added features appealing to this demographic, such as airline travel certificates, free long-distance calling awards, and "numerous discount offers" that pop up from time to time. This is communicated in the answer to this question.

> NOTE   Lesson for FAQ writers: a commercial FAQ is a marketing extension. No matter how deftly they are written, its answers will only be as effective as the services it describes. A bad FAQ can't rescue an ill-conceived marketing plan, but a good FAQ can make a worthy marketing initiative succeed.

The answer to Question 10, "What are the benefits of having a Senior Member Card," is structured similar to most of the previous answers. There's one exception, as we can see from the second and third paragraphs:

"The annual fee for the American Express Senior Member card is reduced from $55 to $35, after your 62nd birthday.

"You can share the benefits of Senior Membership with an Additional Senior Card...for an annual fee of $20, reduced from $30, after your 62nd birthday."

> NOTE   Lesson for FAQ writers: the lowered fee isn't necessarily why this answer works. It works because these strong sales points were set off in short, separate paragraphs. A paragraph consisting of one brief, pungent statement tends to stand out and get attention. Clearly, the reduced-fee arrangement is a selling point of this card. It also conveys the subtle message that the company values and respects maturity. Like everyone else, senior citizens want to feel appreciated. Communicating this helps achieve the goal.

Come to think of it, there's another lesson here. Let's just suppose for a moment that the "annual fee" paragraph read: "American Express Senior Members will enjoy an annual fee reduction from $55 to $35 after their 62nd birthday." What would be wrong with that answer? It would depersonalize the message. When you are talking to a customer in a FAQ, use "you" rather than third-person memospeak. People like to be spoken to directly. Don't you agree?

Questions 11 and 12 respectively ask about the benefits of having an American Express Corporate Card for Small Business, as well as the regular American Express Corporate Card.

The first three sentences of each answer are almost identical. Here's part of the answer to Question 11:

"The American Express Corporate Card for Small Business supplies a means of tracking business expenditures as diverse as meals, out-of-office phone calls, airline travel, and express delivery services. Your monthly statement tracks your spending. The Small Business Corporate Card also offers discount programs for gasoline purchases, express delivery service, hotel chains, and car rentals."

I'm a small businessperson myself, and do a lot of traveling. When I'm on a road trip, I'm looking for a good meal, make lots of phone calls, sometimes change flight plans, and often must express documents from the road back to my office or to a client. This Card was structured with people like me in mind.

> NOTE   Lesson for FAQ writers: In an answer to a question about a specific product, use the first sentence to emphasize the service benefits.

After the 12th question, the FAQ is interrupted with a section that is sub-headed, "Applying For An American Express Card."

There are marketing minds at work here. The Application instructions are not on a separate FAQ, or even a separate FAQ page. This sub-section literally starts right after the answer to Question 12, so you are likely to see the application data on the same screen as the tail end of the answer.

Since the FAQ which was up when we checked specified phoned rather than online applications, a link to a separate application page wasn't feasible. You'd be asking customers to do two things (click to a "How To Apply" page and then phone the number given). For busy people, that is one too many. Listing the number on the screen works better, because it saves that extra click.

> NOTE   Lesson for FAQ writers: Splitting the FAQ into a "How To Apply" section here is justified. Unless you have a link-accessed option that adds significant value and convenience, make your point within or as close to the main FAQ text as possible.

The last section, "Other Questions About The Card," explains the fee rationale, and interest compilation methods for the Optima Card, as well as billing rights and charge-posting methodology.

NOTE   Lesson for FAQ writers: This section is short on sales value but is a natural extension of the questions future or even current members may have about the company's various products. You need to sell them on your service before you run the fine print. Because of this, the *.com* FAQ writer should almost always put such perfunctory data toward the end.

THE "MICROSOFT WINDOWS 95" FAQ

Formal Name: Microsoft Windows 95 Detailed Questions and Answers.

URL: *http://www.microsoft.com/Windows*

Location on Site: Reachable through the Tech Info & Support icon of the Microsoft Windows portion of Microsoft's corporate Web site.

Length: 67 Questions, 17 Sections, 72K.

What FAQ writers can learn from this FAQ: How to explain the value of a product to different audiences, and how you can use your FAQ cross-market the product with some of your other brands.

The first two sections here define Microsoft's Windows 95 operating system, and then make the case for why you should upgrade to it. See Figure 13.2.

At several other points in this book we've talked about the advantages of the "what is" first question. By now, the strategy should be self-evident. If you are talking about a product, a theory—anything that the majority of people might not be able to define clearly—you need to say what it is. For the record, the answer here is that "Windows 95 is the latest member of the Microsoft Windows family of products, and is the successor to Windows 3.x and Windows for Workgroups 3.x."

This FAQ has an interesting structure. The first question, "What Is Windows 95?," is positioned not only as a separate question, but also as a header to the initial section. The other five questions detail the benefits and features of the product, compare Windows 95 to other Windows systems, detail the hardware requirements, and address version-numbering questions.

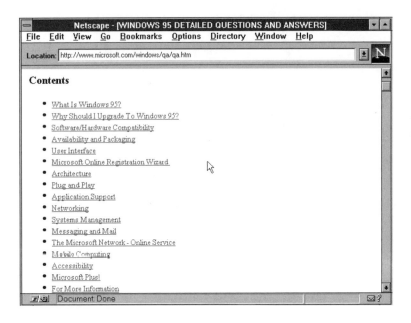

FIGURE 13.2 MICROSOFT WINDOWS 95 FAQ.

Without doubt, the most important of these is the second question in the first section. This is arguably the most mission-critical section of the FAQ. The answer mentions that the system "represents a major step forward in functionality." The second paragraph of the answer introduces some of the technical elements of the Windows 95 architecture, and how they add to that functionality.

> NOTE   Lesson for FAQ writers: "Technobabble lite" is permissible, but only after several sentences describing the functionality advantages the technology behind the product makes possible.

After the introductory section describing the product, the "why should" tack is taken next. Presumably at this stage, the prospect is thinking something like, "Hmmm, sounds interesting, but how will it help me?" It's a big leap across the crevasse from "Hmmmm" to a purchase. As the commercial FAQ writer, you have a bridge to build.

Microsoft positioned Windows 95 for both the individual and corporate markets. Each has different needs, so you don't speak to them in the same language. Putting up separate FAQs would have been one strategy, but probably would have defocused the message. Plus, this is a company which knows the market and realizes that in today's SOHO (Small Office, Home Office) market, the line between individual and corporate users can be blurry.

A detailed look at how the Windows 95 FAQ dealt with both critical market segments is in order. This challenge was dealt with in the "Why Should I Upgrade To Windows 95" section, as follows:

Q. Why would individual customers want to upgrade to Windows 95?

A. The sheer quantity of the improvements included in Windows 95 represents a great value for customers. Top on the list of requested improvements was an easier way to work with the PC. As a result, a new user interface was designed for Windows 95 that helps make computing even easier both for less experienced users and experienced users who want greater efficiency and flexibility.

> NOTE Lesson for FAQ writers: Can you pick out the keywords from the preceding paragraph? There are many, including "great value," "easier way," "greater efficiency" and "flexibility." In the ad business, these upbeat keywords are called "copy points." Ad business? Yes, in a real sense, *.com* FAQs can be an extension of advertising campaigns.

Long filename support is one of many usability improvements in Windows 95. Improving ease of use goes beyond fixing problems with Windows—it encompasses the hardware, applications, and network too. Plug and Play makes hardware configuration automatic, and built-in networking makes starting a new network or connecting to an existing network server such as Novell NetWare and Windows NT Server just as easy.

Microsoft has long known that the eight letter-three suffix file name plan (as in "thisfile.txt.") in DOS and Windows 3.1 wasn't wildly popular. For all their other problems, Apple Computer exploited this limitation for more than a decade by touting the lack of such barriers in its Mac operating system. Microsoft made sure that its code writers got with it and eliminated this problem before Windows 95 was released.

> NOTE   Lesson for FAQ writers: If a product improvement or upgrade takes the air out of the sails of a competitor's advantage, make that point early and often.

"Customers also want greater efficiency and power and to get their work done faster. They want to run more than one application or task at the same time. They want to use their computers to access files, electronic mail, and public-information networks from any location—at work, at home, or on the road. They also want better multimedia, whether for playing MS-DOS based games or for teleconferencing using TV-quality video resolution."

The flexibility advantages having been touted, this was the paragraph to tackle some of the specifics. Once again, this is done by keywords like "efficiency," "power," "faster," "better."

> NOTE   Lesson for FAQ writers: After establishing the fact that the product works, start to specify why it is superior.

In logical order, the next several "bullet grafs" further target the sales points:

- **Preemptive multitasking.** Windows 95 can perform multitasking smoothly and responsively for 32-bit applications.

- **Scalable performance.** The performance improvements that Windows 95 provides over Windows 3.1 increase as the amount of RAM increases, due to the high-performance 32-bit architecture of Windows 95.

> NOTE   Lesson for FAQ writers: Can you pick out the clinchers? "Smoothly," "responsively," "high-performance."

- **Support for 32-bit applications.** Windows 95 supports the Win32 API, which means customers can enjoy a new generation of easier, faster, and more reliable applications.

> NOTE   Lesson for FAQ writers: "Enjoy" is a word that evokes associations of pleasure. Use it when it's appropriate to do so.

- **Increased reliability.** Windows 95 increases protection for running existing MS-DOS and Windows-based applications and provides the highest level of protection for new 32-bit applications for Windows. As a result, an errant application is much less likely to disable other applications or the system.

NOTE Lesson for FAQ writers: Providing you insert qualifiers that diminish the possibilities, negative terms like "errant" and "disable" work well in FAQs.

- **Faster printing.** Windows 95 features a new 32-bit printing subsystem that reduces the time spent waiting for print jobs to finish and improves system response when jobs are printing in the background.

NOTE Lesson for FAQ writers: Users have a need for speed. As long as the claim is true, "faster" works as a bragging point!

- **Better multimedia support.** Just as Windows 3.1 made sound a part of the system, Windows 95 now includes support for video playback. The video system and CD-ROM file system will provide high-quality output for multimedia applications.

- **More memory for MS-DOS-based applications.** The Windows 95 use of protected-mode drivers means customers have more than 600KB free conventional memory in each MS-DOS window, even when they are connected to the network and using a CD-ROM drive and a mouse.

  Breathes there a computer user who has never run up against a memory problem? It's a shared negative experience, war stories about which build a sense of empathy. Now, here comes a product that reduces the risk of memory block.

NOTE Lesson for FAQ writers: What are the relevant complaints and fears of the user base you are writing for? If you don't know, find out and then address part of your FAQ to them.

- **Microsoft Exchange client.** Windows 95 includes the Microsoft Exchange client, a universal client that retrieves messages into one universal inbox from many kinds of systems, including Microsoft Mail, faxes, Internet Mail, The Microsoft Network, CompuServe Mail, and so on.

NOTE   The lyrics to the old Three Dog Night hit might have said "one is the loneliest number you can ever do." But in the computing world, "one" can mean a time-saving consolidation of functions.

- **Support for Mobile Computing.** Users of portable PCs benefit from the built-in support provided by Windows 95 for their hardware, with automatic hardware reconfiguration (through Plug and Play), integrated disk compression, and battery power management. Dial-Up Networking and Briefcase help users stay organized and stay connected while on the road.

NOTE   Lesson for FAQ writers: I'd vote for "built-in" as the key phrase here. "Built-in" connotes an image of convenience, which is what you are trying to sell, right? If I were writing a FAQ, I would make a list of product advantages and structure a good bit of my content around an explanation of these positives.

- **Internet-Ready.** Windows 95 includes the "plumbing" you need to connect to the Internet—support for TCP/IP and PPP dial-up connections are built in, and easy access to the Internet is available through The Microsoft Network. In addition, Microsoft Plus! includes the Internet Jumpstart Kit to give you the tools to browse the Web.

NOTE   Lessons for FAQ writers: Since this FAQ will be read "on" the Internet, the placement of a sales point mentioning Windows 95 "Internet-ready" capability works here. It's also the last bullet and serves as a clincher. Lesson Two: did you notice how the answer introduces other company products? Where applicable and credible, you can use your FAQ to cross-market your other brands.

Companies thinking about ramping up to Windows 95 will have different concerns than the guy running one computer in his home office. This section of the Windows 95 FAQ makes this point well:

Q. Why will companies want to upgrade to Windows 95?

A. Companies are moving to Windows 95 because it helps reduce their PC support burden, helps increase their control over the desktop, and helps increase the productivity of their end users. Numerous studies have shown that as much as 80 percent of the cost of owning a PC over the long term is associated with support costs. This includes installing, configuring, and managing the PC, and training the PC user. The Gartner Group has concluded that Windows 95 will likely lead to significantly lower total cost of ownership compared to MS-DOS and Windows 3.1 (PC Research Note: Personal Computing Costs: A Windows 95 Model, Aug. 15, 1994). Their model estimates the support savings is $1,180 per user per year. Over the five-year ownership period assumed in the analysis, this translates into savings of nearly $6,000 per user.

NOTE   Lesson for FAQ writers: When practical, quoting respected third-party research to make a point can be very effective.

"Windows 95 includes numerous features designed to reduce the costs of supporting PCs and PC users, including the following:"

"Reduce the costs." The people from Redmond are really into those "copy points," now aren't they? As in the "individual" section, these advantages are bulleted:

- **A simpler, more intuitive user interface that can reduce training requirements for novice users and enable experienced users to learn new tasks with less help.** The Start button, taskbar, Windows Explorer, wizards, a new Help system, and more, make Windows 95 easy to learn and make functionality easy to discover.

NOTE   Lesson for FAQ writers: A double-edged sword exists when you try to explain how sophisticated a product is. It might be natural for the FAQ reader to then think, "Gee, how am I gonna teach this to my people?" Nip this thought in the bud with counter-phrases like "simple," "intuitive," and "reduce training requirements."

- **Built-in networking support that is easier to set up and configure and is faster and more reliable to use.** Whether you're running NetWare or Microsoft networks using NetBEUI, IPX/SPX, or TCP/IP protocols, and using NDIS or ODI drivers, Windows 95 has integrated support for your network client, protocol, and driver. Additional networks are added easily. Windows 95 includes 32-bit clients for both NetWare and Microsoft networks that are fast and reliable and require no conventional memory. A Windows 95–based PC can have multiple network clients and transport protocols running simultaneously for connecting heterogeneous systems. In addition, Dial-Up Networking in Windows 95 makes it easy to access information on the network from remote locations in an easy, reliable, and secure manner.

NOTE   Lesson for FAQ writers: The last of the three main brag points is "secure." You've just given your readers some basic specs but then explained that accessing the network is "easy." If I'm a corporate reader, the immediate red-flag question is "Yes, but is it secure?" You've addressed that concern immediately. Diffusing objections without being defensive is a tough task on a FAQ (and in life as well) but you've done it.

- **Plug and Play device installation to automate the difficult process of adding devices to a PC.** Windows 95 supports the industry-standard Plug and Play specification to enable automatic installation and configuration of add-on devices. If you install Windows 95 on the system you have today and purchase a Plug and Play add-on device, you are able to install that device by just plugging it in and turning on your system. Plug and Play takes care of the messy details of installation and configuration. Plug and Play also enables innovative new system designs that support such capabilities as hot docking and undocking.

NOTE   Lesson for FAQ writers: "Messy" is a negative word. The thrust of this point seems to be to diffuse a negative. Have your marketing people done focus group studies about what "musts to avoid" your customers have on their minds? If so, find out what they are, and insert them into your FAQ in the context of something your product helps a user avoid.

- **System-management capabilities that simplify remote administration and enable new system-management applications.** Windows 95 features an infrastructure for the management of PCs that leverages a hierarchical database of system-configuration information, called the Registry. The Registry holds all the pertinent information about the system; hardware, software, user preferences, and privileges—and provides access to its contents over the network through a variety of industry-standard interfaces, including SNMP, DMI, and Remote Procedure Call. This infrastructure simplifies many administrative tasks by including tools for remote configuration of the desktop and enables a new generation of sophisticated system-management applications for managing the desktop, performing hardware and software inventorying, and supporting software distribution.

NOTE   Lesson for FAQ writers: Variations on the word "simple" were used twice in this last graf "Simple" and its syntaxical relations are valid counterpoints in a graf with lots of jargonistic alphabet soup.

- **System policies that enable an administrator to control a desktop configuration.** Windows 95 supports policies, which are settings an administrator configures to define the operations that users can access on their PCs. Policies also can be used to define the appearance of the desktop. For example, the administrator can set a policy to disable the MS-DOS Prompt and the Run commands, to prevent users from arbitrarily running applications.

NOTE   Lesson for FAQ writers: By noting how Windows 95 helps the administrator, the FAQ focuses in on decision makers who will have the authority to buy the product. Know your audience, but since you are talking to a corporate demographic that isn't necessarily limited to administrators, the third person works better here than the second person "you" (a more appropriate appellation for a section of a FAQ targeted to individuals).

- **Support for shared PCs and roving users.** Windows 95 can present different configurations, depending on who has logged into the PC. This option enables users to log on to different machines on the network and see their personal configurations. Many users can choose to use the flexibility of saving desktop settings by password and logon name; for example, for a multi-user workstation on which one user requires large-print or high-contrast settings due to a vision impairment.

NOTE   Lesson for FAQ writers: Now that you've got the administrator's attention, you have to convince them that the product will work flexibly across the enterprise.

- **Built-in agents for automating backup of desktop systems.** Windows 95 includes the software required to back up a desktop system using a server-based backup system. The Backup Agents included with Windows 95 work with the most popular server-based systems.

The pitch comes next:

"In addition to reducing support costs and increasing control over the desktop, Windows 95 helps make end users more productive. In usability-test studies, users of Windows 3.1 are able to perform a series of typical tasks that they perform today in 25 percent less time using Windows 95. These tests did not take into account many of the tasks that users would like to perform but which are too difficult today. These include installing a CD-ROM drive and sound card, or retrieving a file from the desktop system or the network while using the computer at home or traveling on business. By making these capabilities much more accessible, Windows 95 enables customers to be even more productive using PCs."

NOTE   Lessons for FAQ writers: Find studies that make your point. The more favorable stats in these studies, the better. Then, as in the above, end with an upbeat, clinching phrase.

The rest of the Windows 95 FAQ tackles configurability, architecture, application, networking, and mobile computing issues.

THE HOLOCAUST FAQ

Formal Name: Five Questions About the Holocaust

URL: *http://www/ushmm.org*

Location On Site: Linked from the Learning About the Holocaust icon on the U.S. Holocaust Museum Web site Home Page.

Length: Five Questions, 6KB.

What FAQ Writers can learn from this FAQ: How to deal with very sensitive issues in a calm but forthright manner.

On first thought, a FAQ about the Holocaust might seem out of place. FAQs are usually about software, or consumer products, or government, right?

Not necessarily. The beauty of the Internet is in the ideological diversity of opinions. You find Web sites and newsgroups put up by mainstream political candidates, and people who believe they are descended from space beings. Online there are Marxists and skinheads, unreconstituted hippies and aggressive, free-market Libertarians.

The Internet is also a place to learn about history. Keep in mind that history spawns frequent questions: "Why did Queen Isabella back Columbus?" "Who really killed JFK?" Yet for many, no question is as topically centered on the dark side of the human experience as "Why did the Holocaust happen?"

The United States Holocaust Memorial Museum in Washington, D.C. has heard this question asked many times. As long as there are human beings on this planet, the question will need to be posed. Now that we have the World Wide Web, we have another forum to ask it in. Looking at this content strictly on its merits as a FAQ is personally difficult but it's our mission here. Refer to Figure 13.3.

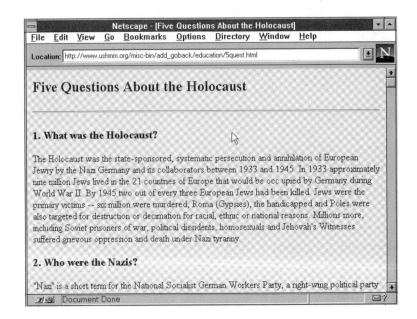

FIGURE 13.3 THIS FAQ ABOUT THE HOLOCAUST TELLS A POIGNANT STORY WITHOUT RESORTING TO NAME CALLING.

As FAQs go, this one is short. The "five questions" are:

1. What was the Holocaust?

   [The first question is a variant of "what is," a good setup phrase for almost any FAQ.]

2. Who were the Nazis?

   [Since the rest of the FAQ draws reference to the Nazis, this is the logical place for the term to be defined.]

3. Why did the Nazis want to kill large numbers of innocent people?

   Without any doubt, this is the toughest question to answer. The temptation to throw around accurate terms like "evil" would have been irresistible. No matter how justified, perjoratives work best when they are explained and annotated as thoroughly as can be. Here's how the Holocaust FAQ did it:

The Nazis believed that Germans were "racially superior" and that there was a struggle for survival between them and "inferior races." Jews, Roma (Gypsies) and the handicapped were seen as a serious biological threat to the purity of the "German (Aryan) Race" and therefore had to be "exterminated." The Nazis blamed the Jews for Germany's defeat in World War I, for its economic problems and for the spread of Communist parties throughout Europe. Slavic peoples (Poles, Russians and others) were also considered "inferior" and destined to serve as slave labor for their German masters. Communists, Socialists, Jehovah's Witnesses, homosexuals and Free Masons were persecuted, imprisoned and often killed on political and behavioral (rather than racial) grounds. Sometimes the distinction was not very clear. Millions of Soviet Prisoners of War perished from starvation, disease and forced labor or were killed for racial political reasons."

NOTE   Lessons for FAQ writers: You may have learned this in debate class. Note the rationale of your enemy and then deflate it. Showing that you know something about what you object to qualifies you better as someone to refute it.

4.   How did the Nazis carry out their policy of genocide?

5.   How did the world respond to the Holocaust?

The answers to these questions are also soberly phrased, with little invective. The case is stronger that way.

THE HOME/WORK SOLUTIONS, INC. FAQ

Formal Name: The Home/Work Solutions, Inc. FAQ.

URL: http://www.4nannytaxes.com/faq.htm

Location on Site: Linked from the Nanitax, Inc. Home Page

Length: 15 questions, one section, 9.5KB.

What FAQ writers can learn from this FAQ: How to explain detailed financial and legal issues concisely but authoritatively.

Earlier in this decade in the U.S., a considerable firestorm erupted when it was revealed that several candidates for national political appointments had committed a technical violation of the tax laws by employing "illegal aliens" as domestic help and not paying withholding taxes on their wages. The controversy resulted in a loosening up of the tax laws, but not until many thousands of Americans realized that they, too, might be in violation of those same statutes. Because of these fears, they, and many more otherwise good citizens, asked their attorneys and accountants if their own related situations were being handled correctly.

There are still some gray areas in "Nanny Law," the persistence of which caused Home/Work Solutions, Inc., a consultancy based in Sterling, VA, to launch a Web site with a FAQ devoted to this issue.

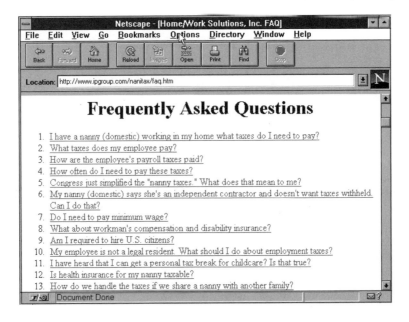

FIGURE 13.4 THE HOME/WORK FAQ IS A MODEL FAQ FOR BUSINESSES SELLING THEIR EXPERTISE IN A GIVEN AREA.

This FAQ is a model for every small consulting firm, financial planner, legal practice, or accountancy that specializes in and wishes to communicate its expertise in a particular area. Despite the complicated nature of this particular subject, no question takes up more than two lines on the screen and most answers are only one paragraph long. I preach about the importance of relevant first questions. The FAQ kicks off with these two questions and answers:

Q. I have a nanny (domestic) working in my home. What taxes do I pay?

A. In general, the Internal Revenue Service requires payroll tax filings by a domestic employer who pays a household employee more than $1000 cash wages in a calendar year. These payroll tax obligations that [sic] may include:

- Social Security & Medicare Taxes (7.65% of Gross Wages)
- Federal Unemployment Tax (FUTA) (0.8% of Gross Wages or less in Most Circumstances)
- State unemployment and disability insurance taxes levied on the employer.
- Advance payment of the earned income credit for eligible employees.

NOTE   Lessons for FAQ writers: Very few things are airtight in this world, so think about using such qualifying phrases as "in general." You don't want people or businesses affected by that rare exception to brand your FAQ—and, by extension, your company—as inaccurate. Also, we'll forgive them once, but **please** have your FAQ copyedited before you post.

Q. What taxes does my employee pay?

A. Your employee contributes to or pays:

- Social Security & Medicare Taxes (7.65% of Gross Wages Collected and Remitted by Employer)
- Employee Disability/Unemployment Taxes where required.
- Federal/State Income Taxes.

Those first two questions detail the parameters. After that, the FAQ gets into the mechanics. Subsequent questions cover such topics as how often the tax is to be paid, whether minimum wage laws apply (they generally do), and if workmen's compensation and disability insurance is required (it depends on the state).

On some FAQs, the last question is as important as the first. Let's see what this company did and why it works:

Q. Do the rules ever change?"

A. Yes. Many rule changes resulting from the Federal 'simplification' are still being defined. Home/Work Solutions' professionals keep current with these changes and notify clients accordingly.

The last Q-A makes a marketing point. Since the previous 14 answers have established the company's expertise, the claim works in the last paragraph. If it had been stated in an earlier answer, the claim wouldn't have had as much credibility.

NOTE   Lessons for FAQ writers: Empty your barrels before you position your service or company as experts in a field. Also, by positioning this topic as one where the rules "are still being defined," the FAQ writer invites subsequent site visits and by implication, direct consultation. Very few facts are cast in stone. If your topic is subject to new discoveries, changes, or revisions, put that into your FAQ. Such a note is a fancy way of saying "it's a complicated world out there, so please stay in touch."

THE MAGNAVOX FAQs

Formal Names: Television Frequently Asked Questions, Audio Frequently Asked Questions, Home Security Frequently Asked Questions, Computer Frequently Asked Questions, Magnavox Frequently Asked Questions.

URL: *http://www:custsupport.faqs.html*

Location on Site: One combined FAQ. Reached from a selection on the "Customer Support" menu, which, in turn, is reached from the Home Page.

Length: Total of 33 questions in five FAQs that follow consecutively on the same FAQ page. 23K.

What FAQ writers can learn from this FAQ: How a company with one brand name but many different products can publish a FAQ that gives enough space to the product performance assets of each division, while not compromising on the market value of the core marquee.

These kinds of Web sites work because of the overlap between electronics devotees and Internet-accessors. I'm not only talking about major company sites, but even those put up by local retailers, consultants, and third-party service providers. If you put up any kind of technocentric Web site you'll be discussing complicated topics that spawn lots of questions. For this reason, you'll need a FAQ. See Figure 13.5.

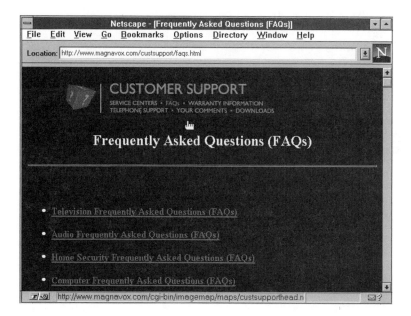

FIGURE 13.5 THE MAGNAVOX FAQ ADDRESSES QUESTIONS ABOUT SEVERAL COMPANY BRANDS.

I find it interesting that the relatively short Magnavox "company" FAQ is the last of the five FAQs in this section. That's because of the decision to focus on the brands first. After all, people don't go into an electronics store thinking "I want a Magnavox." Their thoughts are more along the lines of "I want a television," then perhaps specifying Magnavox as their choice.

First, a word about FAQ "architecture." In an exception from the norm, the FAQ questions are not listed before the body text. I'm neutral on this. If you don't set the stage, then your first couple of questions better work. In the Magnavox Television FAQ, they do. The first two answers on this FAQ work in significant mentions of unique product features, as well as links where one can find out more information about these capabilities.

Here's how this FAQ turned these features into a plus:

Q. I've heard about a feature called Smart Sound in Magnavox televisions. What is it and how does it work?

A. Smart Sound is the Magnavox feature that virtually eliminates the annoying volume changes you hear when watching a TV program and a commercial announcement appears. A special circuit looks at the incoming television audio signal and either lowers or raises the volume of that signal to maintain a single comfortable volume level.

NOTE   Lesson for FAQ writers: Entice them early with special product assets, but don't glaze their eyes over with too much "gee whiz." Not at the start.

Q. I've heard that Magnavox makes a television set with a built in "homing device" to help me find my remote control. Is this true?

A. Yes. Magnavox has a feature called Remote Locator which when activated will send out a signal to your remote control causing it to beep. Simply press the power button on the TV keypanel and the television will send out an RF (radio frequency) signal which instructs the remote to beep. It works from as much as 50 feet away and will even go through walls and doors. When you locate your remote simply press any button on it and the beeping will stop.

Who among the readers has never lost a remote? As you might suspect, I'm a gadget freak, but I have no idea where mine is. I have to get up to change the station. I call it channel-surfing aerobics. Here, a link to "Remote Locator" gives me more info.

> NOTE Lesson for FAQ writers: The real beauty here is in the "Q." The term "I've heard" works because it uses the first person and sets up the site as an information-central resource equipped to either verify or debunk rumors. "Is this true" functions for the same reasons. You don't need a product site for these phrases. Such a FAQ question works with anything that is in the slightest way subject to change, revision, or skepticism.

Most of the following seven questions on this FAQ deal with operational specifics. The four-question Audio FAQ, which comes next, deals almost exclusively with configuration advice.

With 14 questions, the Magnavox Home Security FAQ is the bulkiest. This is justified because of the stakes involved. You can have a state-of-the-art television or audio system but if your home isn't secure, than those other products might wind up as stolen goods to be fenced in some Third World hot shop.

Questions 2-14 of the Home Security FAQ deal with operational issues. As we learned in Chapter 11, migrating some of this to a FAQ can save dollars spent on customer support. Because the solution is only a click rather than 10 minutes of on-hold time away, this strategy also ensures customer goodwill.

The main punch of this FAQ is in the first Q-A. Let's see why:

Q. Why did my new Magnavox home security system telephone someone on my "call list" even though my alarm never went off? A friend says he got a call from my system which played the message I recorded announcing that my security alarm was going off. When he called to tell me about it, I was home and my alarm had not sounded.

> NOTE Lesson for FAQ writers: Almost everyone has heard stories about balky home security systems. By relating such a possibility, the writer has injected a sense of empathy. Phrasing a FAQ question to introduce a solution to a common problem is an effective way of connecting with your audience. You'll have them on the hook for your solution, as in the answer to the previous question.

A. Magnavox Home Security systems HST403MS and HST404MS come equipped with a unique safety feature which automatically dials out daily to test your telephone line. This feature is designed to ensure that your system is able to reach whomever you've programmed it to telephone (the monitoring service, or people on your "call list") in the event of an emergency.

You can customize this feature to make it dial out to test your phone line more frequently, less frequently, or not at all. Call the Magnavox Customer Service hotline at 1-800-208-9029 for help customizing your system over the phone.

NOTE Lessons for FAQ writers: There are several. The "empathy problem" strategy was used to introduce unique products positioned to solve the dilemma. The omnipotent first person "you" speaks to the customer directly. Links to special informational pages describing the HST403MS and HST404MS are provided. The hotline number was given as an alternative backup.

Early in the FAQ, you assure the customer that a "human" voice was available to help them. Some customers want the kind of human hand-holding that consonants and vowels on a computer screen just can't give.

The first part of the short, four-question Computer FAQ follows this model. The initial answer gives three tech support phone numbers and also has two links.

THE "TRIATHALON" FAQ

Formal Name: Frequently Asked Questions

URL: The *Rec.Sport.Triathalon* newsgroup. Also posted to the Web site http://fas.sfu.ca/0h/cs/people/GradStudents/zaiane/personal/triafq.html

Location on Site: Threaded Posting within the newsgroup.

Length: ten questions, 33 KB.

What FAQ writers can learn from this FAQ: How a detailed FAQ doesn't need many questions. How a good FAQ answer can smoothly walk the reader through a detailed, step-by-step process. Tricks of writing a FAQ for a specialized audience.

I've known a few triathletes. They are the ultimate physical fitness buffs. Training for and competing in marathon-length running, cycling and swimming events, they push their bodies to the max on a regular basis.

The first thing you might wonder is how these specimens get their bodies into such good shape. Funny, because that is the fourth question, "How Do I Train?" The first two questions, "What are typical events in a summer triathlon?" and "What are the standard distances?" are, of course, related to the "what is" type of question I recommend for the launch of most any FAQ. They define the concept.

The answer to the "How Do I Train?" question is about 2,000 words. That's longer than just about any FAQ answer I've ever read because of the way it is divided. There are sections on "Getting Started," "A Plan," "Base Building," "Intensity," "Peaking," "Racing," and [whew!] "Recovery." The end of this mega-answer lists two references for further reading. See Figure 13.6.

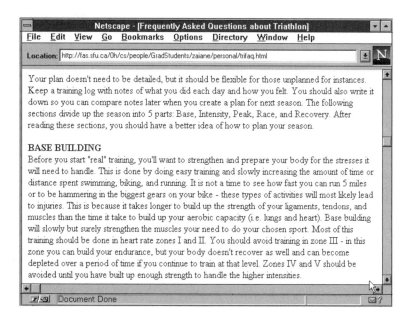

FIGURE 13.6 THE "TRIATHALON" FAQ IS AN EXCELLENT EXAMPLE FOR FAQS THAT EXPLAIN STEP-BY-STEP PROCESSES.

For any competitor, the day of the event is a special time.

There are more than one thousand Web sites and newsgroups devoted to active-competition sports and hobbies. They may be put together by sponsoring organizations, sporting goods retailers, physical therapists, fans, or participants. Preparation and strategy are at the essence of most of these interests. When you talk about preparation and strategy you are dealing with detail. Imparting details is one of the key functions of a FAQ.

Keep in mind that in these FAQs you are talking to a very tuned-in, high-affinity readership. You don't want to dumb-down, but wish to communicate with them at peer-level. Some of your readers will be long-time practitioners. If they brand you as not being on their knowledge level, you will be forever scorned by the same people you want to relate with or sell to.

Todd Jensen, who wrote the "Racing" section of the "Triathalon" FAQ knows this. With an eye toward overcoming some of the obstacles I've just mentioned, let's take a look at his expertly written text.

"Depending on the distance of the race, you need to take a few easy days or more to allow your body to be fully recovered and refueled for the race. Everyone is different—some people need weeks of rest, others can train right up to the day of the race and still perform well. A good sign of how rested you are is your morning heart rate. If it's higher than normal or your legs feel heavy and sluggish, you probably should train lightly or not at all in order to be prepared for the race. A good rule of thumb for longer distance races such as marathons or Ironman triathlons is to reduce your training time with two weeks to go before the event to about 70%, and with one week to go reduce your training even further to about 30% of your normal time."

NOTE   Lesson for FAQ writers: When giving advice, furnish numbers as quantifiers.

"If you're racing every weekend, you really don't need to worry about adding much Intensity to your workouts during the Racing season. Races can be your hard workout—train lightly to keep active and to keep your endurance between races. If you're not racing much, you need to keep doing some hard workouts or race simulation to keep in race-shape."

> NOTE   Lesson for FAQ writers: It's almost subtle, but by reading this you can "tell" that the writer has been through this experience many times.

The next section of this answer lists "helpful hints" for the day of the race. These are given in chronological order. Note the implied, "I know what you're going through" tone. Chronology is important for **any** FAQ answer where a series of sequential steps is outlined. Your FAQ doesn't have to be sports-related for this advice to apply.

- Plan and pack what you are going to wear and use during the race the night before. Create a checklist to make sure you haven't forgotten anything.

- Arrive early enough to the race site so you can scout out the transition area and course. You may want to even do this the day before if it is a long race or you are unfamiliar with the area.

- Leave more time than you think you will need for setting up in the transition area, warming up, and waiting in line for a port-a-john.

- Swim starts can be scary, especially if you are not used to swimming in the open water. Be prepared to get pushed, shoved, kicked, and swam over if you want to keep up with the pack. If you feel nervous about the close body contact, start off to the side or back."

> NOTE   The next eight points discuss specific competition strategies for the swimming, bicycling, and running portions of the triathlon. Let's skip to the last two bullet points, which are most instructive for FAQ writers.

- The run turns into a survival session for a lot of people, but try to keep moving and think positive thoughts.
- Finish strong.

> NOTE   Lesson for FAQ writers: When germane, end with a note expressing comradeship and fellowship. If you are going to sell to a specialized interest group, you'll want to be respected as an equal and seen as a friend.

THE "AMERICAN QUARTER HORSE ASSOCIATION" FAQ

Formal Name: AQHA Frequently Asked Questions

URL: *http://www.aqha.org*

Location On Site: Accessed from the AQHA Web site Home Page.

Length: 23 questions, 10 sections

What FAQ writers can learn from this FAQ: How to write a FAQ for an association Web site and use the FAQ to promote membership.

The Quarter Horse industry is involved in several different activities, from research about genetics and breeding to the staging of several equestrian and racing events each year. Like many association FAQs, this document is written for people with a certain level of knowledge. Given the perceived snootiness of some in the horse set, the writers have avoided the expected "What is a Quarter Horse?" type of question and go right to substance.

There's an assumption here that by visiting the site, you either are a member of AQHA or are at least thinking about joining. That's why the first section, on Membership, contains three basic questions (see Figure 13.7).

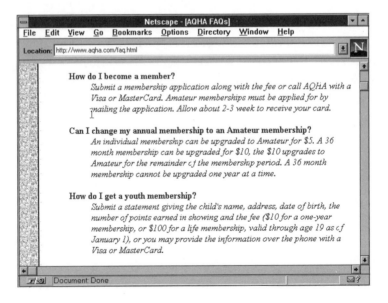

FIGURE 13.7 ASSOCIATION FAQ WRITERS LOOKING FOR A MODE MIGHT WANT TO READ THE "AMERICAN QUARTER HORSE ASSOCIATION" WEB FAQ, PICTURED ABOVE.

1. How do I become a member?
2. Can I change my annual membership to an Amateur membership?
3. How do I get a youth membership?

Each answer clearly describes the particular procedure.

The next seven sections of this FAQ are:

- Transfer, with three Q-As describing the specific procedure for transferring ownership of horses registered with AQHA;
- Duplication and Corrections, 3 Q-A's, detailing how to get a duplicate or corrected copy of your horse's registration certificate;
- Registration, 1 Q-A plus a detailed chart noting the process and fees involved in registering a newborn foal;
- HYPP, 1 Q-A detailing where horses can be genetically tested for HYPP (Hyperkalemic Periodic Paralysis, a genetic muscular disorder)
- Incentive Fund, 4 Q-A's outlining the specifics of an association-sponsored breeding contest program;
- Stallion Breeding, 5 Q-As about how to file and fill out breeding reports on Quarter Horse stallions members might own;
- Shows, a four-part Q-A about rules, qualifying rules and schedule information for several AQHA horse shows.

> NOTE   Lesson for FAQ writers: Most of these answers are brief, only one or two sentences. Conceivably, there could have been one FAQ question for each of these topics, but breaking them up into subtopics makes for quicker reading and retrieval of the necessary info. If your FAQ contains a lot of rules, regulations and fine print, you may wish to consider this method.

The last section, "Programs and Services," outlines the benefits of membership. Here's a list of AQHA extras and how the FAQ describes them:

INCENTIVE FUND

The Incentive Fund is a multi-million dollar awards program for the American Quarter Horse show industry.

MBNA AMERICA RACING PROGRAM

This purse and bonus awards program is designed to increase racing opportunities for older racing American Quarter Horses.

AMERICAN QUARTER HORSE ASSOCIATION OF PROFESSIONAL HORSEMEN

This is an organization for professionals in the American Quarter Horse industry who agree to uphold ethical standards. benefits available to all members of Professional Horsemen include a referral service for customers who are seeking the service of Professional Horsemen in their area.

AQHA STAR PROGRAM

The objective of this youth education program (STAR stands for Skill, Talent and Achievement Recognition) is to produce young people who are capable of meeting the care, safety, management, nutritional and riding needs of the American Quarter Horse.

BEST OF AMERICA'S HORSE

This program recognizes outstanding American Quarter Horses in virtually every equestrian discipline, from dressage to barrel futurities.

AQHA ON-LINE RECORDS SERVICE

Through this service you can research pedigrees as well as show and race records on your personal computer.

AQHA VIDEO LIBRARY

AQHA offers a collection of educational and entertaining videos for loan or purchase.

> NOTE   Lesson for FAQ writers: If you are a FAQ writer for an association Web site, check to see what amenities come with membership. These can be very effective sales tools. You then might want to make this a section of your FAQ, introducing it with a question like: "What benefits will membership in (fill in the name of your organization here) bring?"

THE "CALIFORNIA LEGISLATIVE INFORMATION" FAQ

Formal Name: California Legislative Information on the Internet

URL: *http://www.leginfo.public.ca.gov* Location On Site: A Freestanding FAQ

Length: 20 questions in 10 sections, counting an Overview and Glossary; 70KB.

What FAQ writers can learn from this FAQ: How to explain to citizens or customers ways to gain access to storehouses of online data. Gain their trust.

Over the last several years, public-opinion polls have told us that an increasing number of Americans mistrust government. One reason for this is the feeling that government is non-responsive and out of touch.

There are more than 35,000 city, county, state and federal jurisdictions in the U.S. alone. In turn, most of these have several departments and bureaus. The majority of data stored by these agencies are public documents and records. Terabytes of digitized information is being put on line every day, but there's so much that the average modem-equipped citizen doesn't have a clue about how to get to the knowledge they need. Whether you are running a government Web site, or just a site with lots of archival information on it, you owe your visitors a digital road map.

The State of California's Legislative Counsel Bureau, which oversaw this FAQ, has done a superb job of turning their FAQ into a road map. If you are a FAQ writer for a public agency, you might wish to adapt the FAQ's Table of Contents as a template for yours:

1. INTRODUCTION

    1.1 What Help is Available?

    1.2 What Assistance is Available?

    1.3 What Access Methods are Available?

    1.4 What Legislative Information is Available?

    1.5 What Other Services are Available?

The first three parts of the Introduction describe transfer methods for getting this information. Within this section, there's an informative discussion on File Transfer Protocol.

NOTE   Lessons for FAQ writers: Because of the general nature of governments, there will be a wide variety of skill levels among people looking for information on your government Web site. Some people are already put off by bureaucracy, so don't make matters worse by hitting them with a bunch of over-their-heads technospeak.

For our general purposes, the most instructive models on this site are answers to questions about what information is available. Then, we will quote from a section clearly describing a method to retrieve some specific facts on the site.

Q 1.4. What Legislative Information is Available?

A. AB 1624 (number of the state statute) required that for each current legislative session, the following information be made available over the Internet:

- The legislative calendar
- The schedule of legislative committee hearings
- A list of matters pending on the floors of both houses of the Legislature
- A list of the committees of the Legislature and their members
- The text of each bill introduced, including each amended, enrolled, and chaptered form of each bill
- The history of each bill introduced and amended
- The status of each bill introduced and amended
- All bill analyses prepared by legislative committees in connection with each bill
- All vote information concerning each bill
- Any veto message concerning a bill
- The California Codes
- The California Constitution
- All statutes enacted on or after January 1, 1993

NOTE   Lesson for FAQ writers: On any FAQ for a data-intensive Web site, detail what the site offers. People will want an expectation of what they can find before they take the time to look for it.

Ordinary citizens and special-interest groups alike will go to legislative Web sites to check on bills currently under consideration. This doesn't only happen at the state level, but on the county, school board, and city council level as well. Webmasters for those sites may wish to establish site sections for this timely data. That's what California has done. Here's how the FAQ advises citizens how to get at this data:

"The bill information for Senate bills and Assembly bills is contained in the bill directory (*/pub/bill*). The bill directory points to four index files and two sub-directories. The two sub-directories point to additional sub-directories that are grouped in numerical ranges of 50 Senate bills and 50 Assembly bills.

The index files include two files of Senate bills (one sorted by author and one sorted by bill number) and two files of Assembly bills (one sorted by author and one sorted by bill number).

The index files also include the topic for each bill listed in the file."

A list of directories and files contained in the bill directory follows.

NOTE   Lesson for FAQ writers: If there is a thicket of subject trees and branches on your site, tell how they are organized and grouped before you describe what is on them. You don't want visitors to get ahead of themselves.

Now, you've learned how to write a FAQ. In the Appendices, we'll list and briefly review some other good FAQs by category and location. We'll also provide a glossary of Internet terms, as well as a list of the qualities a worthy FAQ should have regardless of where it's posted.

Happy and productive FAQ-ing!

GLOSSARY

To a beginner or even a user with intermediate knowledge, the Internet can be a rough place to get your bearings. Part of the initial learning curve is mastering the technical jargon that all users must know.

You may be a FAQ writer for a new site, and you may be unfamiliar with some Internet terms; conversely, you might use these words in everyday language but have difficulty translating them for the new visitor likely to come to your FAQ page.

If you are a FAQ writer, you should not automatically assume that all of your readers will understand the Internet's expanding universe of buzzwords and buzz phrases. If, for example, you are writing a Frequently Asked Questions list for a banking site where encryption technology is used to safeguard electronic transactions, you'll want to explain the term the first time you use it.

Using brackets on first reference may work, but don't overdo it; too many bracketed definitions slow down the readability of the text. The FAQ is there to establish the site as an attractive and navigable place. Brackets after every word interrupt the reader's concentration. Besides, brackets {as in this is a bracketed phrase} are ugly.

If you must introduce terms that aren't commonly understood, a "What Is?" question and answer sequence might work better for your FAQ. Should you find it impossible—even after soul-searching—to avoid jargon, then consider either putting a small glossary on the FAQ or linking to a glossary directly from a FAQ answer. The glossary page might contain two glossaries: one for Internet terms and the other for words specific to the topic of your site.

Here's a beginners-level glossary of common Internet terms. Some of the definitions include suggestions as to how FAQ writers can use them in FAQ answers. Feel free to include them in your FAQ, wherever relevant.

ASCII   Stands for American Standard Code for Information Interchange. Every upper- and lowercase letter in the Latin, or Western, alphabet is represented by a two- or three-digit number.

backbone   In this reference, a major Internet network pathway.

baud rate How fast a modem is, or how many bits of data it can process per second. A 28,800-baud modem can process 28,800 (or sometimes more) bits per second.

BBS   A bulletin board system. These can also be Web sites, but many serving specialized interests are dial-up only. In turn, some of these can be accessed through an Internet connection via **Telnet**. Others require you to dial their modem directly. In your FAQ, you may wish to provide **links** to BBSes that explain your topic further.

bps   Another indicator of modem speed. Since a letter has eight bits, a 14,400-bits-per-second (bps) modem will handle up to 2000 screen characters per second. However, because there are spaces between words and modem line quality can fluctuate, the actual figure is somewhat lower.

browser   A software utility that reads and then "translates" an Internet page onto a user's computer screen. Depending on how the page was written and the capabilities of the browser program, the page may come across as straight text, as a Web page with graphics, or as a graphic Web page with additional sound and motion video capabilities.

bytes   A collection of eight bits that form one letter or punctuation mark. The word *frequently*, for example, would contain 10 bytes. With spaces added between sentences, this Glossary is approximately 12,300 bytes long.

client
A software program that lets a user access a remote computer. A user clicking to your Web site, for example, would use a client like the Netscape 3.0 browser to reach your server.

Common Gateway Interface
Also called *CGI*, an electronic mail or other utility that, when accessed, pulls up a screen that allows the user to transfer information to your Web site. CGIs can be used for everything from polling customers to requesting specialized data.

cyberspace
Once a cool term to describe the universe of electronic communication and information retrieval. Still applies, but now is a cliché.

domain name
Your newsgroup or Web site address. Two hypothetical examples would be *www.widgetworks.com* or *alt.fan.tuvok*.

electronic commerce
A range of transactional capabilities possible through cyberspace. Examples are ordering software directly from a Web site or checking your bank balance online.

Email
Stands for electronic mail; messages of text or graphical components sent from one computer to another either over the Internet or over a proprietary network like an online service or a dial-up connection.

encryption
The process of coding sensitive data so it cannot be read except by authorized users. Frequently used in electronic commerce to shield sensitive information—such as credit card numbers—from being intercepted by unauthorized third parties.

FAQ
That's why we're here! Stands for Frequently Asked Questions, a collection of questions and answers describing the site's purpose, content, and how users can "navigate" around the site. Some FAQs also contain basic information about Internet or World Wide Web issues that directly affect the site's functionality.

firewall   A software program that protects a collection of computers from general access by unauthorized users. In a bank setting, for example, the Web site and its FAQ will be "outside" the firewall but individual customer account records will be "inside" the firewall and not accessible to people visiting your site.

Gopher   A text-only Internet site. Gopher programs appeared several years before the Web's emergence and were used primarily by sites with large volumes of archived material. Gopher's are still viable as a text-based repository of information. Now, many Web sites "mirror," or copy, data stored on Gopher servers.

host   Can mean a company that houses and makes accessible the information and utilities on your Web site. Hosting services frequently rent a given amount of "space" per month. Some even design and prepare content for Web sites.

HTML   Stands for HyperText Markup Language, the type of commands inserted into Web documents to specify how a site should look and where a link might be included. Unless you ask your browser to read the source code of a Web document, an HTML command will not appear on a user's screen.

HTTP   HyperText Transfer Protocol, a communications sequence for transferring World Wide Web documents across the Internet.

hypertext   A word or phrase linked to another Web site, Gopher page, or newsgroup. On some Web browsers, appears as an underlined section, i.e., http://www.att.com.

Internet   The full range of interconnected Web, Usenet, Gopher, FTP, Listserv, and other sites.

intranet   A network based on Internet protocols, but usually not accessible to the outside world. These can often be found behind firewalls. Since a company intranet may be accessed by thousands of employees, this may also be a place for a FAQ page.

ISDN   Integrated Services Digital Network, a high-speed data transfer system using specially configured phone lines. Some Web sites that are rich in content are designing special applications that these 128,000-bps connections will be better able to handle than slower 28,000-bps modems can.

InterNIC   A central database where new Web sites are registered.

ISP   An Internet Service Provider. These can be national, regional, or local companies that, for a monthly fee, make Internet access possible.

Java   A programming language that allows Web sites to transfer mini-programs, or *applets*, to customer browsers. Java applets are appearing in FAQs. One example might be using ocean waves to set an appropriate mood on a FAQ page that describes how to book a room at a seaside resort.

Link   An underlined word or phrase on a Web site that carries a special code that will enable a Web browser to move to the highlighted site or section when the link is clicked by the user.

Listserv   A mailing list, often for a specialized topic. Usually free, these lists require a simple online registration process. Then, unless the list is moderated for the quality of posts, most E mail messages received by the Listserv are posted and E mailed to subscribers' computers. If there is a Listserv similar in topic to your site or newsgroup, you may wish to mention it in a FAQ question, such as "Where can I go for more information?"

mail-to   A hyperlink at the end of a Web page that triggers a Web browser's electronic mail program. The program then comes up on the screen. If the user has configured the browser's mail server properly, a message can be directly uploaded to an address on your site. A typical mail-to on a FAQ might be, "If you have questions that aren't answered in this FAQ, send mail to: *webmaster@anysite.com.*

maintainer   In FAQs, the manager, or maintainer of the list. Their tasks include processing new posts, keeping up with news related to the site's general topic, and handling electronic mail. Used far more often in the Usenet than in the Web community

MIME   Multipurpose Internet Mail Extensions. These can be graphics files sent by a Web browser's electronic mail utility.

newsgroup   Discussion groups on Usenet. It doesn't necessarily mean that the content is "newsworthy," however!

POP   Point of Presence. If a visitor from Portland, OR, is using an Internet Service Provider like Netcom to log on to the Web and visit your site, he or she probably configured his or her computer to dial a local Netcom number, or "POP."

posting   A message received and archived by a newsgroup or Web site. A newsgroup FAQ is also a posting.

server   In Internet-speak, a computer and/or software program that contains information stored on your Web site. A site visitor's computer uses client software to read the Web page information stored on your server.

spamming   One of the more irritating aspects of online life. Certain programs let a user with a commercial or ideological message access hundreds of newsgroups with a few keystrokes. These result in simultaneous postings, most of which are despised by conscientious Netizens.

Telnet   A command used to transfer from one site to another. Users often use Telnet to read their electronic mail when they are on the road.

URL   Uniform Resource Locator, or Internet site address. On a Web site for the hypothetical North Missouri Life Insurance Co., the FAQ's URL could be *http://www.nor-molif.com/faq/html.*

Usenet   The area of the Internet for newsgroups.

World   The group of Internet servers and pages that enable text,
Wide Web   graphics, sound, and moving images to be transferred between computers and presented in an integrated fashion.

SOME USEFUL FAQS

The most effective path to learning often involves watching how the given process is done. If you want to improve your public speaking skills, you study tapes of quality orators. Budding baseball players watch video clips of .300 hitters and pick up techniques.

If you are a new FAQ writer—or an experienced one wishing to better your craft—there are hundreds of worthy FAQs to choose from.

In this Appendix, I've tried to include FAQs that either perform at least one FAQ-related function extraordinarily well or are in themselves indispensable resources for FAQ writers. The balance of these are commercial Web site FAQs, but there are other Web and Usenet FAQs as well.

In no particular order, here are a dozen "four-star" FAQs you can learn from:

- The "Microsoft Windows 95" FAQ: A superb FAQ that explains a complicated operating system to several different audiences. Doesn't get overly technical at the expense of the new user, but doesn't pander to the lowest common denominator, either. URL: *http://www.microsoft.com/Windows*.

- "Five Questions About the Holocaust": There are thousands of Internet sites that deal with political and social issues. As befits the free-wheeling nature of Internet content, the rhetoric on some of these sites can be very impassioned. FAQ writers for such pages can take a look here at how an advocacy group managed to discuss a highly sensitive issue without resorting to yelling and name-calling. URL: *http://www/ushmm.org*.

- "Home/Work" FAQ: If you are writing a FAQ for the Web site of a professional service such as an accounting or law firm, you can turn your page into a marketing tool by placing information on your FAQ that, without too much ego on your part, displays your expertise in a given area. Home/Work takes a gray area of tax law and makes it understandable to everyone. URL: *http://www.ipgroup.com/nanitax/faq.htm*.

- "The Holiday Inn Worldwide" FAQ: If you are selling goods or services on your Web site, you'll need to maintain an archive of what you are offering. Holiday Inn, of course, sells hotel rooms. The FAQ provides an informative and handy link to the reservations database. URL: *http://www.holiday- inn.com/faq.html*.

- The "CheckFree" FAQ: Do you have a back-story marketing theme for your product? On Web sites, this can be done in creative ways without the appearance of contrivance. Customers will smell artifice a mile away. The CheckFree FAQ, for example, uses links to environmental organizations to forge a marketing message that paperless money transfers save trees. URL: *http://www.mc2- csr.com/vmall/checkfree/v20faq.html/*.

- The "Triathlon" FAQ: Regardless of whether your FAQ is on the Web or Usenet, some of the answers might cover explaining a step- by-step process. This can involve anything from installation of a software program to how to build a tent. In its description of the various phases of training desirable before a triathlon competition, this FAQ provides a worthy template. URL: the *rec.sport.triathlon* newsgroup.

- "AQHA Frequently Asked Questions": The *.org* section of the Web is full of association-related Web sites. Because associations gain revenue by promoting membership, curious new site visitors naturally drawn to the FAQ on first visit can be "recruited" in the way this FAQ does. You'll find good peer dialogue here, not a carnival-barking hustle about the benefits of joining the American Quarter Horse Association. URL: *http://www.aqha.org*.

- The "California Legislative Information" FAQ: Governments are compulsive collectors of data, most of which is required to be accessible to the public. A Web or Gopher site is the best place to make these files available, but their sheer size makes getting at them impossible without an M.S. in Library Science. There is also likely to be a wide range of Internet skills in the general public. The smart government FAQ writer for a government site won't throw up his or her hands but will see that expert FAQ writers on this site have managed to make government archive retrieval user-friendly. URL: *http://www.leginfo.public.ca.gov.*

- The "Typing Injury" FAQ: This lengthy but well-organized FAQ proves that medically-related FAQs don't have to be text-only, dry recitations of arcane data. This newsgroup FAQ, with its multiple links and photos of ergonomically friendly keyboards, shows you how to import Web-quality production values into your news-group FAQs. URL: *http://www.cs.princeton.edu/grad/dwallach.*

- "Fleet Bank Merger" FAQ: Consolidation has spawned multiple mergers in technology-dependent industries like telecommunications, insurance, and banking. When this happens, Web sites must merge as well. The FAQ page for the acquiring company has the extra role of reassuring new, perhaps uneasy, customers. This FAQ measures up to the task without pandering. URL: *http://www.fleet.com/abtfleet/merger/index/html.*

- The "rec.model.rockets" FAQ: Hobbies, particularly in avocations where new developments are frequent, present FAQs with challenges. Keeping the ever-growing collection of information cohesive is not easy. Sometimes, dividing the FAQ is the best solution. But if you divide a FAQ, how do you avoid dissecting it into discombobulated parts that are less than the whole? The rec.model.rockets FAQ solves the problem. URL: the *rec.model.rockets* newsgroup.

- The "Turbotax for Windows" FAQ: Should your product FAQ require several dozen answers, one approach might be to create a brief and simple "super FAQ" of the most common questions. You can put the rest of the Q-A in a larger, main FAQ, as Quicken, maker of this popular tax-preparation program, did on its Web site. URL: *http://www.ww1.gfn.com/turbotax/support/1/ttsuptie.html.*

OTHER RESOURCES

Two FAQs do a superb job explaining the organizational issues, do's, and don'ts of the FAQ-writing process. Much of their advice is best applied to newsgroup FAQs, but Web site FAQ authors will find useful tips, too.

These FAQs are:

- "FAQs: A Suggested Minimal Digest Format": URL: *http://www.cis.ohio-state.edu/hypertext/faq/usenet/faq-format/top.html*.
- "FAQs About FAQs": URL: *http://www.med.umich.edu/cgi- bin/uncomp/faqs/about-faqs*.
- The "FAQ Maintainers Listserv" is also heavily newsgroup-oriented. The postings here aren't likely to be about marketing, but about FAQ list-compilation tools and assembly issues. Still, it won't cost you anything to subscribe, which you can do by sending an E-mail message to *faq-maintainers@consensus.com*. Type the word **subscribe** in the first line of your message.

REVIEW SITES

Several site-review services rate the quality of Web sites. Dozens of new ratings are added each week. Sometimes, FAQ pages get reviewed separately. More often they are mentioned within the context of a more general commentary on a site. Each of the three main review services is keyword-searchable. Log on once every two or three weeks, and then enter the word **FAQ** or **Frequently Asked Questions** as a search term. You can also ask the site search engine to only pull up citations that have gotten at least a three-star rating.

If you do this, you'll get a list of reviewed FAQs/sites that match your search request. Each will contain either the full text or an excerpt of the review, as well as a hyperlink to the site or the FAQ itself. This is a good way to keep track of what the experts think are the best new FAQs going up on the Internet today.

Two of these services are:

I Guide, http://www.iguide.com

Point, http: //www.point .com

TEN THINGS EVERY FAQ
SHOULD HAVE

1. A reason for existence, or enough relevant material on the site that would lend to a Question and Answer Format.

2. Grammar and spelling must be precise. Nothing deflates authoritativeness quicker than dumb typos and misplaced modifiers.

3. The FAQ must be accurate. If you, the FAQ writer, are not sure how a scientific process works, what an agency does, or if your branches are open until 6 or 7 p.m. on Friday, *ask*.

4. One person should be ultimately responsible for it. A FAQ by committee is fine, but there needs to be someone in charge in case of a tug of war over content.

5. A FAQ must be easily locatable. On Web sites, a Home Page FAQ icon works best. If that isn't feasible, use a link directly from the Help page. Under no circumstances should you force the site visitor to drill down through six submenus before they *finally* reach the FAQ. At the same time, it's a good idea to put key icons for the rest of your Web site at the bottom of each FAQ page.

6. The FAQ can't rust away while the rest of the site is updated often. FAQs in fast-changing fields need frequent updating. Nothing is more maddening than reading a FAQ question about a marketing promotion that happened three months ago.

7. "What is?" is almost always a good opening FAQ question.

8. A FAQ should follow a logical organizational sequence and not go off on topical tangents.

9. Think links. You can add value to your FAQ by pointing to other sources of information on your site or elsewhere.

10. Listen to your public. On commercial Web sites, there should be a mechanism for common questions fielded by support personnel to be added to your FAQ. An equivalent ethic should be followed by newsgroups, where FAQ maintainers should constantly monitor threads to see if they contain inquiries that should be added to the FAQ.

URL Listings

Chapter 1

1.1 News.answers FAQ archive

http://www.cs.ruu.nl/cgi-bin/faqwais

1.2 News.answers FAQ archive directory

http://www.cs.ruu/nl/wais/html/na-bng/alt.html

Chapter 2

2.1 FAQ About FAQs

http://www.cs.ruu.nl/wais/html/na-faq/faqs-about-faqs.html
Copyright, 1995, 1996 by Russ Hersch

2.2 Silicon Graphics Studio Central FAQ

http://www.studio.sgi.com/Products/StudioCentral/qanda.html
Copyright 1995, 1996, Silicon Graphics, Inc.

2.3 c/net Member Services FAQ

http://www.cnet.com/Community/Mservice/faq.html
Copyright 1996, CNET, Inc.

2.4 Parapsychology FAQ
http://eeyore/lv-hrc.nevada.edu/~cogno/para3.html
Copyright 1995,1996, Dean Radin

Chapter 3

3.1 Deja News Research Service
http://www.dejanews.com/
Copyright 1996 Deja News Research Service, Inc.

3.2, 3.3 Vocaltec Internet Phone FAQ
http://www.vocaltec.com/faq.htm

3.4,3.5 MIT SIPB FAQ
http://www.mit.edu/sipb/office-manual/FAQ.html

3.6 TurboTax for Windows Most Frequently Asked Questions
http://www1qfn.com/turbotax/support/1/ttsupt1e/html
Copyright Intuit Inc., 1996

Chapter 4

4.1 OKI VRML FAQ
http://www.vag.vrml.org/VRML_FAQ.html

4.2 c/net Member Services FAQ
http://www.cnet.com/Community/Mservice/faq.html
Copyright 1996, CNET, Inc.

Chapter 5

5.1 Magnavox FAQ
http://www.magnavox.com/custsupport/faqs.html
Copyright 1995 Philips Consumer Electronics Company

5.2 Netcom FAQ
http://www.netcom.com/support/faq.html

5.3 rec.model.rockets Newsgroup FAQ
http://www.cs.ruu.nl/wais/html/na-dir/model-rockets/general.html

5.4 OKI VRML FAQ
http://www.vag.vrml.org/VRML_FAQ.html

5.5 news.answers archives
accessible through http://www.cs.ruu.nl/cgi-bin/faqwais

Chapter 6

6.1 Anonymous FTP FAQ
http://www.macworld.com/q/@316951ymwslx/netsmart/anonftpfaq.html
Copyright 1993-1995, Perry Rovers

6.2 Misc.invest Newsgroup FAQ
http://www.cis.ohio-state.edu/hypertext/faq/usenet/
investment-faq/general/
Copyright 1996, Christopher Lott

6.3 CNN Web site Help Page
http://www.cnn.com/feedback/help.index.html
Copyright 1996, Cable News Network

6.4, 6.5 The Roaster FAQs
http://www.natural.com/pages/products/roaster/roasterfaq.html
Copyright 1995-1996, Natural Intelligence, Inc.

6.6 RSA Data Security FAQ
http://www.rsa.com/rsalabs/faq/faq_rsa.html
Copyright 1993 RSA Laboratories

6.7 RSA Data Security FAQ on Disk
not on Web site, but distributed on a floppy disk.
Copyright RSA Data Security, Inc.

Chapter 7

7.1 Language Journal of Linguistic Society of America
http://semlab2.sbs.sunysb.edu/Language/faq.html

7.2 rec.autos.makers.chrysler FAQ
http://www.cs.ruu.nl/wais/html/na-bng/rec.autos.makers.chrysler.html

7.3 Deja News Search Engine
http://www.dejanews.com
Copyright 1996 Deja News Research Service, Inc.

7.4 OpenText
http://www.opentext.com
Copyright 1996 OpenText Corporation

7.5 Motoresearch Incorporated FAQ
http://www.carsurvey.com/
Copyright 1995 Motoresearch Incorporated

Chapter 8

8.1 Example of an e-mail link.

8.2 The Mentos FAQ
http://www3.gse.ucla.edu/~cjones/mentos-faq.html

8,3, 8.4 Internet Phone FAQ
http://www.northcoast.com/savetz/savetz.html
Copyright Kevin Savetz

8.5 The Windows NT Internet Phone FAQ
http://198.105.232.7:80/kb/faq/backoffc/win-nt/
Copyright 1996, Microsoft Corporation

8.6 The Stephen King Dark Tower FAQ
alt.fan.authors.stephen-king Newsgroup

8.7 The RealAudio Help Index
http://www.realaudio.com/help.html
Copyright 1995,1996, Progressive Networks

8.8 Kennedy Space Center FAQ
http://www.ksc.nasa.gov/

8.9 Sci.bio.food-science Newsgroup FAQ
http://www.cs.ruu.nl/wais/html/na-dir/sci/food-science-faq/.html

Chapter 9

9.1 Fleet Bank Merger Questions
http://www.fleet.com/abtfleet/merger.index.html
Copyright 1996, Fleet Bank

9.2 NCR Logo FAQ
http://www.ncr.com/qa.html
Copyright 1996, NCR Corporation

9.3 AT&T Toll-Free 888 FAQs
http://www.att.com/business/FAQ/faq5_1_1.html
Copyright 1995, AT&T

9.4 Apple Cyberdog FAQ
http://cyberdog.apple.com/features/generalfaq.html
Copyright Apple Computer, Inc., 1996

9.5 Lotus FAQs for Notes R4.0
http://www.lotus.com/csswww/R4Faq.htm

9.6 Quarterdeck Product Patches
http://arachnid.qdeck.com/qdeck/support.techlist.html
Copyright 1996, Quarterdeck Corporation

Chapter 10

10.1 Wells Fargo Helpful Tips
http://wellsfargo.com/nav/hlp

10.2 Games Domain Direct Download FAQ
http://www.gamesdomain.co.uk/gdfaq/gdfaq.html

10.3 Security First Commonly Asked Questions
http://www.sfnb.com/infodesk.caq.html
Copyright Security First Network Bank

10.4 Sprynet FAQ
http://www.sprynet.com/customer/sprynet.html

10.5 CheckFree FAQ Safegame
http://www.mc2-csr.com/vmall/checkfree/v20/faq.html

10.6 CheckFree Ecology Page
http://www.mc2-csr.com/vmall/checkfree/v20/ecology.html

10.7 TechWeb FAQ
http://techweb.cmp.com/techweb/docs/faq.html
Copyright 1996 CMP Media, Inc.

10.8, 10.9 Typing Injury FAQ
http://www.cs.princeton.edu/~dwallach/tifaq/general.html

10.10 All About Java

http://www.javasoft.com/allabout.html

Copyright 1996, Sun Microsystems

10.11 JPEG Image Compression FAQ

http://www.cis.ohio-state.edu/hypertext/faq/usenet/jpeg-faq/top.html

Chapter 11

11.1 USA Today

http://www.usatoday.com/leadpage.about.htm

Copyright 1996, USA Today

11.2 StarSight FAQs

http://www.starsight.com/mktgfaqs.html

11.3 CMP TechWeb FAQ

http://techweb.cmp.com/techweb/docs/faq.html

Copyright 1996, CMP Media

11.4 Eastman Kodak FAQ

http://www.kodak.com/customers/customers.shtml

(main FAQ directory)

Copyright 1996, Eastman Kodak Company

11.5 Holiday Inn FAQ

http://www.holiday-inn.com/faq.html

Copyright 1996, Holiday Inns, Inc.

11.6 US West Yellow Pages FAQ

http://www.uswest.com/yellow_pages/FAQ's.html

Copyright 1995, US West, Inc.

Chapter 12

12.1 Quarterdeck Patch

http://arachnid.qdeck.com/qdeck.products/MagnaRam/magnaram_
    patch.html

Copyright 1996, Quarterdeck Corporation

12.2 Lotus Support Technote

http://www.lotus.com/css/notes.htm

12.3 Oracle PowerBrowser FAQ

http://www.oracle.com/products/websystem/powerbrowser/html/
    faq.html

Copyright 1996, Oracle Corporation

12.4 MindSpring FAQ

http://www.mindspring/com/faq

12.5 Netscape Navigator FAQ

http://home.netscape.com/eng/mozilla/1.1/faq_nav.html

Copyright 1996, Netscape Communications Corporation

12.6 Netscape Server Software FAQ

http://home.netscape.com/eng/server/1.1/faq

Copyright 1996, Netscape Communications Corporation

12.7 Xcellenet Facts and FAQs

http://www.xcellenet.com/remote/facts/

12.8. Broderbund FAQs

http://www.broderbund.com/support/faqs.html

Copyright 1996, Broderbund Software

12.9 Novell NetWare Client 32 for Windows 95 FAQ

http://netwire.novell.com/home/client/c3295/faq.htm

12.10 Digital LinkWorks FAQ

http://www.digital.com/.i/info/linkworks/faq.html

12.11 IBM Software Developers FAQ

http://www.software.hosting.ibm.com/is/sw-servers/ss1faq_
    developer.html

Copyright 1994, 1995, 1996, International Business Machines

12.12 IBM Software Servers FAQ

http://www.software.hosting.ibm.com/is/sw-servers/ss1faq_
    servers.html

Copyright 1994, 1995, 1996, International Business Machines

Chapter 13

13.1 Frequently Asked Questions about American Express Cards

http://www.americanexpress.com/corp/connecting/cards.html

Copyright 1995, American Express Company

13.2 Windows '95 Detailed Questions and Answers

http://www.microsoft.com/windows/qa/qa.htm

Copyright 1996, Microsoft Corporation

13.3 Five Questions About the Holocaust

http://www.ushmm.org/misc-bin/add_goback/education/5quest.html

13.4 Home/Work Solutions FAQ

http://www.4nannytaxes.com/faq.htm

Copyright Home/Work Solutions, Inc.

13.5 Magnavox FAQs
http://www.magnavox.com/custsupport/faqs.html
Copyright Philips Consumer Electronics Company

13.6 Frequently Asked Questions About Triathalon
http://fas.sfu.ca/0h/cs/people/GradStudents/
zaiane/personal/trifaq.html

13.7 American QuarterHorse Association FAQs
http://www.aqha.com/faq.html

13.8 California Legislative Public Access Guide
ftp://leginfo.public.ca.gov/pub/public_access_guide

Index

E

F

R

S